Wittgenstein on Internal and External Relations

Also available from Bloomsbury:

Analytic Philosophy: The History of an Illusion, Aaron Preston
Applying Wittgenstein, Rupert Read (edited by Laura Cook)
Bertrand Russell's Bundle Theory of Particulars, Gülberk Koç Maclean
Dialectic of the Ladder: Wittgenstein, the 'Tractatus' and Modernism, Ben Ware
Portraits of Wittgenstein, edited by F. A. Flowers III and Ian Ground
The Bloomsbury Companion to Analytic Philosophy,
edited by Barry Dainton and Howard Robinson
The Bloomsbury Companion to Philosophy of Language,
edited by Manuel García-Carpintero and Max Kölbel
The Later Philosophy of Wittgenstein, David Pole

Wittgenstein on Internal and External Relations: Tracing All the Connections

Jakub Mácha

Bloomsbury Academic
An imprint of Bloomsbury Publishing Plc

BLOOMSBURY
LONDON • OXFORD • NEW YORK • NEW DELHI • SYDNEY

Bloomsbury Academic
An imprint of Bloomsbury Publishing Plc

50 Bedford Square
London
WC1B 3DP
UK

1385 Broadway
New York
NY 10018
USA

www.bloomsbury.com

BLOOMSBURY and the Diana logo are trademarks of Bloomsbury Publishing Plc

First published 2015

Paperback edition first published 2016

British Library Cataloguing-in-Publication Data
A catalogue record for this book is available from the British Library.

ISBN: HB: 978-1-4742-4214-1
PB: 978-1-3500-1437-4
ePDF: 978-1-4742-4212-7
ePub: 978-1-4742-4213-4

Library of Congress Cataloging-in-Publication Data
Mácha, Jakub. Wittgenstein on internal and external relations : tracing all the connections / Jakub Mácha.– 1 [edition].
pages cm
Includes bibliographical references and index.
ISBN 978-1-4742-4214-1 (hb)– ISBN 978-1-4742-4213-4 (epub)– ISBN 978-1-4742-4212-7 (epdf) 1. Wittgenstein, Ludwig, 1889-1951. I. Title.
B3376.W564M1455 2015
192–dc23
2015010318

Typeset by Fakenham Prepress Solutions, Fakenham, Norfolk NR21 8NN

Der Denker gleicht sehr dem Zeichner.
Der alle Zusammenhänge nachzeichnen will.
Wittgenstein, Ms 153a, p. 90v[2], 1931

Contents

Preface and acknowledgments

I follow Wittgenstein's term 'album' in the Preface of the *Philosophical Investigations*, so this book can be labeled an album too—meaning an album of themes, items, problems, or questions that have caught my interest while reading Wittgenstein's writings. It is my own album of Wittgenstein's remarks that I have collected in a certain order that, I hope, reveals an important strand in Wittgenstein's thinking that has been neglected in Wittgenstein scholarship thus far.

My plan or strategy is to look at Wittgenstein's writings from a certain perspective—from a perspective that focuses on the distinction between internal and external relations. A relation is *internal* if it is unthinkable that its terms should not possess it, and it is *external* otherwise.[1] This book is intended to capture the landscape (re)presenting Wittgenstein's engagement with this distinction. Seen from this perspective, this distinction appears to be one of the most fundamental distinctions that Wittgenstein drew in his writings. I have assembled Wittgenstein's remarks in such a way that the fundamental character of this distinction will become apparent.

Although the character of this study is exegetical, I try to keep a slight distance from his writings. I have assembled Wittgenstein's remarks in a different way from how he himself (or his editors) did and have placed emphasis on some problems that may be tangential to his concerns. I admit that I have tried to extract a workable philosophical view or, rather, a coherent set of views from Wittgenstein's *Nachlass*.

It is often proclaimed by so-called *resolute* readers that Wittgenstein did not provide any philosophical theory (of language, mind, perception and so on). His achievements have to be seen as residing more in a therapeutic approach to philosophy. Although I am sympathetic to such readings, I must insist that there still remains something in Wittgenstein's philosophy (the early as well as the later) that can be called a theory. This attempt at setting out a theory is neither about the world nor about knowledge nor about language. It is a theory of how to analyze a philosophical text in order to get rid of any philosophical problems that emerge due to the unsurveyable character of natural languages. It is Wittgenstein's method of analysis. Wittgenstein is, in my view, the real godfather of analytic philosophy. Despite the fact that the goal of logical or philosophical analysis has shifted from the kind of Tractarian 'concept-script' of the *Tractatus* to surveyable representations in his later philosophy, the main traits of his analytical method remained unchanged throughout his philosophical career. The main thesis that I am advancing in my book is that **Wittgenstein's method of analysis rests on the distinction between internal and external relations.** I do not hesitate to call Wittgenstein's method of analysis a kind of *philosophical theory*, although this clashes with Wittgenstein's desire not to offer theories. Drawing this distinction is not theoretically neutral. It presupposes various views, primarily concerning the nature of modality (necessity, thinkability, or conceivability). This theory is not, however, a theory of a primary order. It introduces a procedure for how to deal with other philosophical theories—a sort of transcendental theory.

The present book has the following structure: it proceeds chronologically in its main outline. Part II summarizes the philosophical background against which the distinction between internal and external relations emerged. Hegel and Bradley are addressed in Chapter 4. Russell and Moore—Wittgenstein's direct teachers and colleagues—are the subject of Chapter 5. Part III is devoted to Wittgenstein's early writings, i.e., to the texts that precede the *Tractatus Logico-Philosophicus* and to the *Tractatus* itself. Chapter 6 distills the definition of the notions of internal and external relations from these texts. The subsequent chapters in this part are all highly interlinked. You can read them in any order and you can skip some of them. If you are not concerned with Wittgenstein's early writings or with Wittgenstein's philosophical development, feel free to skip Parts II and III entirely. Part IV deals with Wittgenstein's later writings from 1929 up to his death in 1951. Its structure is similar to the previous part. Chapter 10 provides some definitions of internal and external relations in these texts. The following chapters explore various themes from Wittgenstein's later philosophy in which the distinction between internal and external relations is important. The subsequent chapters are independent of each other, although there are some connections and continuities. So, for instance, Chapter 12 continues the discussion of intentionality from Chapter 11. I do not explicitly distinguish between the so-called middle Wittgenstein of the early 1930s, the Wittgenstein of the *Philosophical Investigations*, and the *third* Wittgenstein. But at some points, there are recognizable shifts in Wittgenstein's thinking that need to be taken into consideration. Accordingly, sections 11.1–11.3 discuss Wittgenstein's account of intentionality from the early 1930s, whereas section 11.4 offers a somewhat more complex analysis from *The Blue Book*. Chapter 13

'Rules and their applications' is subdivided into two sections. The first one is devoted to Wittgenstein's notion of a rule that can be traced back to his calculus model of language from the early 1930s. The second section pays attention to the final stage of Wittgenstein's thinking, which is sometimes labeled the third Wittgenstein. Part V gives the rationale for Wittgenstein's method of analysis based on the distinction between internal and external relations. Please feel free to skip the footnotes, which provide additional thoughts or references to thoughts that lie outside the main concerns of this book. Sometimes I bring up parallels and analogies to the ideas of other thinkers and philosophers that Wittgenstein might have not been directly acquainted with or that emerged later after his death.

A major part of this book was written during my stay at the Wittgenstein Archives at the University of Bergen in 2013, where I had many opportunities to discuss some of the content of this book with the staff of the Archives and with numerous guests. I am most grateful to Professor Alois Pichler, Director of the Wittgenstein Archives, and I would like to thank him for his friendly hospitality throughout my stay, which has made this book possible. I would also like to thank the following people for their helpful comments and useful corrections of the earlier versions of some of the material presented here: James Klagge, Herbert Hrachovec, Peter Baumann, Modesto M. Gómez Alonso, Wilhelm Krüger, Alois Pichler, Deirdre Smith, Ondřej Beran, Dinda Gorlée, Peter Hacker, Gisela Bengtsson, Christian Erbacher, Maja Jaakson, Bernard Linsky, Kenneth Blackwell, Sorin Bangu, Karl-Friedrich Kiesow, Josef Petrželka, Andrew Napthine. My apologies to anyone I may have forgotten.

During 2011–13, I received support from the Czech Science Foundation (Grant № P401/11/P174), for which I am most grateful. I also wish to thank the Faculty of Arts, Masaryk University, for a period of research leave, for generous support, and for a stimulating working environment. I am grateful for permission to the Master and Fellows of Trinity College Cambridge to use a quote from Ms 153a, p. 90 as the epigram and to reprint the duck-rabbit figure in Chapter 17.

List of abbreviations

AWL	*Wittgenstein's Lectures: Cambridge 1932–1935*. Ed. A. Ambrose. Oxford: Blackwell, 1979.
BBB	*The Blue and Brown Books*. Oxford: Blackwell, 1958.
BT	*The Big Typescript. Ts 213*. Ed. and trans. C. G. Luckhardt und M. A. E. Aue. Oxford: Blackwell, 2005.
CV	*Culture and Value*. Ed. G. H. von Wright in collaboration with H. Nyman, trans. P. Winch. Oxford: Blackwell, 1980.
LA	*Lectures and Conversations on Aesthetics, Psychology and Religious Belief*. Ed. C. Barrett. Oxford: Blackwell, 1966.
LFM	*Wittgenstein's Lectures on the Foundations of Mathematics, Cambridge 1939*. Ed. C. Diamond. Sussex: Harvester Press, 1976.
LWL	*Wittgenstein's Lectures: Cambridge, 1930–1932*. Ed. Desmond Lee. Oxford: Blackwell, 1980.
LWPP I	*Last Writings on the Philosophy of Psychology*. Vol. 1. Ed. G. H. von Wright and H. Nyman, trans. C. G. Luckhardt and M. A. E. Aue. Oxford: Blackwell, 1982.
LWPP II	*Last Writings on the Philosophy of Psychology*. Vol. 2. Ed. G. H. von Wright and H. Nyman, trans. C. G. Luckhardt and M. A. E. Aue. Oxford: Blackwell, 1992.
M	Wittgenstein's Lectures in 1930–33. In PO, pp. 46–114.
MDC	M. O'C. Drury. Conversations with Wittgenstein. In *Recollections of Wittgenstein*. Ed. R. Rhees. Oxford: Blackwell, 1981, pp. 112–89.
Ms	*Wittgenstein's Nachlass. The Bergen Electronic Edition*. Oxford: Oxford University Press, 1998–2000, manuscript.

NB	*Notebooks 1914–16*. Ed. G. H. von Wright and G. E. M. Anscombe, trans. G. E. M. Anscombe. Oxford: Blackwell, 1961.
OC	*On Certainty*. Ed. G. E. M. Anscombe and G. H. von Wright, trans. D. Paul and G. E. M. Anscombe. Oxford: Blackwell, 1969.
PG	*Philosophical Grammar*. Ed. R. Rhees, trans. A. J. P. Kenny. Oxford: Blackwell, 1974.
PGL	*Wittgenstein's Lectures on Philosophical Psychology 1946–7*. Ed. P. T. Geach. New York: Harvester, 1988.
PI	*Philosophical Investigations*. Ed. G. E. M. Anscombe and R. Rhees, trans. G. E. M. Anscombe. Oxford: Blackwell, 1958.
PO	*Philosophical Occasions 1912–51*. Ed. J. Klagge and A. Nordmann. Indianapolis: Hackett, 1993.
PPO	*Public and Private Occasions*. Ed. J. Klagge and A. Nordmann. Lanham, Boulder, New York, Oxford: Rowman and Littlefield, 2003.
PR	*Philosophical Remarks*. Ed. R. Rhees, trans. R. Hargreaves and R. White. Oxford: Blackwell, 1975.
RFM	*Remarks on the Foundations of Mathematics*. Ed. G. H. von Wright, R. Rhees, G. E. M. Anscombe, revised edition. Oxford: Blackwell, 1978.
ROC	*Remarks on Colour*. Ed. G. E. M. Anscombe, trans. L. L. McAlister and M. Schättle. Oxford: Blackwell, 1977.
RPP I	*Remarks on the Philosophy of Psychology*. Vol. I. Ed. G. E. M. Anscombe and G. H. von Wright, trans. G. E. M. Anscombe. Oxford: Blackwell, 1980.
RPP II	*Remarks on the Philosophy of Psychology*. Vol. II. Ed. G. H. von Wright and H. Nyman, trans. C. V. Luckhardt and M. A. E. Aue. Oxford: Blackwell, 1980.
TLP	*Tractatus Logico-Philosophicus*. Trans. D. F. Pears and B. F. McGuinness. London: Routledge & Kegan Paul, 1961. [Sometimes using trans. by Ramsey and Ogden or my trans.]

Ts	*Wittgenstein's Nachlass. The Bergen Electronic Edition*. Oxford: Oxford University Press, 1998–2000, typescript.
UW	Ursache und Wirkung: Intuitives Erfassen / Cause and Effect: Intuitive Awareness. In PO, pp. 370–426.
VW	*The Voices of Wittgenstein*. By Ludwig Wittgenstein and Friedrich Waismann, ed. G. Baker. London: Routledge, 2003.
WWK	*Ludwig Wittgenstein and the Vienna Circle*. Conversations recorded by Friedrich Waismann. Ed. B. McGuinness. Oxford: Blackwell, 1979.
Z	*Zettel*. Ed. G. E. M. Anscombe and G. H. von Wright, trans. G. E. M. Anscombe. Oxford: Blackwell, 1967.

All references to Wittgenstein's manuscripts and typescripts are quoted from *Wittgenstein's Nachlass. The Bergen Electronic Edition*. Oxford: Oxford University Press, 1998–2000 and referenced according to the von Wright catalogue: G. H. von Wright, *Wittgenstein*. Oxford: Blackwell, 1982 by Ms or Ts number followed by page number. The original punctuation and spelling is retained in quotations. If not stated otherwise, italics are in the original.

1

Introduction

1

Wittgenstein's method of analysis: 'I'll teach you differences.'

What is the method of analysis? Traditionally, at least since Kant, philosophical analysis has aimed at resolving a whole into its parts. The godfathers of analytic philosophy—Frege, Russell, and Moore—understood the concept of analysis in this sense. In the manuscript the *Theory of Knowledge*, Russell takes analysis to be 'the discovery of the constituents and the manner of combination of a given complex.'[1]

The important thing here is that in the works of these philosophers, another conception of analysis is implicit. With the aid of a formal language, analysis now reveals the underlying logical form of language, which might be obscured in ordinary language. In other words, starting with the surface grammar[2] of ordinary language, analysis aims at uncovering its 'logical form.' Russell's theory of descriptions is a good example here. Unlike with proper names, definite descriptions that appear in the position of a grammatical subject have to be analyzed away. The surface 'grammar,' however, does not discriminate between proper names and definite descriptions. Thus, a logically relevant distinction might get lost in the surface grammar of ordinary language. The aim of logical analysis is to uncover and fix such logically relevant distinctions.

Wittgenstein follows Russell exactly on this point: 'Russell's merit is to have shown that the apparent logical form of the proposition need not be its real form.'[3] For Wittgenstein, as he interprets it, the theory of descriptions deals with one particular logical distinction (namely, the distinction between proper names and definite descriptions). His goal—at least in the *Tractatus*—was to clarify the logic of our language, which means developing a logically adequate language (whose grammar would be captured by a concept-script or a *Begriffsschrift*).[4] One thing is to provide a logical notation for our natural language and another to construct a new formal language. The latter was Frege's aim, the former Wittgenstein's. In what follows I will frequently speak of a logically adequate language. This expression should cover both a formal language and a natural language whose logical form is transparent. In such a language, the surface grammar would match the logical grammar and thus the distinction between them would effectively collapse. The idea of a single logically adequate language, which would embody the general form of every proposition, was abandoned in Wittgenstein's later work. Logical analysis is no longer like a chemical analysis which enables us to see the hidden structure of a proposition; what remained is the idea that some expressions have to be substituted for others in order to clear away any misunderstandings caused by false analogies between the different areas of language:

> Our investigation is therefore a grammatical one. Such an investigation sheds light on our problem by clearing misunderstandings away. Misunderstandings concerning the use of words, caused, among other things, by certain analogies between the forms of expression in different regions of language.—Some of them can be removed by substituting one form of expression for another; this may be called an 'analysis' of our forms of expression, for the process is sometimes like one of taking a thing apart.[5]

False analogies and ipso facto philosophical misunderstandings may be caused by ambiguous words and sentences. It was Wittgenstein's intention to tackle such logical ambiguities.[6] To do so, first, one has to detect an ambiguity and, second, there has to be a rule or a test to resolve the ambiguity. Sometimes it is enough simply to point out that an expression that is causing problems is ambiguous. But even then this presupposes a generic logical distinction that makes it possible to detach the separate meanings. This distinction would be a key that allows us to say that a given expression means this as opposed to that. In this book, I am going to examine one important distinction in Wittgenstein's works—namely, the distinction between internal and external relations.[7]

But I would like to assert an even stronger claim—that the distinction between internal and external relations is one of the most fundamental distinctions that drives Wittgenstein's method of analysis. The most conclusive evidence stems from the *Tractatus* where Wittgenstein writes that he introduces 'these expressions in order to indicate the source of the confusion between internal relations and relations proper (external relations), which is very widespread among philosophers.'[8] Later, he continues with the thinking that philosophy or metaphysics has obscured the distinction between conceptual and factual statements: 'Philosophical investigations: conceptual investigations. The essential thing about metaphysics: it obliterates the distinction between factual and conceptual investigations.'[9] The distinction is employed here in order to be able to indicate a certain widespread confusion among philosophers. It allows us to ask about the philosophical claim: does the author mean an internal relation or an external relation here?[10]

The general lesson behind Wittgenstein's method of analysis remains unchanged. Two forms of expression are identified that look the same in ordinary language. The aim of analysis is to show, however, that they are different. Here is the most explicit expression of this conception of analysis (reported by Drury):

> Hegel seems to me to be always wanting to say that things which look different are really the same. Whereas my interest is in showing that things which look the same are really different. I was thinking of using as a motto for my book a quotation from King Lear: 'I'll teach you differences.'[11]

Hegel's leading methodological maxim is to unify all differences. Wittgenstein wants to see himself as turning Hegel on his head, which might be an allusion to Marx's treatment of Hegel as Marx's intention was the 'turning of Hegel on his head.'[12] But Marx still stood, in a sense, within Hegel's system. Marx's philosophical method is basically the same as Hegel's. The real—as it were methodical—turning of Hegel on his head comes only with Wittgenstein.

The radicalism of Wittgenstein's approach—in comparison with Frege or Russell—consists in his insisting on this general methodological principle and resisting the urge to formulate any underlying philosophical theory. Wittgenstein's claim that 'All philosophy is a "critique of language"'[13] indicates that philosophy—a philosophy of the future which is invoked in the *Tractatus* 6.53—is neither about the world and its essential features, nor is it about the essential features of language. What all philosophy is actually about is how to deal with other accounts of the world and language. Philosophy is a second-order or transcendental theory as indicated in my Preface.[14]

2

Why relations matter

The traditional distinction between essential and accidental properties is well known. It rests on the commonsense intuition that if some properties of an entity were taken away from it, it would no longer be the same entity. Such properties are essential to the entity. Things get complicated, however, when we consider that some properties are relational properties (whose characterization involves reference to another thing or things). Relations can be seen as generalized properties (i.e., properties are unary relations). The crucial question is: does an analogous distinction apply to relations?

It is comprehensible when two things (particulars, e.g., material objects) are related by a relation that is accidental (e.g., the relation of being close to each other). But are we able to imagine two things that cannot but be related by a certain relation? Why would we then treat these two things as separate objects if we cannot conceptually separate them? Such a relation must be *internal* in the sense of holding among parts of a whole. Even then, there is some doubt as to whether such a picture is not self-contradictory.[1] Do internal relations hold between particulars at all or are all relations merely external? The latter claim is sometimes call the doctrine of external relations.

There are several historical factors leading up to this subject matter.[2] At the beginning of the twentieth century, philosophers like Russell and Moore tried to solve the problem of the unity of a proposition by employing a unifying relation between the proposition (or its constituents) and the judging mind. This means that the mind ensures that a proposition (for instance, 'The river is moving') is not merely a conglomerate of elements (river, to be, moving), but a coherent whole. Such a relation is on the one hand a constituent of the proposition and on the other hand something that ensures the unity of the whole proposition. It turned out that external relations could not do this unifying job, because nothing unifies the unifying relation with its terms.

A similar problem emerges if one takes facts to be entities that make propositions true. Initially, Russell and Moore did not distinguish between them.

Propositions were identical with the facts that make them true (this is the *identity theory of truth*). The constituents of a proposition are not linguistic entities. So among the constituents of the proposition 'The apple is red' are a certain apple and the color red. But later on Russell and Moore were forced to distinguish between judgments and the facts that make them true. Then, however, there emerges the question about the nature of the relation between a proposition and a fact that makes it true. And again, it turned out that external relations are bad candidates for this task, because then all truths would be accidental.

The third cluster of problems concerns Bradley's Regress Argument, which leads to the view that there are no relations at the ontological base and finally to ontological monism. If there are no relations in any ontologically significant sense, then reality is a single whole, i.e., ontological monism is the ultimate account of reality.

The notion of an internal relation might be helpful in saving pluralism. If two terms are internally related, there is no need for any further unifying relations. The fact that these two things are internally related is grounded in these very things, in their natures. The internal relation does not add anything to the complex consisting of these two terms and is in this sense only an *apparent* relation.[3] There is, furthermore, no need for any relation connecting a term with the internal relation, because internal relations are grounded in the natures of their terms. Hence, the infinite regress of instantiations of additional unifying relations is avoided.

The price to pay for this turn is divorcing the linguistic form (i.e., the surface form) from the logical form (i.e., the true form) of predication. As already discussed in the previous chapter, such a discrepancy must be surmounted by logical analysis. Another problem is what the ultimate form of predication, i.e., the general form of the proposition, actually determines. Does this form reflect any (necessary) properties of the world or is it imposed during the course of logical analysis?[4]

Why do internal and external relations in Wittgenstein matter so much? The distinction between internal and external relations imposes a metaphysical burden or—as one would say today—imposes ontological commitments with respect to the nature of reality and the nature of modality. This is obvious in Bradley, Russell, and Moore. Wittgenstein employs the internal/external distinction primarily as a heuristic tool, eventually freeing it from any metaphysical burdens—if not in the *Tractatus*,[5] then certainly in his later work. The general lesson I would like to draw is how a metaphysical distinction—far from being regarded as nonsensical—can be transformed into and employed as an analytical heuristic tool.[6] Wittgenstein was still wholeheartedly maintaining Frege's Third Principle ('Never to lose sight of the distinction between concept and object.')[7] when he wrote: 'Philosophical investigations: conceptual investigations. The essential thing about metaphysics: it obliterates the distinction between factual and conceptual investigations.'[8]

This is, for me, what analytic philosophy is most significantly about.

3

What is wrong with the internal/ external distinction

There is something inherently misleading about the distinction between internal and external relations. The first thing is that this terminology is historically laden. It had been used by Wittgenstein's predecessors and contemporaries to formulate various philosophical theories and doctrines. The expressions 'internal relation' and 'external relation' had been used in several different senses in philosophy. Rorty, following A. C. Ewing, summarizes the historical provenance at the beginning of the twentieth century:

> [T]he meanings given to 'internal' ranged from a very weak sense, in which to say that a relation *R* which *X* bore to *Y* was internal to *X* meant merely that '*R* makes a real difference to *X*,' to a very strong sense, in which it meant that 'from a knowledge of *Y* and *R* we could infer with logical necessity that *X* possesses a certain determinate or relatively determinate characteristic other than the characteristic of standing in the relation in question.'[1]

Even philosophers within a single tradition have occupied the opposite poles of this range. Moore subscribed rather to the weak sense of 'internal relation' while Wittgenstein's notion of an internal relation is closely connected to logical necessity. Such ambiguities have distorted the discussion of this topic. It is, then, somewhat surprising that Wittgenstein took the distinction between internal and external relations as one of the central concepts of the *Tractatus*. At the beginning of the 1930s, Moore reported that

> [Wittgenstein] used it 'only because others had used it'; and he proceeded to give a slightly different formulation of the way in which the expression had been used, *viz.* 'A relation which holds if the terms are what they are, and which cannot therefore be imagined not to hold'.[2]

In Wittgenstein's later writings, the internal/external distinction seems not to be as central as in the *Tractatus*. However, this distinction is still there and what has changed is rather its verbal expression. Instead of 'internal relation' Wittgenstein now uses 'grammatical relation' or 'conceptual relation' and instead of 'external relation' he uses 'factual relation.'[3, 4]

Such ambiguities affect more or less every philosophical notion. But there is a second and more serious reason why the difference between internal and external relations may be misleading. Distinguishing between internal and external relations suggests that there must be some external relations and some internal relations among all relations. But this is misleading according to Wittgenstein. The class of all relations is not divided into external and internal relations. Wittgenstein says occasionally that only external relations are proper while internal relations are called improper.[5] Internal relations are, strictly speaking, not relations at all. The modifier 'internal' operates like 'fake' or 'apparent.' It is like the class of horses, which is not divided into real ones and wooden ones. We can, of course, distinguish between internal and external relations, but we have to keep in mind that only external relations are proper relations. Wittgenstein expressed these concerns about this distinction at the beginning of the 1930s. He is reported as saying that internal relations are 'entirely different from other relations' and that 'the expression "internal relation" is misleading' because internal relations and external relations are categorially different; they 'belong to different categories.'[6]

What exactly is the source of this categorial difference? There is almost pervasive evidence in Wittgenstein's *Nachlass* indicating that the difference stems from the nature of the things that are related. Internal and external relations have categorially different relata. Internal relations hold between concepts (or properties, qualities, universals) while external relations hold between objects (or particulars). This delimitation is implicit in Wittgenstein's early writings, but is obscured by his shifting uses of the words 'object,' 'property,' and 'relation.' In the later texts, these shifting uses are anchored in the notion of a language-game. What is a factual (external) relation in one language-game can be a grammatical (internal) relation in another language-game.[7]

We have to clarify now in what sense internal relations are said to be *improper*.[8] Something is an improper *X* if it has most but not all of the characteristic properties of *X*, but still resembles *X*. So which essential characteristics of relations do internal relations lack?[9] A proper relation should relate two (or more) *distinct* terms. These terms should be distinct objects of thought. We should be able to refer to them independently of each other. However, the crux of the *assertion* of an internal relation is to say that its terms are not independent of each other. These terms are indistinguishable in the respect that is captured by the internal relation. Then, however, we lose the reason[10] for taking these terms to be distinct entities. In an important sense, these terms are partially or wholly identical. Every internal relation wears its identity on its sleeve, which may give rise to all the perplexities and paradoxes of identity.[11] These paradoxes emerge primarily if we consider the identity or dependence of objects as opposed to the identity and dependence of concepts. Saying that two objects are identical or not independent is *prima facie* baffling because we can then ask whether there are two objects or only one. On the other hand, saying that two concepts are identical is easily comprehensible; it might mean that they are synonymous, co-referential, or the like.

Wittgenstein once called identity the very Devil.[12] It is no exaggeration to say that identity posed one of the main problems that Wittgenstein struggled with throughout his philosophical career. In an early notebook entry, he tells us: 'To say of two classes that they are identical means something. To say it of two things means nothing.'[13] Later in the *Tractatus* we are told: 'That identity is not a relation between objects is obvious.'[14] Wittgenstein was preoccupied with the *Law of Identity* in his later work as well. In one of the most important passages of the *Philosophical Investigations*, where the problem of rule-following culminates, he writes:

> 'A thing is identical with itself.'—There is no finer example of a useless proposition [...]. 'Every coloured patch fits exactly into its surrounding' is a rather specialized form of the law of identity.[15]

The idea behind this remains unchanged. Identity is not a relation between (material) objects. In this sense, internal relations cannot be relations between objects either. This is also the reason why internal relations are improper for Wittgenstein.

We do not find any explicit argument against internal relations in Wittgenstein. Obviously, he was not as hostile towards this notion as Russell and Moore were.[16] Resolute readers of Wittgenstein, however, tend to see internal relations as nonsensical, as a kind of misunderstanding, as an incoherent notion. But where exactly does the problem lie? Is it something problematic about the internal relations themselves or is it problematic when they get confused with external relations? Diamond argues for the latter option when she says that the problematic thing about a logical (i.e., internal) relation is 'that we may misunderstand its role.'[17] McManus seems to argue that any asserted internal relations are inherently muddled even if they are not confused with external relations:

> … the person who hears an 'internal relation' assertion as telling him something has to be confused, and that is what someone who asserts such assertions is getting at. These assertions are moves *within* a person's confusion […].[18]

Internal relations for McManus only have a signaling function, indicating that something is not quite right about our language and understanding. Although this account may find some support in the *Tractatus*, it is wholly inconsistent with Wittgenstein's later work in which internal relations are grammatical relations. All mathematics, for instance, is based on internal relations.[19] Does the McManus account imply that every expression of a grammatical rule or every arithmetical statement is a move within one's confusion? In Part IV of this book, and especially in the concluding Part V, rather different bounds of sense for the expressions of internal relations will be proposed. A statement of an internal relation is nonsensical when it is used reflexively without any underlying external relation that would account for a difference between the relata. Such statements are, in fact, expressions of the pure identity '*a* is *a*.' I will call this methodological principle the *maxim of no reflexive uses of internal relations*.

The argument here proposes that assertions of internal relations—when intended and recognized as such—may have a positive function in clearing up the confusion. When one arrives at an asserted internal relation, the assertion may be taken as a kind of a reminder or as an *imperative*. An internal relation assertion may thus be intended to remind one that there is a logical or grammatical rule that should have been followed. But it may also be intended as an invitation to amend or to improve one's manner of expression. An asserted internal relation may be understood as an invitation to incorporate the relation into one's logical notation (in the *Tractatus*) or into the grammar of a language-game (in the later philosophy). Chapter 19 sums up several ways of introducing new grammatical rules, such as defining and learning a new expression, introducing a new standard of measurement, proving a mathematical statement, presenting a novel work of art, and much more.

If an imperative has been successfully carried out and the confusion surmounted, there is then no point repeating the imperative. There is no point ordering someone to 'Come here!' if they are already here. If the logical grammar of our language is clear, there is no point repeating any logical or grammatical rules. As McGinn formulates it: 'once Wittgenstein's remarks have achieved what they are intended to achieve, they can be completely left behind.'[20] Obviously, in a logically adequate language like that which is strived for in the *Tractatus*, an internal relation could not even be expressed. And analogously, if a language-game were wholly surveyable, there would be no need to express its grammatical rules. The distinction between internal and external relations collapses away eventually when there is no confusion anymore and therefore no need for any logical analysis.

II

Prelude

The aim of Part II is to present possible sources of Wittgenstein's thinking in terms of internal and external relations. While he claims in the *Tractatus* to settle 'the disputed question "whether all relations are internal or external,"'[1] Wittgenstein is obviously referring to the dispute over relations which was led by Russell and Moore on the one hand and by the so-called British idealists, especially by Francis Bradley, on the other.

Russell ascribed to Bradley the view that all relations are internal while he himself advocated the opposite view that all relations are external. I am going to argue in Chapter 5 that Russell's interpretation of Bradley's position is wrong. Wittgenstein followed Russell in his assessment of the core of the debate, but in doing so he did not embrace Russell's doctrine of external relations. One must conclude that Wittgenstein was closer to Bradley than to Russell or Moore. Moreover, Wittgenstein was more sensitive to Bradley's arguments concerning the nature of relations in his early philosophy and some Bradleyan (or Hegelian points) points can be found in his later philosophy as well.[2]

4

Hegelianism and British idealism

Idealism can be characterized very roughly as a mind-dependence of reality or a concept-dependence of objects. Let me give a voice to some critics of idealism who are important in the present context. Russell understands idealism as 'the doctrine that whatever exists, or at any rate whatever can be known to exist, must be in some sense mental.'[1] Moore says that 'Modern Idealism, if it asserts any general conclusion about the universe at all, asserts that it is *spiritual*.'[2] To put it in terms of relations: reality is internally related to mind or experience.[3] All objects are conceptually related and these relations are essential to its relata, i.e., to these objects. This statement undermines the very distinction between concepts and objects.

British idealism—a philosophical movement at the turn of the nineteenth and twentieth centuries—is not easy to characterize in terms of a single doctrine or a single philosophical strategy or method. With some reservations one can say that the British idealists were, although rather unorthodox, followers of Hegel.[4] The exponents of the early phase of analytic philosophy—Russell, Moore, and to some extent Wittgenstein—did not sharply distinguish between Hegel's views and the views of his British followers.

Nevertheless, a good starting point for our historical presentation of the distinction between internal and external relations would be Hegel. In §1 I contrasted Wittgenstein's method of analysis with Hegel's synthetic method. Hegel's method of dissolving (aufheben) all conceptual distinctions leads ultimately to monistic ontology. Hegel was indeed an adherent of the doctrine of internal relations. He writes in his *Logic*: 'Everything that exists stands in correlation, and this correlation is the veritable nature of every existence.'[5] To *adequately* understand the veritable nature (i.e., the essence) of every single thing, one has to understand its relations to every other thing and, in the end, to the whole, to the Absolute. To put the doctrine in negative terms: we cannot isolate or abstract one single thing out of the whole and understand it *adequately* in isolation.[6]

The crucial point of this doctrine is the requirement for adequate understanding. Our practical requirements for adequate understanding are limited. On the one hand, we can get along with obviously lower requirements for adequate understanding in daily practice. One can manage to understand what a table is with knowledge of a restricted number of its relations to other things. On the other hand, one cannot understand what a particular table is without any understanding of several other things. One cannot understand what a table is without understanding what tables are for, i.e., without understanding its role in human practice.

Practical considerations can provide hints both in favor of and against the doctrine of internal relations. Wittgenstein is led by practical considerations in his reflections about the doctrine. For his and Hegel's argument in favor of the doctrine, see §17.1.

4.1 Bradley's metaphysics

We do not know to what extent Wittgenstein was acquainted with Bradley's or any other idealist's works.[7] It may be the case that Wittgenstein read only those parts of Bradley's works that were quoted by Russell or Moore. Because Wittgenstein's affinities to Bradley's views concerning the nature of relations are apparent, we have to address them in this study. Before doing so, I am going to briefly sketch the outlines of Bradley's metaphysics.

Bradley's ontology consists of one single substance, which is the Absolute or Reality-as-a-whole. From an epistemological point of view, he then distinguishes between Appearance and Reality.[8] Reality is everything, including our Appearances. Appearances are abstractions from Reality; they are partial views or aspects of Reality. Here comes the analogy to a painting by Candlish:

> Appearances thus contribute to Reality in a fashion analogous to the ways in which segments of a painting contribute to the whole work of art: detached from their background, they would lose their significance and might in isolation even be ugly; in context, they can themselves be beautiful and make an essential contribution to the beauty and integrity of the whole.[9]

Everything human beings experience, every judgment, every object, every relation, becomes a mere Appearance. Appearances are not individual or independent substances. The only substance is the Absolute or Reality. Appearances are not substances because their being depends on something else—namely, of course, Reality. Although Appearances are real (in the sense that they belong to Reality), they are epistemologically deficient. Appearances are, however, not wholly real; they are real to the extent that they qualify Reality. Bradley says of Appearances that they are unreal and not real: so, for instance, causality and change are unreal; time and space are unreal; bodies are unreal, nature is unreal,[10] but relations are also unreal.[11] One can conclude that Appearances are both real and unreal.

The (amount of) Reality of Appearances is a matter of degree. This is to understand that human knowledge is always a matter of degree. Bradley conceives of our knowledge in terms of judgment or predication. No judgment is quite real; every judgment depends on something else. In his terminology: '[T]he condition of the assertion must not fall outside the judgement.'[12] We can try to include such conditions into the judgment, but we never succeed entirely. For example, take the judgment:

(1) This apple is red.

This judgment depends on many factors: on the meanings of its constituents, on the context of the deictic act of the speaker, and on other relevant factors. One can try to include all of this in the judgment:

(2) This apple is red where 'apple' means 'pomaceous fruit of the apple tree', 'red' means 'the color of blood', and I am referring to the object lying on the table in front of me.

Although this judgment is more accurate than the previous one, the problem remains. (2) depends on even more conditions than (1). Hence, we can never make (1) quite true.[13] The upshot is that 'in the end, no possible truth is quite true.'[14] Bradley dismisses traditional two-valued logic: every truth is one of degree. Of course, our everyday judgments can be said to be either true or false. The distinction between true and false is a matter of degree *in the end*. The adverbial term 'in the end' is used here in Bradley's idiosyncratic sense with respect to the Reality of a judgment. This view is sometimes called the doctrine of degrees of truth.

What is judgment for Bradley? Judgment cannot be identified with any linguistic entity like sentences. Judgment consists in taking an idea—a *mere* idea as Bradley puts it[15]—and saying that the idea is related to Reality. The *ultimate* subject of every judgment is Reality: 'All judgement [...] predicates its idea of the ultimate Reality.'[16] The idea is indicated by the grammatical subject and the predicate. Bradley calls the grammatical subject a 'special' or 'limited' subject.

In any judgment 'S is P' we are asserting, in fact, S(R)P, which is to read: '[In] Reality, being what it is, P can qualify S and together they both qualify the larger reality which is their condition.'[17] The content of a judgment always exceeds the content of its special subject. That is why no judgment can be wholly true. 'The judgement, as it stands, can therefore [...] be both affirmed and denied. It remains conditional and relative only.'[18] Every judgment, like (1) for instance, can be true in some context and false in another.

It is further important to make clear how Bradley understands the notion of truth. What is his theory of truth? We have seen that judgment (2) can be truer than judgment (1) (provided that there is indeed a red apple on my table). This is to understand that (2) is nearer to Reality than (1). In Bradley's idealist metaphysics there is, however, no room for any kind of correspondence. Appearance is not a pendant of Reality. A judgment is true to the extent that its special subject together with its special predicate is *identical* with its ultimate subject, which is Reality. This means that a judgment is true insomuch as it is identical to Reality. Bradley can be said to be an adherent of the identity theory of truth. Since no judgment is wholly true, no judgment is wholly identical with Reality. When a judgment is becoming truer, i.e., more identical with Reality, Reality then gradually swallows its character. The judgment disappears in Reality. It is like committing a 'happy suicide' as Bradley puts it.[19] Bradley's account of truth, thus, turns out to be ultimately eliminativist.[20]

After the nature of Appearances comes the definition of Reality-as-a-whole. Every attempt to characterize Reality is, however, condemned to fail because such an attempt has to be carried out within the framework of judgment.[21] Judgments, however, are Appearances which are abstractions from Reality. Reality transcends our intellect. But this is only a negative characterization. Bradley, however, strives for a positive account of Reality or the Absolute.

How can Bradley characterize Reality without using the framework of judgment? There is a kind of human experience which lies outside any judgment. Bradley calls this kind of experience 'feeling' or the 'feeling base': 'This Reality is present in, and is my feeling; and hence, to that extent, what I feel *is* the all-inclusive universe.'[22] The point is that feeling is free from any distinctions and relations.[23] Bradley goes on to argue that conceptual distinctions and, what is most important, relations are unreal in order to come to his most famous thesis, namely ontological monism: 'Reality is one.'[24] If relations belonged to Appearance only, the ultimate Reality would be a single and uniform whole. Bradley's argument for the unreality of relations (in Bradley's idiosyncratic sense) is the subject of the next section.

4.2 Bradley on relations

Bradley's published views on relations went through several changes or, more precisely, amendments over time. His account of relations in *Appearance and Reality* is, to say the least, obscure. The clearest account is to be found only in his posthumously published essay 'Relations,' though this had no impact on the debate over internal and external relations.[25] It is, therefore, no surprise that Russell and Moore misunderstood Bradley's views to some extent.

Bradley provided several arguments in favor of the unreality of relations. Only some of them make use of the distinction between internal and external relations.[26] Bradley's main argument for the unreality of relations proceeds in two steps: he argues that (i) external relations are unreal and (ii) internal relations are unreal. The conclusion is, then, that all relations are unreal. First, I am going to give an overview of Bradley's understanding of the internal/external distinction. Then I will provide a definition of external relations followed by an argument against their reality. Finally, I will present a definition of internal relations and an argument against their reality.

Bradley called relations external or internal[27] in at least two senses. In an informal sense, a relation is external to a judgment if it is not part of that selfsame judgment. An internal relation is, then, part of this judgment. 'Internal to' means in this sense 'to be part of' whereas 'external to' means 'not to be part of.'[28] These definitions include hardly any metaphysical significance. However, Bradley came up with a much deeper notion of internal and external relations than this.

The externality and internality of relations is for Bradley a matter of degree. A relation can be partly internal and partly external. A merely internal relation and a merely external relation are the limiting cases of a scale. Bradley's argument leads, however, to the conclusion that these limiting points are impossible: 'No relation is *merely* intrinsic or external, and every relation is both [of these].'[29] Here is Bradley's most explicit definition of an external relation:

> What should we mean [...] by a relation asserted as simply and barely external? We have here, I presume, to abstract so as to take terms and relations, all and each, as something which in and by itself is real independently.[30]

Bradley defines here a relation that is 'simply and barely external,' i.e., wholly external (and not internal at all). A relation is external if this relation and its terms are independently real. Let us take a relational fact *aRb*. Relation *R* is external if *R* and its terms *a* and *b* are independently real. We have to take the expression 'independently real' in Bradley's sense. How do we find out whether a thing is capable of existing independently of another thing? In a polemic note to Russell, Bradley proposes the following criterion:

> I am still in doubt as to the sense in which according to Mr. Russell relations are external. The terms are to contribute nothing, and so much I understand. But I still do not know whether Mr. Russell takes the relations apart from any terms to be thinkable.[31]

Hence, a thing that is capable of existing independently must be *thinkable* independently.[32] Relation *R* would be, thus, external if we were able to think of this relation *R* without relating its terms *a* and *b* and furthermore without these terms being related by *R*. In other words, we must be able to think of *a* and *b* as independent objects and to think of the relation *R* without relating it to any particular terms. In today's fashionable terminology, an external relation can be thought of as a case of *relatedness without relation*. Neither the relation nor the terms can do the task of relating. Neither of them can be thought of as the reason for the existence of the relational fact *aRb*:

> And we must, if so, assume that their coming or being together in fact, and as somehow actually in one, is due in no way to the particular characters of either the relations or the terms. [...] Undeniably the fact is somehow there, but in itself it remains irrational as admitting no question as to its 'how' or 'why'. Or, if you insist on a reason, that would have to be sought neither in the terms nor the relation, but in a third element once more independently real and neither affecting, nor again affected by, either the relation or the terms.[33]

This explanation already contains a germ of an argument against the possibility of external relations. This argument is known as Bradley's Regress Argument. The gist of the argument is as follows: suppose a relational fact *aRb* where *R* is an external relation. Making use of spatial metaphors, we can say that *R* must be something that exists between its terms. We may now wonder how *R* is connected to these terms or how *R* affects them. In order to explain this we have to postulate the new dyadic relations R_1 and R_2 as doing this job.[34] R_1 relates *a* and *R* and R_2 relates *R* and *b*. The original relational fact *aRb* is now decomposed into two relational facts aR_1R and RR_2b. Relations R_1 and R_2 are, however, external relations (for if they were not, *R* itself would not be a merely external relation). The original problem of explaining how a merely external relation can relate its terms still remains unsolved. It is clear that postulating other external relations runs into an endless regress.

There is another strategy for resisting this regress, however. Suppose that the terms *a* and *b* have different aspects and that some of these aspects are *not* essential to these terms. Let a_1 be an accidental aspect of *a*. It is thinkable that *a* lacks the aspect a_1 and so let us call this case *a'* (i.e., where *a* is deprived of a_1). The aspect a_1 can be compatible with relation *R*. The reason why *R* relates *a* can thus be explained by reference to a_1. Recall that this scenario is possible even though *R* is an external relation and *a* is an independent object. The same explanation can be presented with regard to the term *b*. Hence, the relational fact *aRb* can be explained by *a*'s aspect a_1 and *b*'s aspect b_1.

The price that we pay for this explanation is the disruption of the unity of the terms. Term *a* is now composed of *a'* and a_1. The aspect a_1 is, in fact, a relational property of *a*. Aspect a_1 becomes an external relation between *a'* and *R*. We have to ask now how *a'* is related to a_1. The regress is here again because *a*'s 'unity disappears, and its contents are dissipated in an endless process of distinction.'[35] This strategy thus transposes the original problem of explaining the relational fact *aRb* into the problem of explaining the unity of the terms.[36]

What are the conclusions of Bradley's Regress Argument? The argument shows *prima facie* that wholly external relations are self-contradictory and thus impossible. What about relations which are partly external and partly internal? Although such relations are not wholly contradictory, they contain a contradiction. This means, however, that they are unreal, i.e., they belong to Appearance. And finally, does this argument lead to the doctrine of internal relations? It depends how we understand this doctrine. If the doctrine says that all relations are *merely* internal, then the argument yields no such conclusion. If, however, what is meant by the doctrine is that all relations (if there were any) must be partly internal, we can then accept this conclusion.

In order to prove the unreality of all relations, Bradley still has to show that there are no merely internal relations. The definition of internal relation is as follows:

> Relations would be merely internal if, the terms being taken as real independently, each in itself, the relations between them (as a class, or in this or that particular case) in fact arose or were due merely to the character of the terms as so taken.[37]

Two features of internal relations follow from this definition: first, internal relations (in contrast to external relations) cannot stand alone without relating to their terms. Bradley has stressed this feature again and again: an internal relation 'essentially penetrates the being of its terms' or must 'affect, and pass into, the being of its terms.'[38] There is no internal relatedness without relation. Second, an internal relation holds in virtue of the *character* of its terms. The character (or nature) of a term must be understood as *all* its non-relational properties.[39] We might further say that these terms together make up a systematic or genuine unity. A change of one term would modify the relation and the other term. On the one hand, the terms must be conceivable as different entities and, on the other hand, they are parts of a perfect unity. Internally related things can be described as a perfect 'identity-in-difference.'[40]

Let me proceed to Bradley's argument against merely internal relations. As we have already seen, Bradley employs spatial metaphors in order to characterize the relationship between relations and their terms. Although merely external relations are 'between' their terms, they fail to be 'together' with their terms on pain of falling into an infinite regress of postulating other relations. Internal relations show the opposite defect. They are 'together' with their terms. They fail, however, to be 'between' them. In Bradley's words:

> An actual relation [...] must possess at once both the characters of a 'together' and a 'between', and, failing either of these, is a relation no longer. Hence our terms cannot make a relation by passing themselves over into it bodily. For in that event their individuality, and with it the required 'between', would be lost. All that we could have left would be another form of experience, no longer relational, which qualifying directly our terms would have ceased to be terms.[41]

A wholly internal relation is wholly 'together' with its terms. Such an internal relation is supervenient on all the properties of its terms. The relation, thus, can have no other properties but those that are supervenient on the properties of its terms. This means, however, that a wholly internal relation is not 'between' its terms. Vallicella makes this point aptly: 'They [internal relations] are "between" their terms as *relations*, but not "between" their terms as *internal*.'[42] The problem is that if the terms stood in a wholly internal relation, we could not distinguish between them, i.e., they would lose their individuality. Then, however, if there were no distinct terms, there would be nothing to relate. The (originally binary) relation would become a property of the whole, consisting of both terms.[43]

Let me restate the point in a more formal way. As argued in the case of external relations, a relation must somehow be connected with its terms or at least some aspects of its terms. Let *aRb* be a relational fact and *R* an internal relation. Above, we considered the possibility of a case where *R* was an external relation that is compatible with *a*'s aspect a_1. In our present case, where *R* is an internal relation, the aspect a_1 must be comprised of the whole term *a*. The same holds for *b*'s aspect b_1. The relational fact *aRb* actually becomes a non-relational predication *R*(*ab*) or

(3) *ab* is *R*.

As we have seen in the previous section (p. 21), no predicative judgment can be wholly true. There is always an external condition on its truth. The judgment (3) always qualifies a part of Reality. The property R is external to the whole of ab, or in other words, ab is not wholly identical to R. The judgment (3) has to be restated as

(4) *ab* is an *R*.

And this judgment in fact has the form

(5) Reality is such that *ab* is an *R*.

What seems to be a perfect unity, a perfect system, or a perfect whole, is always an abstraction from a larger part of Reality. We can consider two examples of a systematic unity: a living organism and a perfect work of art. We may presume that a living organism exhibits a significant degree of systematic unity. Each part of the organism has a function within the whole and each part depends on each other part. An analogous consideration may be applied to a great work of art. Each part (tone, brushstroke, syllable, and so on) fits together with other parts and with the whole. There is nothing superfluous. But no living organism is thinkable entirely outside its environment or biotope; and no work of art can be taken as such outside of its society and culture.[44] Hence, if one claims that this is a living organism or that is a great work of art, these judgments always qualify a larger part of reality which is not expressed in the surface form (4) of these judgments. There is always an external condition, e.g., the environment or culture. Every living organism is only a living organism within its environment; every work of art is only a work of art within its culture.[45]

The conclusion is that wholly internal relations are impossible, for judgments expressing them cannot avoid external conditions. We may be tempted to think of Reality as a perfectly internally related system, as a perfect identity-in-difference. But then the terms of such relations would have to be independent substances which would be opposed to these relations. These oppositions are, however, abstract differences that cannot be wholly true. Bradley can conclude, therefore, that '"internal" relations, though truer by far than external, are, in my opinion, not true in the end.'[46] Merely internal as well as merely external relations are self-contradictory. Every relation is both internal and external[47] and belongs to Appearance. In other words, all relations are unreal.

In the remainder of this section, I want to focus on the issue of what the terms of relations in question are, or more precisely, what kinds of terms are supposed to be related here. Do we speak about relations between particulars (objects, things, and so on) or between universals (concepts)? Bradley is sometimes unclear concerning the nature of related terms when he is speaking, for instance, about the relation between practice and life, desire and will, imagination and play, or humanity and the universe. These examples suggest that relations between universals are his main focus. However, Bradley speaks of relations between things or objects, especially when the internal/external distinction is employed.[48]

We have to realize that if the unreality of relations should result in ontological monism, i.e., in the view that Reality is one, then the term must be realities, at least *prima facie*. The view that Reality is one can be taken negatively as meaning that Reality is not made up of particular building blocks (atoms, objects, things, and so on). We are interested in the purported relations between these building blocks.

Furthermore, if one accepted Bradley's arguments that merely internal and merely external relations are self-contradictory, then one could not give any examples of such relations. All examples would then be negative examples of relations that are *not* merely internal or external.[49] It is surprising, then, that some commentators of Bradley's works have offered plenty of examples of internal relations. So Wollheim, for instance, says that 'the relation "being married to someone" is internal to him [a husband]. Similarly the relation of being disloyal to one's country is internal to a traitor.'[50] In a similar manner, Pears claims that

> A relation is internal if the proposition attributing it to an individual is true *a priori*. [...] [T]he proposition that a particular husband is married, or a particular wife is married, is true *a priori*, because it is guaranteed by definition.[51]

To reduce internal relations to *a priori* truths or to truths that are guaranteed by definition is an *ignoratio* to Bradley's arguments.[52] Truths by definition are conceptual truths. Internal relations would hold, then, between concepts, e.g., between the concepts of husband and wife. As we have seen above, even such seemingly internal relations cannot escape external conditions and, thus, are both internal and external.

Do, then, the relations under consideration hold between particulars? Some authors have interpreted Bradley's writings in this way with some textual support.[53] If this were so, how could we account for Bradley's example of a relation between red-hairedness and a red-haired man? Red-hairedness is a universal property and if we insisted on its particularity, we would be forced to accept something like the *trope theory*, which postulates concrete properties.[54] Even though this line of argument is not wholly unpromising, there is, I think, a less complicated and simpler explanation available.

As indicated at the beginning of this chapter, the distinction between concepts and objects is not an either-or choice in the idealist framework. As Appearances, concepts as well as objects are abstractions from Reality. That is to say: Reality unites concepts with objects. In Bradley's words: 'The immanent Reality, both harmonious and all-comprehending, demands the union of both its characters in the object.'[55] An object's character, as we already know, is comprised of all properties of the object. A character abstracted from the object can be taken, then, as a concept. At any rate, objects are continuous with concepts. To put it another way, the distinction between objects and concepts is a matter of Appearance. As argued above, relations are Appearances, but their terms are Appearances too. They are all 'abstractions and mere ideal constructions.'[56] Every term is, in Bradley's system, always partly an object and partly a concept, and these parts are connected.

By having an entity which is always continuously between an object and a concept, we can abstract away an object, leaving a concept (or rather a part of the object's character), and we get a term of an internal relation. Such a relation is, however, internal to a certain degree; it is, at best, more internal than external. If we abstracted away a great deal of the object's character, we would get an abstract object that can be a term of an external relation. Once again, such a relation would only be more external than internal, for we cannot abstract from the character completely. All these examples of 'conceptual' relations given by Wollheim and Pears are, thus, examples of relations that are internal rather than external.

I have discussed the issue of the nature of terms in detail, since this becomes central for Wittgenstein. The distinction between concepts and objects is available to him (although with some reservations in the *Tractatus*). In his later works, the nature of related terms determines the internality or externality of a relation. Conceptual relations are internal, while external relations hold between objects.[57]

5

Russell and Moore

Both Russell and Moore offered several arguments against the views and doctrines involving internal relations that they (more or less justifiably) attributed primarily to the idealists and to Bradley. By rejecting these doctrines, they introduced their own claims, mostly involving external relations. This rough description may give the impression that one side favored internal relations over external relations and the other side the other way around. The nature of their disagreement is, however, more complex.

5.1 Arguments against internal relations

We have to clarify what exactly Russell and Moore are arguing against. What are the claims they attribute to the idealists' camp and which they then subject to analysis in turn? Russell and Moore attribute to their opponents the so-called axiom (or doctrine or dogma) of internal relations. This is how Russell formulates the axiom: 'Every relation is grounded in the natures of the related terms.'[1] Let us suppose that Russell and Bradley more or less agree in their definitions of internality or, at least, that their definitions are compatible.[2] The axiom of internal relations thus reads:

(6) Every relation is internal.

As we have seen above in §4.2, the internality of a relation is a matter of degree for Bradley. This axiom can mean either

(7) Every relation is *merely* internal (i.e., not external at all).

or it can mean

(8) Every relation is internal *to some degree* (i.e., not entirely external).

Only the latter, weaker claim can be attributed to Bradley; moreover, it is only an intermediate claim in his proof of the unreality of all relations. But neither Russell nor Moore really noticed that internality is a matter of degree and, hence, they could not distinguish between (7) and (8). For them, a relation is either internal or external.[3] This is a serious flaw in their discussion. Russell and Moore actually provide arguments against (7), as we are going to see. Then, however, they draw their conclusions as if they have provided arguments against (8). They imply that some or even all relations are merely external.

Let us now move to Russell's and Moore's arguments in more detail. The first argument was elaborated by Russell primarily in *The Principles of Mathematics*. As we saw in §4.2, an internal relation can be reduced to a property of the whole of all its terms.[4] Hence, an internal relation *R* that holds between *a* and *b* can also be reduced to the property *R'* of the whole of *ab*. The relational fact *aRb* is, then, equivalent to the subject-predicate fact *R'*(*ab*).[5] The whole (*ab*) is, however, equivalent to (*ba*).[6] As Russell puts it: '(*ab*) is symmetrical with regard to *a* and *b*, and thus the property of the whole will be exactly the same'[7] in the case of *aRb* as in the case of *bRa*. This means, however, that internal relations must be symmetrical. From the axiom of internal relations it follows, therefore, that all relations are symmetrical. Russell argues now that because there are—as a matter of fact—asymmetrical relations (like the relation of something being greater than something), the doctrine of internal relations hence cannot be true.

Russell's objection turns around the problem of explaining the evident asymmetry of some relations (given that the axiom of internal relations holds true). If we take the weaker reading of the axiom (8), there is an obvious way of explaining the asymmetry. On this reading, every relation may be partly internal and partly external and a relation gets its asymmetry due to its partial externality. Russell's objection holds only for relations that are wholly internal; and therefore he has to presuppose the stronger reading of the axiom of internal relations (7) in his argument. Furthermore, Russell's argument is in the end based on our commonsense conviction that there are asymmetrical relations like 'greater than.' Bradley would also admit that there are such relations, but they belong to Appearance only. He would hardly admit, however, that the axiom of internal relations (7) holds true for Appearances, i.e., that every relation is merely internal in Appearance.

As we saw in §4.1, the grammatical or apparent form of a judgment is, for Bradley, not equivalent to its real form. The ultimate subject of every judgment (subject-predicate or relational) is Reality-as-a-whole. The grammatical subject is only a *limited* or *special* subject and the grammatical predicate is only a *limited* predicate. Let us take the subject-predicate judgment 'Hugo is tall.' Its real form is expressed as 'Reality is such that Hugo is tall.' The same transposition can also be applied to the relational judgment:

(9) Hugo is taller than Guido.

which is in fact

(10) Reality is such that Hugo is *taller than Guido*.

This judgment is, however, different from

(11) Reality is such that Guido is *taller than Hugo*.

In other words, although the ultimate subject of every judgment is Reality, the difference between the limited subject and the limited predicate is preserved. The limited predicate of (10) is 'taller than Guido,' not 'Guido'; and the limited predicate of (11) is 'taller than Hugo.'[8] The reason why this is so is the (partial) externality of every judgment. No judgment is capable of a complete unification of its limited subject with its limited predicate and of this semi-unified whole with Reality. Hence, Bradley's account of judgment is able to handle asymmetrical relations in the same way as it is able to handle symmetrical relations.

Let us turn now to the next argument. The previous argument was based on the commonsense belief that there are asymmetrical relations. But Bradley's ultimate claim that there are, in the end, no relations would therefore be disproved by the existence of any relation (whether symmetrical or asymmetrical). If, as Russell says, 'the axiom of internal relations is equivalent to the assumption of ontological monism and to the denial that there are any relations,'[9] then the existence of any relation would refute Bradley's position. And Bradley is willing to admit this:

> Asymmetrical relations are said to disprove Monism, because Monism rests on simple inherence [i.e., predication] as the only way in which there is [any] ultimate reality.
>
> The argument, if right, is improperly limited – because *any* relations, *if so*, disprove Monism.
>
> But Monism does not rest on simple inherence as the one form of reality. It even (in my case) says that that form is unsatisfactory (see *Appearance*).

> In short, far from admitting that Monism requires that all truths can be interpreted as the predication of qualities of the whole, Monism with me contends that all predication, no matter what, is in the end untrue and in the end unreal [...].[10]

Bradley argues in *Appearance* and *Reality*[11] that relations presuppose qualities and *vice versa*. The subject-predicate form presupposes the relational form, namely a relation between the subject and the predicate. No commonsense belief can *prima facie* prove or disprove anything about Reality, because commonsense beliefs are about Appearances only. This argument can also be seen as a *reductio ad absurdum* of the previous argument that invoked asymmetrical relations.

What the disagreement is really about is the ontological status of relations, and not the way they appear to us. Relations played an important role in Russell's accounts of judgment and predication[12] at that time. Russell had proposed several theories aimed at explaining the unity of the proposition by invoking a binary relation between the other constituents of the proposition or a multiple relation between the other constituents and the judging mind. Here it is important that such a relation is a real constituent of the proposition among the other terms. If relations were unreal, Russell's binary or multiple relation theories of judgment would then be unsatisfactory. These theories would explain predication by referring to a relation which is not wholly real. Such a relation must be explained by something else. Something would therefore be missing in Russell's account if Bradley were right. The root of the disagreement between Russell and Bradley lies also in their general theories of judgment.

The third and last argument I shall now focus on is the most promising one in my eyes. The previous arguments focused on whole classes of relations (on asymmetrical relations or on all relations). This argument focuses on a single relation, namely the relation between a part and the whole. If the axiom of internal relations holds true, this relation must be internal as well.

The part-to-whole relation is, of course, an asymmetrical relation, i.e., it is different from the whole-to-part relation which is a typical example of an internal relation. A particular stamp collection, for example, would no longer be the same collection if some stamps were taken away from it. The inverse relation (part to whole) does not seem to be an internal one. A particular stamp remains the same stamp whether it is a part of a collection or not.[13]

Both Russell and Moore admit that the whole-to-part relation is internal: 'every relational property of the form "having *this* for a spatial part" is "internal" in our sense.'[14] They argue, however, that the opposite part-to-whole relation is not internal, but purely external. This position is, in fact, a fundamental feature of ontological atomism. Each object is what it is regardless of its placement among other objects. The nature of each object is independent of the relations it bears to other objects.

The argument aims to demonstrate that if a part were internally related to the whole, then the distinction between part and whole would collapse. Let me first state Russell's brief version of this argument:

> In a 'significant whole,' each part, since it involves the whole and every other part, is just as complex as the whole; the parts of a part, in turn, are just as complex as the part, and therefore just as complex as the whole. Since, moreover, the whole is constitutive of the nature of each part, just as much as each part is of the whole, we may say that the whole is part of each part. In these circumstances it becomes perfectly arbitrary to say that *a* is part of W rather than that W is part of *a*.[15]

If two objects were internally related, we could reconstruct the nature of one object from the nature of the other object.[16] If a part were internally related to a whole, this part would be as complex as the whole. Then, however, this part would contain the whole. The entire situation of a whole having parts would be unintelligible, which leads us to the conclusion that there is no complexity whatsoever.

Let me restate this argument in Moore's terms. He argues in §22 of the *Principia Ethica* that internal relations between a part and the whole are unintelligible. Suppose there were an organic whole whose parts would not be what they are but for the existence of the whole. These parts would also be internally related to the whole. Moore argues that this situation is self-contradictory. The parts of such a whole cannot be distinct objects of thought. For if we tried to name a part of the whole *W* by a predicate *a*, the whole would figure in the definition of this predicate. When we assert that something is *a*, we could also assert that the same thing is *W*. This means, however, that *W* is a part of *a*. This is contradictory unless *W* is identical with *a*. This implies that we cannot successfully assign a name to an internal part of a whole.

I think that this is by far the best argument that Moore and Russell offered against internal relations. Moreover, I think that Bradley and the other idealists would accept this line of argument and echoes of it can be found in

Wittgenstein's *Tractatus* as well as in his principle that internal relations can only be shown, but not said (the *doctrine of showing*). Moore concludes from this argument that the part-to-whole relation must be external. Furthermore, I maintain that the argument is valid not only for the part-to-whole relation, but for a large class of internal relations between objects. This argument does not affect those internal relations that are analytic in the sense that they hold in virtue of being in language. That is also the case for the whole-to-part relation, which is internal in spite of this argument. This argument nevertheless allows for the important conclusion that all relations *between objects* are external. This is the doctrine of external relations.

Moore concluded his extreme pluralism from this argument against the intelligibility of internal relations. This argument is, however, a double-edged sword. External relations are, for Bradley, not an alternative to internal relations. External relations are even more unintelligible or unreal than internal ones, a view which Bradley supports by his Regress Argument.[17] Bradley's radical conclusion is that there are, in the end, no relations at all; and thus no distinct objects that could be related. The one and only object is Reality-as-a-whole. Hence, this third argument cannot help us to resolve the choice between pluralism and monism.

5.2 In favor of external relations

The rejection of the axiom of internal relations leads us to the opposite view that *there are some* external relations. And there is indeed enough textual support for this claim in Russell and Moore. Russell says, for instance, that

> *there are* such facts as that one object has a certain relation to another, and such facts cannot in general be reduced to, or inferred from, a fact about the one object only together with a fact about the other object only.[18]

Moore says quite explicitly that 'some relations are purely external'[19] and similar claims can be found in Russell too. I would like to focus now on a different claim that has often been ascribed[20] to Russell and Moore, namely the claim that

(12) *All* relations are (merely) external.

Russell, in his early paper 'The Classification of Relations' (1899), indeed wrote explicitly that 'all relations are external.'[21] But on a closer look at his argument, we see that he derives this claim from the irreducibility of relations to pairs of predicates of their terms. No relation *a*R*b* is, for Russell, reducible to the pair of predicates α(*a*) and β(*b*). This is so because every relation presupposes the relations of diversity between their terms. Such a pair of predicative statements cannot guarantee that the terms *a* and *b* would be distinct.[22] Russell stresses that he is retaining Bradley's phrasing in describing his view that all relations are external. If so, however, then from this argument it follows only that there are no relations which are purely internal or that all relations are partly external. We have here an instance of the first argument against internal relations that has already been presented in the previous section. Russell only denies (7) by his argument, but he continues his argument as if he has denied (8).

The general claim (12) must be taken with additional qualifications. According to Bradley, Russell 'defends a strict pluralism, for which nothing is admissible beyond simple terms and external relations.'[23] Russell protests, however, that this is not what he himself means by the doctrine of external relations. He derives this internal/external distinction from the notion of reducibility, as we saw above. However, he says, even within the same text (*The Philosophy of Logical Atomism*), that

> Particulars [belong to] an inventory of the world, that each of them stands entirely alone and is completely self-subsistent. It has the sort of self-subsistence that used to belong to substance, except that it usually only persists through a very short time, so far as our experience goes. That is to say, each particular that there is in the world does not in any way logically depend upon any other particular.[24]

This quotation may give rise to the impression that there are only mutually independent particulars. These particulars are simples. Any complexity is to be located in complexes, i.e., in facts. If so, no internal relations between simples would be admissible and hence all relations between simples would be external. Russell is indeed committed to this doctrine. This doctrine is, however, restricted to relations between simples (let us call this the *restricted* doctrine of external relations as opposed to the *unrestricted* doctrine mentioned above). Relations between complexes and facts[25] are not affected by this doctrine. For instance, the relation between a whole and its parts may still be internal in spite of the doctrine.

As we can see, the main motivation for the ascription of the doctrine that all relations are external lies in Russell's (and Moore's) general metaphysical insights rather than in their direct arguments. There is, furthermore, another general view that might motivate the unrestricted doctrine of external relations.

Let us proceed to the case of relations between propositions. Like Bradley, Moore and Russell held, at a particular stage of their thinking, that (true) propositions are identical with the facts they express. The identity of a fact is constituted solely by the fact itself. This view is sometimes labeled *the identity theory of truth*. If, however, there were no internal relations between objects, then there would be no internal relations between propositions. A fact could happen to be related to another fact; but this relation could not be constitutive of this very fact. The consequence is that the relation of logical entailment is also an external relation. But then Russell and Moore would be committed to the view that logical relations are accidental; propositions are what they are independently of the logical relations in which they stand. Although this view seems to be unpromising, let us try to make some sense of it.

This account, I would like to argue, does not imply that logical entailment is an external relation.[26] The restricted doctrine of external relations together with the identity theory of truth implies that all relations between propositions *that directly stand for facts* are external. But propositions that directly stand for (or are identical with) facts are just elementary propositions. Thus, Moore and Russell are committed to the view that all relations between elementary propositions are external.

This view does not, however, render logic external. Logic is, for Russell explicitly, about *complexes*—or *molecular propositions* which are actually identical with complexes. In his manuscript *Theory of Knowledge*, Russell writes: 'Belief in a molecular proposition gives what is most distinctive in the process of inferring.'[27] At least some relations between complexes or structures are clearly internal. Consider the whole-to-part relations which are obtained between a complex and its part (which may also be a complex as well). So, therefore, the relations of inference between $(p \vee q)$ and q can be taken as an instance of the whole-to-part relation. In §7.3 I am going to show that Wittgenstein fully developed this idea in the *Tractatus*.

To sum up the various doctrines of external relations that Russell and Moore are committed to:

(13) There are external relations.
(14) All relations *between simples* are external.
(15) All relations between elementary propositions are external.

In Chapter 7, I shall argue that Wittgenstein endorsed in the *Tractatus* the existential claim (13) and the universal claim (15). He, however, admitted that there might be internal relations between simple objects. (14) cannot, therefore, be attributed to Wittgenstein.

III

Wittgenstein's early writings

6

Definitions of the internal/external distinction in the early writings

The aim of this chapter is to investigate how Wittgenstein defines the distinction between internal and external relations in his early texts, i.e., his pre-Tractarian texts, and, of course, in the *Tractatus* itself. We have to make clear how Wittgenstein defines this distinction before it can be employed to explain or illuminate various problems. Hence, only remarks that may contribute to our understanding of the notion of internal and external relations are going to be addressed in this chapter. Remarks that employ the internal/external distinction in order to throw light on other problems will be addressed in subsequent chapters.

6.1 Pre-Tractarian texts

In Wittgenstein's earliest texts, the *Notes on Logic*, which he dictated to or elaborated with Russell, there is no occurrence of the internal/external distinction. The first occurrence is to be found in Wittgenstein's notes that he dictated to G. E. Moore in Norway in April 1914. Here is Wittgenstein's very first remark concerning the distinction:

> *Internal* relations are relations between types, which can't be expressed in propositions, but are all shewn in the symbols themselves, and can be exhibited systematically in tautologies. Why we come to call them 'relations' is because logical propositions have an analogous relation to them, to that which properly relational propositions have to relations.[1]

Many ideas are expressed in this remark. Let us try to untangle them. The terms of internal relations are types of entities. This means that internal relations are relations holding between universals. Wittgenstein will stand by this feature of internal relations throughout his philosophical career and later it becomes even more important than it is in his early texts.[2]

A second idea is that internal relations cannot be expressed in propositions; they can only be shown in the notation of a logically adequate language (a kind of *Begriffsschrift*). The external/internal distinction is, thus, closely connected to the distinction between saying and showing from the outset. These two distinctions are, however, not identical. All internal relations can only be shown, but surely not everything that can be shown can be conceived of as a case of an internal relation. Or at the very least, it is not straightforwardly clear how to apply the internal/external distinction in ethics or to Wittgenstein's reflections about the sense of the world.

There is also a close connection here between internal relations and logical tautologies. Again, all internal relations can be transformed into tautologies. Internal relations share with logical tautologies their strict necessity. Moreover, the holding of an internal relation can be proven systematically just as logical tautologies can be deduced from axioms. So, if proposition p is related to proposition q by an internal relation R, there must be a systematic way of transforming p into q. In other words, there must be a formal operation O that transforms p into q so that $O(p) \leftrightarrow q$ is a tautology.

Internal relations are opposed to proper relations which can be expressed by means of a proposition. Internal relations are (somehow) improper; whereas external relations are relations of a proper nature. The external relation that, for example, Wittgenstein admired Frege can be *expressed* in a (proper, i.e., empirical) proposition 'Wittgenstein admired Frege.' This is analogous to an internal relation being *shown* in a logical proposition, i.e., in a tautology. In De Morgan's law $\neg(P \wedge Q) \leftrightarrow \neg P \vee \neg Q$, for instance, the internal relation between $\neg(P \wedge Q)$ and $\neg P \vee \neg Q$ (where P and Q are propositions) is shown. The systematic operation of transforming one of these expressions into the other occurs here.

Wittgenstein insists that internal relations hold among universals. This is, however, often obscured by his mode of expression. Consider the following remark: 'The agreement of two complexes is obviously internal and for that reason cannot be expressed but can only be shewn.'[3] Taken literally, this remark makes the claim for an internal relation between two complexes, including complexes of particular things. This would, however, be a misunderstanding. Two complexes agree on two conditions: they have the same structure and their simple parts mutually agree. To have the same structure is tantamount to having the same form. Hence, there must be agreement between the forms of the complexes, which is something universal. The second condition amounts to identity between the concepts that describe the simple parts (identity is thus one case of an internal relation). This is so because two simple entities can be the same only in the sense that they fall under the same general concept. Hence, this remark can be read as claiming that an internal relation of identity holds between concepts, but it does not commit Wittgenstein to relations between objects.

This idea of internal agreement between complexes can now be extended to the idea of partial agreement. Wittgenstein says that: 'The proposition that is about a complex stands in an internal relation to the proposition about its component part.'[4] Following on from the elaboration in the previous chapter, this remark says that a description of the form of a complex stands in an internal relation to a description of the form of its part. In short, the form of a complex contains a form of its part. This is to say merely that a complex contains its part. We could also conclude that for Wittgenstein (and likewise for Moore[5]) the relation between a whole and its part is always an internal one. The internal agreement of two complexes is thus rendered as a special case of the whole-to-part relation.

Before moving any further, let us stop for a moment and illustrate how to transform this whole-to-part relation into a logical tautology. Let us suppose a complex consists of two parts *M* and *N*. This can be described as $(m \wedge n)$, where the proposition *m* stands for 'There is *M* here' and *n* for 'There is *N* here.' Here we have a tautology that $(m \wedge n) \rightarrow n$. To put this briefly, the fact that there are *M* and *N* here implies that there is *N* here.[6]

There is also another important essential feature of internal relations, namely that there are 'no hypothetical internal relations.'[7] Wittgenstein's explanation of this is as follows: 'If a structure is given and a structural relation to it, then there must be another structure with that relation to the first one. (This is involved in the nature of structural relations.).'[8] In the light of Wittgenstein's equating of internal relations with structural relations in the *Tractatus*,[9] we do not need to be disturbed by Wittgenstein's shifting terminology here. Internal relations are necessary in the sense that if there is one structure and an internal relation that relates this structure to another structure, there must *necessarily* be the other structure (or structures in the case of relations with more members). This means that the internal relation gives an unequivocal way of transforming the former structure into the latter one. In terms of formal operations, this feature means that if a structure *s* and an operation *O* are given, then there is an unequivocal way for this operation to be applied to the structure, i.e., it is possible to calculate $O(s)$ unequivocally.

Wittgenstein's account of the distinction between internal and external relations that has been outlined here is very sketchy. Fundamentally, it says only that internal relations express a sort of tautology that obtains between universals[10] and that one term can be transformed into the other by a formal operation. This account is incomplete for at least two reasons: it is restricted solely to binary relations and there is no specification for how to transform an internal relation into a logical tautology. This is supplemented in the *Tractatus* (or in those manuscripts from which the *Tractatus* was composed[11]).

6.2 The Tractatus

In the *Tractatus* Wittgenstein gives an explicit definition of the notion of an internal property:

> A property is internal if it is unthinkable that its object should not possess it.[12]

Wittgenstein supplies two addenda (in parentheses) to this definition. The first is an example of an internal relation:

> This shade of blue and that one stand, eo ipso, in the internal relation of lighter to darker. It is unthinkable that *these* two objects should not stand in this relation.[13]

The second addendum is:

> Here the shifting use of the word 'object' corresponds to the shifting use of the words 'property' and 'relation.'[14]

As in the previous section, we should not take this definition too literally in the sense that internal relations hold exclusively among Tractarian simple objects. The expression 'object' in the definition should be understood without any commitments as a term or a relatum. Next, the definition of internal property is suitable for defining internal relations too. Hence, a relation is internal if it is unthinkable that its objects (or terms, or relata) should not possess it.

Before examining this definition, let me say a few words about the example Wittgenstein gives. The internal relation between two color shades is paradigmatic for him. He repeatedly uses this example in his later texts, most prominently in his conversations with members of the Vienna Circle[15] or in his last manuscripts on colors.[16] The relata of this internal relation are neither concrete things that have these colors, nor expressions denoting these colors. We can take as an example two stones. One has a midnight-blue-colored surface, the other one is sky-blue. The relation of being darker between these two stones is an external one. It is thinkable that the color of the first stone may fade so that this stone will cease to be darker than the other stone. The same can be said of the relation between the expressions 'midnight-blue' and 'sky-blue.' These have concrete occurrences (as color patches) on the pages of this book, and it is thinkable that the color of some of these patches could fade. And finally, the lightness relation between the color shades 'midnight-blue' and 'sky-blue' is an internal one. The reason for this internality could be that, for instance, in the HSV color space sky-blue has a brightness of 92 percent, whereas midnight-blue has a brightness of 44 percent. It is unthinkable that 92 is less than 44. Note that no psychological considerations can be brought in as a counterexample here. If someone nevertheless insisted that midnight-blue is not darker than sky-blue, they must either understand some other colors under these terms, or understand the relation of being darker in some other sense, i.e., their intuitive notion of darkness and brightness would be different from that of the HSV color space. Internal relations can thus be exhibited in true mathematical statements and, at the end, in tautologies.[17]

The crucial notion in the definition used here is that of thinkability, or rather of unthinkability (Undenkbarkeit). We can rule out the psychological notion of thinkability which Wittgenstein certainly did not have in mind. There are (at least) two other ways to understand this notion. A straightforward reading would be that 'unthinkable' means 'impossible' or 'inconceivable.' A proposition is impossible if one cannot conceive or entertain this proposition. But there are no impossible propositions, so we cannot say of a proposition that it is impossible or unthinkable. What is meant here is rather this: every attempt to put certain signs together must fail. These signs cannot be assembled into a sign expressing a proposition, i.e., into a propositional sign. Hence, although we cannot say of a proposition that it is unthinkable, we can say of certain signs that when put together, they cannot express any proposition.

A relation is internal if it is impossible that its relata could not be related by this selfsame relation. This definition can be rephrased by saying that a relation is internal if it is necessary for its relata to stand in this relation. This is in agreement with the previous definition which states that internal relations can be systematically exhibited in tautologies. A not holding of an internal relation is just as unthinkable as it is unthinkable that a tautology is not true.

There is, however, a more technical understanding of the notion of thinkability. Wittgenstein says that '"A state of affairs is thinkable": what this means is that we can picture it to ourselves.'[18] Since no pictures are true *a priori*,[19] no tautologies are thinkable in this technical sense. If so, the notion of an internal relation would be self-contradictory, for internal relations are supposed not to be unthinkable, but as they cannot picture a state of affairs they are unthinkable as well.[20]

A possible way out is to show that Wittgenstein, strictly speaking, makes only the following claim: 'What is thinkable is possible too.'[21] We cannot, however, infer from this claim that what is necessary is unthinkable. Wittgenstein speaks of the thinkability of states of affairs and leaves open for now whether there are other realms of thinkability or unthinkability. The immediately following remarks, however, may shed light on this issue. Here we are going to delimit what cannot be thought: 'We cannot think anything unlogical.'[22] Something illogical is simply something which contradicts logical laws; and this is the same as claiming that a contradiction is true. And again, this delimitation does not touch upon the question of whether logical tautologies are thinkable or unthinkable. It would be strange, however, to claim that we cannot think or entertain both contradictions and tautologies. This interpretation is further supported by Wittgenstein's claim that 'Propositions can represent the whole of reality.'[23] Such propositions are, precisely, logical tautologies.

These considerations lead to the conclusion that Wittgenstein's own technical definitions of thinkability and unthinkability allow for tautologies being thinkable and contradictions being unthinkable. By the same token, internal relations can be located within the realm of the thinkable just as logical tautologies can—except that they touch the borderline between the thinkable and the unthinkable. Hence, the Tractarian definition of internal relation does not need to be rendered self-contradictory.

This definition of internal properties and relations occurs in the context in which Wittgenstein describes what propositions and reality have in common, and this is their *logical form*. But a proposition cannot represent its logical form. In order to be able to talk (in a certain sense) about logical forms (and about their parts, i.e., their formal properties), Wittgenstein introduces the saying/showing distinction and the closely connected external/internal distinction. Tractarian objects and states of affairs have formal properties just as (complex) facts have structural properties. These properties can be relational properties or they can be mutually related. Wittgenstein now stipulates that these properties and relations are internal:

> Instead of 'structural property' I also say 'internal property'; instead of 'structural relation', 'internal relation'.[24]

These terminological stipulations allow us to broaden the scope of inquiry. This talk of structural or formal properties and relations can be taken to be the same as talk of internal relations. So when Wittgenstein talks of, for instance, 'the structure of a picture,'[25] we can take him to be talking of the internal properties of (or internal relations within) a picture.[26] Another example is the remark from the *Notebooks* discussed a few pages above where Wittgenstein talks of 'the nature of structural relations.'[27]

Wittgenstein's definition of the internal/external distinction is supposed to match or follow the definitions given by the idealists on the one hand and by Russell and Moore on the other. This is clearly Wittgenstein's aim when he writes: 'I introduce these expressions in order to indicate the source of the confusion between internal relations and relations proper (external relations), which is very widespread among philosophers.'[28] We can surmise therefore that the confusion Wittgenstein had in mind was the obscuring of the internal/external distinction in the surface grammar of our natural language. Nevertheless, several remarks later he writes: 'Here we have the answer to the vexed question "whether all relations are internal or external." '[29] Wittgenstein is, of course, referring to the controversy about relations as examined in Chapters 4 and 5.

What is the answer Wittgenstein gives us exactly? The answer, which is spread over the remarks ranging from 4.122 to 4.1251, is that the obtaining of an internal relation cannot be expressed (or said or asserted) by means of propositions. The obtaining of internal relations can only be shown[30] in propositions that are concerned with the relevant relata. So Wittgenstein would side with Russell and Moore here that all relations are indeed external, but with the reservation that all relations *that can be expressed by a proposition* are external. He admits, however, contra Russell and Moore, that internal relations are nevertheless not nonsensical. They are part of the symbolism[31] of a logically adequate language and they are thus shown in such a symbolism.

What I have presented thus far is, of course, not a solution to the problem as to whether all relations are internal or external. I take it here that Wittgenstein is proposing a terminological stipulation that allows him to enter into conversation with his predecessors by subsuming the problem in question under his distinction between saying and showing. Any answer to the question whether there are internal relations at all, or what their status is, depends (in the

Wittgenstein of the *Tractatus*) on an understanding of the idea that something can be shown, but not said.

6.3 Summary

The following (though not necessarily independent) characteristics of internal relations can be found in Wittgenstein's early texts:

1 Internal relations are such that it is unthinkable (or impossible) that their relata do not possess them.
2 Internal relations hold between concepts or universals.
3 Internal relations can be exhibited in tautologies.
4 The identification of a term of an internal relation is, *eo ipso*, the identification of all other terms. This characteristic, of course, does not apply to internal properties.
5 The external/internal distinction is an instance of the more general saying/showing distinction.
6 Internal relations can also be labeled as structural or formal relations.

7

The doctrine of external relations

Like Russell and Moore, Wittgenstein was committed to the doctrine of external relations, but in a different sense than his mentors. Although he shared with Moore and Russell the view that all relations between elementary propositions are external, he also allowed for internal relations between propositions and simple objects. Moreover, he sided with Bradley on the issue of the unreality of all relations. Finally, I shall argue in this chapter that despite the doctrine of external relations, Wittgenstein conceives of logical entailment as being based on internal relations and, hence, as necessary.

7.1 Elimination of signs for relations

Wittgenstein would have accepted Moore's argument against the intelligibility of internal relations, which was discussed earlier in §5.1. Wittgenstein introduces the internal/external distinction 'in order to indicate the source of the confusion between internal relations and relations proper (external relations).'[1] This implies that internal relations are somehow improper for Wittgenstein.

I shall now argue that signs for relations cannot occur in fully analyzed propositions. One of the aims of the analysis proposed in the *Tractatus* is to eliminate any signs for relations. The immediate conclusion of this claim is that signs for relations are not names, and relations are not simple objects. One of the tenets of the picture theory is that relations between the elements of propositional signs signify relations between the elements of a signified fact. In the *Notes on Logic* Wittgenstein writes: 'Thus facts are symbolised by facts, or more correctly: that a certain thing is the case in the symbol says that a certain thing is the case in the world.'[2] By this remark we can understand that the symbolizing fact and the symbolized fact have to be in accordance. They have to contain the same combinations of things, where the things from the symbolizing fact (i.e., the names or signs for complexes) correspond to the things from the symbolized fact. This insight—surely quite revolutionary—is sometimes called the *symbolic* or *linguistic turn*. At this point, it is important to say that relations within the symbolizing fact express relations within the symbolized fact. The picturing relationship is a relation between facts.

This remark from the *Notes* is further developed in the *Tractatus* at 3.14s where Wittgenstein argues that '[a] propositional sign is a fact.'[3] Relations between things should be signified by spatial relations between the elements of a propositional sign: 'the spatial arrangement of these things will express the sense of the proposition.'[4] Hence, propositional signs are capable of representing relations by their spatial structure, i.e., by the spatial arrangement of their elements—in a logically adequate notation.

The key remark, which expresses Wittgenstein's eliminavistic strategy, then immediately follows:

> Instead of, 'The complex sign "*aRb*" says that *a* stands to *b* in the relation *R*', we ought to put, 'That "*a*" stands to "*b*" in a certain relation says that *aRb*.'[5]

Let us assume for a moment that the signs '*a*' and '*b*' stand for simple objects, i.e., that they are names. In this case, then, a sign for a relation is contrasted with a sign for an object. I take it here that Wittgenstein is proposing a refinement to our mode of expression. It is inadequate to analyze the complex sign '*aRb*' into its simple parts '*a*,' '*b*,' and '*R*.' The sign for the relation '*R*' should now be eliminated from our notation or should disappear in the process of analysis. That which in a logically inadequate notation is signified by *aRb*, should be signified in a logically adequate notation by a certain concatenation of the names '*a*' and '*b*.' This specific relation is signified by a spatial arrangement of '*a*' and '*b*' within the propositional sign.

The relation between '*a*' and '*b*' is a structural relation within the propositional sign. 'Structural relation' is synonymous for Wittgenstein with 'internal relation.' The sign for relation *R*, which might have been an internal or an external relation, has to be eliminated in favor of an internal relation within the signifying fact. Wittgenstein expresses exactly this idea in one of his conversations with Waismann. Wittgenstein says there that external relations give us only incomplete descriptions of a situation and then goes on to say:

> If we describe the state of affairs completely, the external relation disappears. But we must not believe that there is then any relation left. Apart from the internal relation between forms that always obtains, no relation need occur in

> the description, and this shows that in fact *relational form* is nothing essential; it does not depict anything.[6]

This is no argument against the intelligibility of relations, though. Wittgenstein maintains, however, that signs for relations can be eliminated in logical analysis and are therefore not necessary in a logically adequate notation. Then, however, according to Wittgenstein's version of Occam's maxim, if a sign is not being used, it is meaningless.[7] No sign for relations is used in a logically perfect language. Therefore, signs for relations are meaningless in such a language.

In order to complete the argument that relations cannot be the constituents of facts along with objects, we need to show that internal relations cannot be named, i.e., that there are no names for internal relations. This insight is tantamount to the earlier claim by Wittgenstein that there is 'no name which is the name of a form.'[8] We have to realize that a name of a logical form would be a logical constant. This claim is, hence, a part of the meaning of Wittgenstein's *fundamental idea* that there are no logical constants.[9] I follow Gregory Landini here in equating this fundamental idea with the *doctrine of showing*.[10] What arguments could Wittgenstein offer in favor of these fundamental claims or doctrines?

The doctrine of showing is, however, not a philosophical thesis. It is, rather, a sort of guiding philosophical principle which is related to Frege's distinction between concept and object, or between unsaturated and saturated expressions. The claim that there cannot be any name of a logical form can be taken as the claim that no saturated expression can refer to something unsaturated since a logical form is always unsaturated.[11] We can even move on to identifying the notions of a logical constant and of an internal property and relation.[12]

Neither external nor internal relations can be named in a logically adequate language. The conclusion of this complex argument is that relations cannot be the constituents of facts. They are not a part of the substance of the world and thus are not real. Wittgenstein can be regarded as siding with Bradley. Relations are unreal for Bradley in the sense that they are not real substances. They are not independent entities; their truth (i.e., whether they are real) depends on something else. They are, thus, not wholly true. For Wittgenstein, relations are unreal in the sense that they are not part of the substance of the world.[13]

There is a long and as yet unresolved dispute concerning whether Tractarian objects include relations. As noted above, I take the argument just presented as evidence that relations cannot be Tractarian objects. All Tractarian objects are, hence, exclusively particulars.[14]

7.2 All relations between states of affairs are external

One of the most important doctrines endorsed in the *Tractatus* is that elementary propositions are logically independent of each other. At 5.134 Wittgenstein writes: 'One elementary proposition cannot be deduced from another.' The justification for this is that there are no logical relations between two situations.[15] Wittgenstein gives a more accurate expression of this independence at 2.062, where he claims that the existence (or non-existence) of one state of affairs (i.e., an atomic fact) is independent from the existence (or non-existence) of another. So given that one state of affairs exists, it is thinkable (conceivable) that another state of affairs exists and it is also thinkable that it does not exist.

An internal relation relates terms that we cannot even conceive of not being related by this very relation. If two things are internally related, it is unthinkable that one of these things exists and the other does not. The existence of internally related things is not independent. But states of affairs are independent in precisely this way. Therefore, they cannot be internally related. There can be no internal relations between states of affairs; to put it another way, all relations *between states of affairs* are external.

Wittgenstein does not give any further justification for his doctrine of external relations. As is well known, Wittgenstein abandoned this view in his 1929 paper 'Some Remarks on Logical Form.' However, several attempts have been made by commentators to justify Wittgenstein's commitment to this doctrine. As we saw in §5.2, Russell and Moore were committed to this doctrine too. Landini provides a detailed argument showing that Wittgenstein arrived at this doctrine by the study of Russell's 'recursive correspondence theory [of truth] according to which only "atomic" facts (as it were) are truth-makers.'[16] M. McGinn argues that

> the demand for the independence of elementary propositions arises out of Wittgenstein's conviction that propositional logic is the essence of all representation as such.[17]

This is, of course, a conviction that Wittgenstein shared with Frege and Russell. If logic and, in particular, logical inference are essentially about complex propositions—as I shall argue below—then elementary propositions, which lack any structure from the point of view of the propositional calculus, must be logically independent. And finally, Michael Kremer argues that the logical independence of elementary propositions is related to Wittgenstein's view that names stand for simple objects.[18]

I do not disagree with these arguments. Wittgenstein was surely inspired by Russell in this respect; and the logical independence of elementary propositions is interconnected with other Tractarian insights as well. I shall follow Kremer and M. McGinn and provide a text-immanent justification of this doctrine from within the *Tractatus*. Suppose we have two states of affairs that are not logically independent. Suppose furthermore that these two states of affairs are combinations of the simple objects *abc* and *cd*. Then, however, one could ask what leads us to think that '*abc*' and '*cd*' are elementary propositions. The dependence of these two states of affairs has to stem from the combinatorial properties of their components, i.e., from the forms of the objects they are composed of. For instance, *abc* implies *cd* because the form of *c* is such that *c* must be combined with *d*. If this were so, any analysis of a complex proposition into a truth-function of elementary propositions '*abc*' and '*cd*' would be flawed. The correct analysis of the situation in question would be that it consists of a state of affairs *abcd*, not of two states of affairs *abc* and *cd*. The logical relation (the implication, for instance) between '*abc*' and '*cd*' has to be incorporated into the elementary proposition '*abcd*.'[19]

The existence of two elementary propositions that are not logically independent indicates that there is something wrong with our analysis. Either one or both are complex propositions and they then need to be further analyzed into their elementary components. Or their dependence lies in the forms of the objects they describe and in such a case they are combined into a single elementary proposition.

The conclusion to this is that presumptive elementary propositions that are not logically independent are not elementary propositions at all. The justification for the doctrine of external relations between states of affairs or elementary propositions is, in my view, terminological. Elementary propositions and states of affairs, which are asserted by elementary propositions, are externally related, because these notions are so defined.

7.3 Logical relations are internal

We now proceed to the relation of logical entailment and logical necessity in general. In claiming that all relations are external, Moore makes one important exception: the one relation that he takes to be internal is the previously mentioned whole-to-part relation.[20] This internal relation is crucial to the method of philosophical analysis which aims to explain a complex whole in terms of its parts. Since (due to the doctrine of external relations) a complex is no more than a concatenation of its parts, nothing gets lost in the process of analysis. Thus, just as Wittgenstein allows for the elimination of the relation *R* in 3.1432, the sign for the complex which relates its parts together may be eliminated here.

I now want to argue for something which Moore merely suggests, which Russell more or less endorsed in the *Theory of Knowledge* manuscript, but which is only fully developed in the *Tractatus*. The main idea is that (propositional) logic is concerned with molecular propositions. More specifically, logic is concerned with the forms of molecular propositions and the relations between these forms which are, of course, internal. Although Moore has not really succeeded in explaining the nature of logical necessity,[21] I believe this explanation would have been available to him too.[22]

First, Wittgenstein conceived of the method of analysis as described above. At TLP 2.0201 he writes that a statement about a complex can be decomposed into a statement about its parts together with a proposition describing the complex. We must not confuse the original unanalyzed proposition about the complex with the proposition describing the form of the complex which comes out in the process of analysis. Wittgenstein says at TLP 3.24 that 'A proposition about a complex stands in an internal relation to a proposition about a constituent of the complex.' The proposition about a complex is, of course, the original unanalyzed proposition. This proposition stands in an internal relation to an elementary proposition that it contains. This internal relation, which holds among the parts of a complex, is the proposition that describes the form of the way the parts are related together. The relation between a complex and its parts is, therefore, the internal relation that (propositional) logic is concerned with. Logic is concerned with the forms of propositions. In an adequate logical notation, the sign for the complex, which aims at describing the form of the complex, should be resolved or eliminated. The form of a molecular proposition should then be clear from the proposition itself.

At TLP 5.47 Wittgenstein introduces his slightly complicated reasoning about molecular propositions: the only way to construct molecular propositions is by applying a function to an argument. This, however, involves all of the logical constants.[23] This is what all propositions have in common with each other and this is the general form of the proposition. The general form of the proposition is, therefore, the form of the construction of a (molecular) proposition. The general form of the proposition is the only general primitive sign that logic deals with.

To put all of these considerations together now: logic deals with the general form of a proposition which expresses, in effect, a form of how logical operations are applied to elementary propositions. This means that logical space (i.e., a space of all possible propositions) is delimited by the general form of the proposition. Although there are no internal relations between elementary propositions, there could be molecular propositions that share the same form or the form of one proposition could be a part of the form of another.[24] Logical relations are, in fact, instances of the whole-to-part relation.[25] Thus, there could be internal relations that hold between molecular propositions. Necessary logical relations like entailment can be explained internally in just this way. The consequence of this is that logical relations can be read off the forms of propositions alone. Rules of inference are thus rendered superfluous.[26]

To conclude, Wittgenstein held in his early writings, like Moore and Russell, that all relations *between elementary propositions* are external. Following Moore and Russell, he took internal relations to be inexpressible by means of a proposition; but he sided with Bradley in conceiving of all relations, internal as well as external, as being unreal. Wittgenstein's conclusion was that relations should be built into our logical notation where they express or show themselves. Wittgenstein claimed he had resolved the question of whether all relations are internal or external.[27] The answer is that all the relations that can be expressed in a proposition are indeed external, and internal relations can be shown in a logically adequate notation. It is, perhaps, no accident that Wittgenstein first came up with his fundamental saying/showing distinction in the *Notes dictated to G. E. Moore* where the internal/external distinction's earliest occurrence is also to be found.

8

The nature of simple objects

Russell and Moore denied any internal relations *between both simple objects and atomic facts*. For Wittgenstein, however, objects are not independent in the sense that only[1] certain combinations of objects are possible in a state of affairs.[2] These possibilities and impossibilities lie in the objects themselves; and Wittgenstein calls this the form of independence and the form of dependence. This form is a part of the nature of an object.[3] To know an object, one must know all of its internal properties.[4] The internal properties which make up the form of an object are always relational properties, because they involve the possibility of being combined with other objects. The relation of being actually combined between two objects is an external one because it is thinkable that these two objects might not actually be combined. However, the opposite relation of not actually being combined might be an internal one if there were two objects that cannot be combined in a state of affairs. The conclusion of this argument is that Wittgenstein (unlike Russell and Moore) allows for internal relations between simple objects.[5]

Wittgenstein uses the metaphor of a *chain* to clarify this sort of dependence: 'In a state of affairs objects fit into one another like the links of a chain.'[6] How do we actually understand this metaphor? Objects are connected without any connecting relations—without any *glue*—as we know from the previous chapter. The links of a chain are connected without any further elements. Objects hang together in virtue of their formal (i.e., internal) properties. But still, it is not clear how these properties can be conceived. A natural suggestion might be that Tractarian objects are like Democritean atoms which have tiny hooks and barbs. Accordingly, the internal properties of the Tractarian objects would be based on, or derived from, their shapes. Some objects would fit together because their shapes are compatible and some would not. However, this view faces a serious objection: why should we take shapes to be internal properties and not external?[7] Saying that simple objects have hooks and barbs implies that they have spatial parts, which casts doubt upon the very idea of a simple object. Then, however, we are forced to take this explanation metaphorically. Simple objects have hooks in some metaphorical sense. But what is this sense? The metaphor of the chain has, then, merely been replaced by the metaphor of having hooks and barbs.

In what follows I would like to provide two different answers to these questions. According to the so-called metaphysical view, internal relations between simple objects lie in the objects themselves. They are *de re* necessary and our language (or a logically adequate language) should mirror these necessities. On the other hand, according to the so-called anti-metaphysical or resolute view, internal relations between simple objects emerge during logical analysis. They hold in virtue of language and are thus *de dicto*.

8.1 The *de re* view

This account of the internal properties of simple objects has been favored by adherents of the so-called traditional or metaphysical interpretation of the *Tractatus*. So Peter Hacker says: 'The logical (metaphysical) forms of states of affairs are language independent—*de re* possibilities do not depend upon our descriptions of them.'[8] The most vigorous advocate of this view is—in my view —Raymond Bradley[9] in his book *The Nature of All Being* (1992). He interpreted Wittgenstein's early philosophy as advancing a robust Leibnizian ontology of possible worlds with S5 modal logic. Here is the most explicit statement of Bradley's view concerning simple objects: 'the logical necessity which binds an internal property to its possessor is de re necessity.'[10] This idea is further developed:

> [T]he formal property of *combinatorial potential* [...] is 'essential' to (2.011), 'part of the nature of' (2.0123(2)), or 'internal' to (2.01231) its possessors. Hence it is a de re necessary modal property of all metaphysically simple objects.[11]

What does it mean exactly that internal properties of simple objects are *de re* modalities? We may follow Hacker in saying that these modalities are language independent. More precisely, the formal properties of combinatorial potential or powers of *metaphysically* simple objects are not derived from the combinatorial powers of names which correspond to these objects. It is in fact the other way around. The internal properties of names mirror the internal properties of simple objects.

The main motivation for this approach is to be found in the following remark from the *Notes Dictated to G. E. Moore*:

> Thus a language which *can* express everything *mirrors* certain properties of the world by these properties which it must have; and logical so-called propositions shew *in a systematic way* those properties.[12]

This claim is not just restricted to the internal properties of simple objects. The wording suggests, rather, that the claim is about the logical forms of states of affairs and the facts which determine the logical forms of logical propositions. This reading is further vindicated in the *Tractatus*, 4.121: 'Propositions cannot represent logical form: it is mirrored in them. [...] Propositions *show* the logical form of reality.' I think, however, that these claims imply that the internal properties of names[13] mirror the internal properties of simple objects. The essential, i.e., the internal properties of simple objects are their combinational powers within possible states of affairs.[14] It is obvious that the primary entities are states of affairs and that their constituents—simple objects—are derivative. The nature of the pictorial relationship now indicates that if logical propositions mirror the logical forms of facts, then the internal properties of names mirror the internal properties of simple objects.

Bradley finds three different meanings or rather 'shifting use[s]' for the term 'object' in the *Tractatus*. Wittgenstein introduces his shifting uses as follows: 'Here the shifting use of the word "object" corresponds to the shifting use of the words "property" and "relation."'[15] Bradley interprets this remark as concerning the respects in which an object is *simple*. In his reading, objects can be said to be simple in a metaphysical, semantic, and epistemic sense.[16] Objects are *metaphysically* simple if they are the ultimate constituents of the world. Wittgenstein says, for instance, that 'we feel that the WORLD must consist of elements.'[17] An object is *semantically* simple if '[*i*]*ts composition* becomes completely *indifferent*'[18] during logical analysis. The structure of the object does not affect any logical entailment. Here is Wittgenstein's example:

> from 'All men are mortal' and 'Socrates is a man' there follows [...] 'Socrates is mortal' which is obviously correct although I equally obviously do not know what structure is possessed by the thing Socrates or the property of mortality. Here they just function as simple objects.[19]

Obviously, the structure of an object may sometimes affect logical entailment and sometimes it does not need to. The same object may sometimes function as a simple and sometimes as a complex. The decisive factor here is how the object is described. Then, however, this notion of simplicity is *de dicto*.

According to the *epistemic* interpretation, simple objects are phenomenological items like points of a visual field. They are akin to Russell's objects of acquaintance. There is some textual evidence for this. Wittgenstein says, for example, that it seems to be possible that 'patches in our visual field are simple objects'[20] or '[w]hen we see that our visual field is complex we also see that it consists of *simpler* parts.'[21] The crucial question now is whether the epistemic notion of a simple object is more fundamental than the metaphysical or semantic one. If so, the decision concerning whether something is a simple object or a complex would be independent of their descriptions. This means, however, that the epistemic notion of simplicity is *de re*. I do not want to address all the arguments for the epistemic interpretation. I would like, rather, to point out that all the textual evidence allows that although some visual patches may be simples, other things may be simples too. This implies that the fundamental criterion of simplicity may be metaphysical or semantic. A visual patch, or more generally, an object of acquaintance is a simple if it is metaphysically simple or if it is referred to by a name.

Therefore, in conclusion, the textual evidence for the epistemic interpretation is very weak. The metaphysical interpretation, which renders the notion of simplicity to be *de re*, is more substantial. It is based, however, on remarks from the *Notebooks*. The most important expression of the metaphysical view comes from the early *Notes* which express a rather immature version of Wittgenstein's later views. Moreover, there are yet more arguments that disadvantage the metaphysical interpretation relative to the semantic one.

In the *Tractatus*, Wittgenstein says that the 'only necessity that exists is *logical* necessity.'[22] If there were any *de re* modalities, as the metaphysical interpretation suggests, logical necessity would include *de re* modalities too. Bradley is, then, forced to the claim that 'the logical necessity which binds an internal property to its possessor is de re necessity.'[23] But, as argued in §7.3, the main idea of the Tractarian logic is that propositional logic is concerned with molecular propositions. This main idea is in apparent tension or, rather, conflict with the idea that the *de re* possibilities of the combination of simple objects are *logical* possibilities. The fundamental idea of the *Tractatus* is that logical constants do not represent.[24] This idea can be taken as saying that there are no logical properties.[25] Bradley's account, thus, is incompatible with the fundamental Tractarian idea.

The metaphysical interpretation of simplicity features in the *de re* account of the internal properties of simple objects. Besides the *de re* internal properties, there are *de dicto* internal properties of complexes. In his later philosophy, Wittgenstein conceives of internal relations as being strictly *de dicto*. Moreover, he makes this insight into one of his main tools for the analysis of language. This metaphysical interpretation forces us to see a deep discontinuity in Wittgenstein's thinking. This puts it at a disadvantage in the light of the fact that there is another interpretation available that conceives internal properties of simple objects as *de dicto*. In the next section I shall provide evidence in favor of the semantic interpretation and the *de dicto* notion of simplicity.[26]

8.2 The *de dicto* view

The most convincing evidence for the *de dicto* account of simples is to be found in the *Notebooks* entries. Here Wittgenstein writes:

> we do not infer the existence of simple objects from the existence of particular simple objects, but rather know them—by description, as it were—as the end-product of analysis, by means of a process that leads to them.[27]

Simple objects are the references of names after some logical analysis has been carried out. What counts as a simple object is thus determined by the process of logical analysis. Such an analysis does not need to be completed in order to result *in a logically adequate language*. The metaphysical view tends to see simple objects as references of names in a logically adequate language (and a language is logically adequate if it mirrors, *inter alia*, the internal properties of metaphysically simple objects). The semantic or *de dicto* view sees the notion of simplicity relative to the actual process of logical analysis. To be simple is not a property of an entity; it is, rather, its function. Some objects can function as simples in the process of logical analysis: 'It functions as a simple object. (What does that mean?)'[28] The criterion of simplicity was mentioned earlier: 'Its *composition* becomes completely *indifferent*. It disappears from view.'[29] Hence, if the composition of a thing is not important at a certain stage of logical analysis, this thing only functions as a simple object at that stage. Thus, metaphysically complex objects, such as for instance a book or a man, can fulfill the role of a simple object.

Wittgenstein gave another criterion for the simplicity of the Tractarian objects in 1930:

> What I once called 'objects', simples, were simply what I could refer to without running the risk of their possible non-existence; i.e. that for which there is neither existence nor non-existence, and that means: what we can speak about *no matter what may be the case.*[30]

Objects are those parts of states of affairs that cannot but exist. Note that this specification of objects is *de dicto*. It says that an object is anything that fulfills a certain condition, *viz.* the condition that it necessarily exists.

Both the specifications of objects, i.e., that their composition is indifferent and that they cannot cease to exist, are equivalent if non-existence of a thing means its decomposition and separation into parts.

Even if its composition is indifferent, such an object nevertheless has internal properties (an internal nature) which are its powers of combining with other objects in a state of affairs. These properties are derived from the combinational powers of the name that refers to this object. Here is Wittgenstein's own example:

> This object is *simple for me*!
> If, e.g. I call some rod 'A', and a ball 'B', I can say that A is leaning against the wall, but not B. Here the internal nature of A and B comes into view.[31]

The objects A and B function as simples here while the relation of *leaning against* and the wall may be simple or complex. The internal natures of A and B are such that A can stand in the relation of *leaning against* to the wall whereas B cannot stand in that relation. Their internal properties are different with respect to that relation. Obviously, they also share certain internal properties, e.g., the combinational power to stand in the relation of *being near* the wall. It may now be argued[32] that the internal nature of simple objects is nevertheless grounded in the *de re* properties of these objects. B cannot be leaning against the wall, because of its round or symmetrical shape. But this is again a *de dicto* relationship between two concepts. Round objects in general cannot lean. This is due to the relationship between roundness and the relation of leaning against.

The notion of simplicity is relative to a certain process of analysis and this is—in my view—the true explanation for the shifting conception of simplicity as mentioned above. What is (treated as) a simple on one occasion may appear to be a complex on another occasion. This is tantamount to the claim that the composition of an object is sometimes indifferent and sometimes not. If the composition matters, then a description of such a complex has to be eliminated in favor of names referring to simple objects. Wittgenstein supplements his fundamental thought about these simple objects with the following claim: 'even if the name "N" vanishes on further analysis, still it indicates a *single common* thing [*Ein Gemeinsames*].'[33] 'Gemeinsames' can also be translated as 'conjoint' or even 'combined.' 'N' would refer to a complex. In the same vein, the sentence is ambiguous because 'Ein Gemeinsames' may apply to a thing (as the English translation suggests); it might, however, also apply to the name itself. On this reading, 'N' is then a name of multiple things; it is an indefinite description in Russell's sense.

I argued in §7.1 that the signs for relations should be eliminated in favor of internal relations within the signifying state of affairs in a logically adequate language. Now we see that signs for complexes should be eliminated too. All that remains after the final analysis are signs for simple objects, i.e., their names. Wittgenstein says, however, in several places that relations and predicates are objects too.[34] How does the account given here mesh with these claims?

My line of answer lies in the following consideration: we have to distinguish relations (and predicates) both *before* analysis and *after* analysis. At 3.1432 Wittgenstein considers the complex expression '*a*R*b*' and explicitly takes *R* to be a relation. This is, however, a sign for a relation in the language to be analyzed. But why is *R* a relation at all? What criterion is available to Wittgenstein here? In general, *R* is a relation because of the logico-syntactical grammar of this language (no semantics is involved here). As this language is not yet analyzed, logical categories of linguistic entities have to be determined *a priori*. This means that at this stage we can only employ preconceived criteria of categorization. What a relation is, is characterized essentially as its role in the combinational system of entities. We can employ here a Fregean criterion (that relations are unsaturated) or a Russellian criterion (that relations unify complexes).[35]

On both accounts, a sign for a relation is a complex sign that has to be eliminated in favor of internal relations within a signifying fact. Wittgenstein says now that even 'if the analysis were completely carried out, its result would have to be a proposition which once more contained names, relations, etc.'[36] Relations are, hence, among the constituents of elementary propositions in a completely analyzed language. Because the constituents of elementary propositions are names, some names express relations (and of course, some do not). There are, as it were, at least two logical kinds of names. And since names act as proxies for simple objects, there are also at least two logical kinds of simple objects—particulars and universals—in the logically adequate language.

The key question at this point is what resources we have to distinguish between these two classes of objects. We can rely only on the essential, which means the internal, properties of these objects. We can distinguish between classes of objects according to their combinational powers. Let me explain this with one example. Suppose we have a class *I* of objects that cannot be combined with each other:

(16) $I \equiv \{a, b, c, d, \ldots\}$

Accordingly, the combinations of these objects like *ab*, *ac*, *bd* are not admissible states of affairs. But there are admissible states of affairs consisting only of a single object from *I*. However, let us suppose there is another class *P* of objects that cannot be combined with each other but can nevertheless be combined with objects from *I*.

(17) $P \equiv \{p, q, r, s, \ldots\}$

Now, therefore, combinations like *pq*, *qs* are not admissible. There are, however, admissible states of affairs such as *pb*, *qa*, *sd*. Finally, let us suppose that a class *R* of objects can be combined only with two or more objects from *I*.

(18) $R \equiv \{\alpha, \beta, \gamma, \delta, \ldots\}$

Inadmissible combinations are now, for example, $\alpha\beta$, αp, αd, while admissible combinations can be αcd, βdb, γbcd, $\delta abcd$. Let me use bracketing to make this logically adequate language more surveyable, which is not vital for its logical function. Admissible states of affairs are now: a, c, $p(b)$, $q(a)$, $s(d)$, $\alpha(c,d)$, $\beta(d,b)$, $\gamma(b,c,d)$, $\delta(a,b,c,d)$.

I have only divided these simple objects into several classes according to their combinational properties. Based on these internal properties, we can treat objects from *I* as individuals, objects from *P* as predicates and objects from *R* as relations.[37] We can thus define what counts as an individual, a predicate (a property, a one-place relation) or a relation. An individual is an object such that it can make up a state of affairs by itself. A predicate is an object such that it can be combined with one other object in a state of affairs. A relation is an object such that it has to be combined with two or more other objects. Although some of these objects are predicates or relations, these objects are nevertheless still simple.

To conclude, the account given here is able to mesh with the following two claims by Wittgenstein: that relations have to be eliminated in the course of logical analysis, and that there can still be relations in fully analyzed sentences (i.e., there are relations among simple objects). What a relation in a language to be analyzed is has to be determined *a priori*. Such relations, then, are complex signs that have to be eliminated in favor of internal relations within states of affairs. What a relation in an analyzed language is is thus determined *a posteriori* by internal properties of simple objects.[38]

9

The picture theory

Wittgenstein famously writes in the *Tractatus*:

> A gramophone record, the musical idea, the written notes, and the sound waves, all stand to one another in the same *internal relation of depicting* that holds between language and the world.[1]

It is obvious that the comparison between language and pictures lies at the heart of the *Tractatus*. What is less obvious, though, is what the aim of this comparison is. What is the point of involving pictures in the *Tractatus*? Does Wittgenstein advance a picture *theory* of representation or meaning, or does he introduce a mere *analogy* between pictures and language? Resolute readers of the *Tractatus* tend to follow Wittgenstein's later retrospective comments and conceive of the involvement of pictures as a mere analogy.[2] Other scholars, however, ascribe to Wittgenstein some substantial claims about the essence of the proposition (and by implication of language and the world) 'which depicts the facts that it describes.'[3]

If internal relations occurred only in the context of a misunderstanding[4] and if they served only to overcome metaphysical claims about language and its relation to the world and thereby play only a purely transitional role, then it would be a mistake to ascribe to Wittgenstein the picture theory of meaning. In short: if internal relations do not possess any positive role, then neither does the picture theory, because it is articulated essentially in terms of an internal relation. So, for example, McManus says that '[a]scribing a "picture theory" of representation to the *Tractatus* is [...] a mistake anyway.'[5] Diamond similarly says:

> the so-called 'picture-theory' of the *Tractatus* is not merely something that fails to fulfill some supposed narrow *Tractatus* criterion of sensefulness. The picture-theory is a story about the relation between propositions and reality; it dissolves from within, since we cannot attempt to grasp what it supposedly conveys without using the relational forms of our language, but what we are being shown is that, used in the way we try to use them, they are empty.[6]

How does such an elucidation come about? Resolute readers take the picture theory as setting a *limitation*[7] on the combinational possibilities of names and elementary propositions, i.e., on their internal properties and relations. Let us restrict ourselves for now to names. Names are, supposedly, independent of each other in the sense that no combination is excluded. The picture theory sets a limitation which separates logical combinations of names from illogical ones. The logical form of the world determines that some combinations of names are logical and permissible while others are illogical and impermissible. But this view is, according to the resolute reading, mistaken. We cannot consistently say that there are any impossible combinations, but this is exactly what the idea of the internal relation of depicting between language and the world is trying to maintain. The role of the picture analogy is different. It helps us to see that according to the context principle, we failed to give meaning to some of the elements of the proposition in question.

> Thus, the picture analogy helps us to see that 'illogical combinations' [...] are problematic just because we haven't given those combinations any sense yet, any role to play in our systems of representation.[8]

This is fair point, but this does not imply that the picture theory is a mistake. An occurrence of 'illogical combinations' of signs indicates that the symbols they stand for do not have the same combinatorial powers as the objects they represent.[9] The picture theory says, *inter alia*, that the combinatorial powers of the corresponding elements must be the same. Obviously, we can arbitrarily combine signs as orthographical units. The point of introducing a logical syntax is so that if we know what a sign symbolizes, i.e., if we treat signs as symbols, illogical combinations are then excluded or, rather, cannot occur.[10] This means that illogical combinations of symbols cannot occur in a logically adequate language. The situation is, however, different in a (possibly logically inadequate) language that is to be analyzed. The point of introducing the picture theory of representation and hence the internal relation of depicting is, on my understanding, to improve the analyzed language in the direction of a logically adequate language. Properly speaking, the combinational powers of objects and names should thus be harmonized. In this sense, the internal relation of depicting then serves as a practical command, an imperative.

9.1 Levels of the pictorial relationship

The pictorial relationship has several distinct levels. Wittgenstein begins with the lowest level of names and objects: 'A name means an object.'[11] The next level consists of elementary propositions and states of affairs: 'The simplest kind of proposition, an elementary proposition, asserts the existence of a state of affairs.'[12] Possibly complex propositions, in turn, are pictures of reality.[13] On the uppermost level, there is the pictorial *internal relation* between language and the world.

The levels of each side of the pictorial relationship are bound by whole-to-part relations, which are, of course, internal. Here is the language side: 'An elementary proposition consists of names.'[14] 'A [possibly complex] proposition is a truth-function of elementary propositions.'[15] Language is the totality of all propositions.[16] The world side is as follows: 'A state of affairs (a state of things) is a combination of objects (things).'[17] 'What is the case—a fact—is the existence of states of affairs.'[18] Reality, a fact, is 'the existence and non-existence of states of affairs.'[19] And finally, '[t]he world is the totality of facts.'[20] Not all these levels are of the same modal status. Names are internally related to *actual* objects. Wittgenstein does not distinguish actual and possible objects. Objects are those entities that we may refer to without any risk of their possible non-existence.[21] Hence, there are no possible objects or names that can possibly refer to objects, i.e., no names that can be empty. On the other hand, elementary propositions depict *possible* states of affairs and complex propositions depict *possible* facts. There is a slight terminological problem with the uppermost level. Language should depict the totality of all possible states of affairs. But Wittgenstein defines the world as the 'totality of *existing* states of affairs.'[22] 'Existing' here means 'actual.' We should thus say rather that language depicts an imagined world [gedachte Welt],[23] for language can contain propositions that are not actually true, i.e., that depict a non-obtaining fact.

This hierarchy begs the question: which level is the most fundamental? Complex propositions are functionally dependent on elementary propositions, and therefore the level of complex propositions and their corresponding facts cannot be fundamental. The world is the mere totality of all mutually independent states of affairs; hence this level is also not fundamental. Only the level of names and objects or the level of elementary propositions and states of affairs can be considered to be fundamental. And indeed, we find both of these suggestions among commentators. Those commentators who tend towards the *de re* account of simple objects, as discussed above,[24] would consider the object level as the most fundamental one, whereas advocates of the *de dicto* account would prefer the level of elementary propositions and states of affairs.

The view that the level of names and objects is the most fundamental one finds some support in Wittgenstein's 1915 *Notebooks*: 'And if the general description of the world is like a stencil of the world, the names pin it to the world so that the world is wholly covered by it.'[25] Accordingly, Raymond Bradley claims that:

> The logically noncontingent features [of states of affairs] are functions of the internal (de re necessary, formal) properties of simple objects (how they *can* combine in possible states of affairs). The logically contingent features are functions of their external properties (how they *do* combine in possible states of affairs).[26]

In short, the internal properties of simple objects and their correlation with names determine the whole picturing relation. However, this view faces several objections. First, this account is inconsistent with the *context principle* which Wittgenstein endorses.[27] Names have meaning only in the context of a proposition. But if the level of names and objects were fundamental, i.e., if their connection determined the picturing relation, then names would possess meaning prior to their involvement in propositions. A name's meaning is the depicted object.[28] The second objection is that it is wholly mysterious how a connection between a name and an object can be established. There would have to be some kind of mechanism that injects meaning into signs and makes them into names. One might think here of something like baptism, or of a mental, though not psychological, mechanism as Hacker states:

> That such configurations, in thought or language, *actually represent* [...] is a function of the will, of the metaphysical self [...]. It is a mental act (albeit of a transcendental self, not of the self that is studied by psychology) that injects meaning or significance into signs, whether in thought or in language.[29]

The point is that if the connection between a name and an object is supposed to be an internal relation,[30] this connection cannot depend on any fact that results from this kind of injecting act. If there is the question of how the connection between a name and an object is established, then it is thinkable that they are not connected. If it is thinkable that two entities are not related, the relation in question is thus external. The upshot is, then, that if the level of names and objects were taken as fundamental, the picturing relationship would be an external relation.

As already said, those who prefer the *de dicto* account of simple objects would tend to prioritize the level of elementary propositions and states of affairs. But the *de dicto* view derives our knowledge of objects from our knowledge of names. And furthermore, names have meaning only in the context of a proposition. This implies that the preference for the level of elementary propositions and states of affairs leads to a further preference for the side of elementary propositions. Hence, the whole picturing relationship would be determined once we knew what the elementary propositions signify.

The picturing relation obtains between the propositional signs and *possible* states of affairs or, more generally, *possible* situations.[31] A propositional sign is *projected* onto a possible situation. Wittgenstein speaks of the method of projection in this context.[32] The whole consisting of a propositional sign and the method of projection both belong to a proposition.[33] A propositional sign (which is an existent state of affairs or even a complex situation) depicts a possible situation. Hence, the picturing relation obtains between two situations. There is no mysterious gap between language and the world. In short, one situation depicts another situation.

Let us look at Wittgenstein's analogy of gramophone records, musical notes, and waves of sound. The method of projection amounts to this: there is a certain general rule for transforming written signs into waves of sound and another rule for transforming grooves on a gramophone record into a musical score and so on. These laws of projection are, Wittgenstein advises us, like the rules of translation from one language into another. They belong to thoughts, which are propositions with sense, in other words, these laws are essentially constitutive of symbols. Consequently, a musical score does not show the slightest similarity with waves of sound if we do not understand it. And to understand a score amounts to knowing or possessing an appropriate method of projection. But we can *derive* the resulting waves of sound from the musical score by means of the projection method.[34] This derivation is akin to a mathematical operation. If we possess the score and the method of projection, we possess or, rather, we *could* imagine the waves of sound (and there are many different methods of projection—i.e., many different ways of interpreting a score). This shows that the relation of depicting is an internal relation.[35]

What, then, is constitutive of a possible (meaning: possibly non-existent in reality) state of affairs that is represented by a proposition? All we need is this same proposition. 'In a proposition a situation is, as it were, constructed by way of experiment [probeweise zusammengestellt].'[36] All thinkable facts are, thus, constructed from propositions. But if the logic of propositions 'deals with every possibility and all possibilities are its fact,'[37] all possible facts are thus constructed by propositions. What is thinkable is possible and what is possible is thinkable.[38] There are no possible facts that are not thinkable, i.e., that are not constructed by propositions. Possible facts are in a certain sense *contained* in propositions. Hence, there are no possible facts outside propositions. It is clear now why the relation of depicting is internal. A represented fact is nothing but a projected propositional sign.

Two problems or questions emerge at this point: The first is how to be sure that what can be represented by a proposition is also possible in reality. The second problem is how a represented fact attains reality. The first problem is this: if the level of elementary propositions is fundamental, how do we harmonize the level of names and objects? More precisely, how do we harmonize the combinatorial powers of names and objects? But it boils down to the question of how to analyze the elementary propositions (after we have analyzed complex propositions as truth-functions of logically independent elementary propositions). As discussed in §7.2, if names correspond to simple objects, elementary propositions must be logically independent of each other. If two seemingly atomic propositions happen not to be independent, some of their parts do not refer to simple objects (they may refer to complexes). This means that the combinatorial powers (i.e., internal properties) of these parts do not correspond to the combinatorial powers of simple objects. This consideration gives us a mere indication that the combinational powers of names do not conform to the combinational powers of simple objects.

The main indication that there is some kind of nonconformity between (the internal properties of) names and objects is given by the fact that we are able to express these internal properties and relations at all. By expressing an internal relation we are trying to express something that cannot be expressed in a logically adequate language. A language in which it is possible to express an internal relation is, thus, not logically adequate. §3 presents the general perspective that expressing an internal relation may be taken as an imperative to improve our language. Such an imperative invites us to improve the logic of our language. In this case, it invites us to coordinate the combinatorial powers of names and objects. It works like this: in an expression of an internal property, a *formal concept* must be employed that is combined with other names. In a logically adequate language, these names cannot be combined with formal concepts and all formal concepts have to be substituted by propositional variables. In Wittgenstein's words:

> The expression for a formal property is a feature of certain symbols.
>
> So the sign for the characteristics of a formal concept is a distinctive feature of all symbols whose meanings fall under the concept.
>
> So the expression for a formal concept is a propositional variable in which this distinctive feature alone is constant.[39]

Wittgenstein also proposes that the distinctive feature should be embodied in a propositional variable. Such a variable is a structured variable where some parts vary and some parts are constant. The distinctive feature corresponds, of course, to the constant part. Let me illustrate this point with an example of an internal relation between two shades of color:

(19) Midnight-blue is darker than sky-blue.[40]

This internal relation asserts a certain relation Φ between two properties Ω1 and Ω2. The expression

(20) $\Omega_1 \Phi \Omega_2$

should be analyzed into:

(21) $[\Omega_1 x.\ \Omega_2 y \supset x \Phi y]$.

This form is not, though, the final analysis. (21) is a propositional variable that ranges over propositions like

(22) $\Omega_1 a.\ \Omega_2 b \supset a \Phi b$,
$\Omega_1 b.\ \Omega_2 c \supset b \Phi c$,
$\Omega_1 a.\ \Omega_2 c \supset a \Phi c$,
...

where *a*, *b*, *c* are names. This analysis is, however, a neat illustration of adjusting the combinational powers of names by means of converting formal properties into propositional variables. Signs for the properties (Ω_1, Ω_2) can be followed only by signs for the objects (*a*, *b*, *c*). A sign for a relation Φ can occur only between the signs for objects, but not between the signs for properties as in (20). It is noteworthy to say that the sign Φ expresses an internal relation in (20), but an external relation in (21) and (22). In an unanalyzed language, the sign Φ may be ambiguous between expressing an internal and external relation. The aim of the analysis presented here is to cope with this ambiguity. The combinatorial powers of Φ are thus adjusted in such a way that the expressing of (20) is impossible.

The second problem concerning how a fact that is represented by a proposition can reach reality is the subject of the next section.

9.2 Language measures reality

Wittgenstein liked the analogy of comparing a proposition with a situation and measuring an object against a yardstick.[41] He writes: 'Proposition and situation are related to one another like the yardstick and the length to be measured.' Later in the *Notebooks*, he writes: 'The proposition is a measure of the world.'[42] The key claim from the *Tractatus* is: '[A picture] is laid against reality like a measure.'[43]

What does this analogy say? A situation that is represented by a proposition is compared to an actual situation in order to find out whether they match. If they do, the proposition is true but otherwise it is false. These situations need[44] not be identical, though; they have to match at certain points. It is essential for a yardstick to have graduating lines. In the analogy, pictures have graduating lines too: 'In a picture the elements of the picture are the representatives of objects.'[45] What we measure are, in fact, the relations between these graduating lines: 'The fact that the elements of a picture are related to one another in a determinate way represents that things are related to one another in the same way.'[46] What lies between these lines is not significant: 'Only the end-points of the graduating lines [Teilstriche] actually *touch* the object that is to be measured.'[47] It is as if the yardstick only has two graduating lines and the outcome of a measurement is bipolar. Either the thing measured is one yard long or it is not. By analogy, a proposition is either true or false.[48]

The graduating lines correspond to names in this analogy. In the concrete act of measurement, these graduating lines are coupled with some points of the measured thing. There is no prior agreement about what is supposed to correspond to the graduating lines while measuring. They can be paired with virtually anything. If the analogy is sound, names do not need to correspond to objects prior to putting a proposition (and the represented situation) up against reality. The correspondence may be established *ad hoc*. In the *Philosophical Remarks* Wittgenstein extends the analogy:

> By application I understand what makes the combination of sounds or marks into a language at all. In the sense that it is the application which makes the rod with marks into a *measuring rod: putting* language *up against* reality.[49]

The analogy is extended as follows. We have to be able to recognize particular lines as graduating lines (marks) on a rod in order to use it as a yardstick. The pictorial relationship allows us to recognize a combination of sounds or marks on a piece of paper as a represented situation. This is the case because we possess a method of projection. The same method enables us to recognize some elements of the *measured* situation as objects that are paired with objects in a *represented* situation and—on that account—with names that occur in the proposition.

What else do the represented situation and the real situation have in common? Wittgenstein's answer is: their *logical form*.[50] But what exactly makes up a logical form? As already indicated above, what we are looking into when measuring is whether the elements of the represented situation are related to each other in the same way as the corresponding elements of the measured situation. In other words, we are trying to find out whether these two situations exhibit the same structure. If so, Wittgenstein can therefore say that 'a proposition describes reality by its internal properties.'[51]

Let us now go back to the analogy to the yardstick. The only elements that matter are its two end-points (more precisely, the graduating lines on the yardstick). The only structure is that these points are one yard (0.9144 meters) distant from each other. A thing is one yard long if it exhibits the same structure of having its end-points in the same relation. We can consider these points as being in Euclidean space, withthe end-points of the yardstick marking a unit vector.

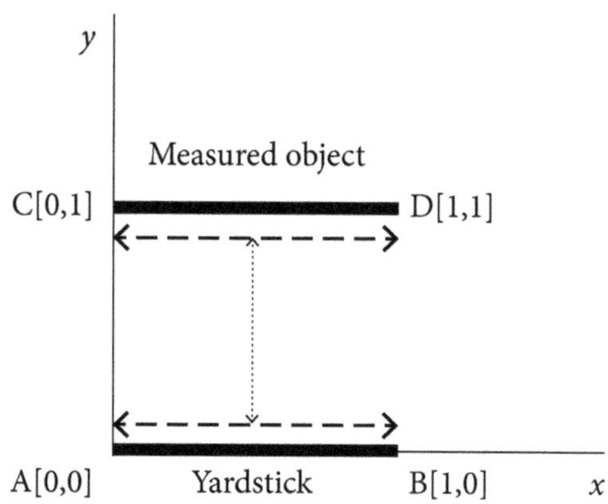

Figure 9.1

The internal properties of the yardstick and the measured thing are marked by the dashed lines, and the internal relation between them is marked by the dotted line. The end-points *A* and *B* of the yardstick stand in the internal relation of having the length of one yard. If the end-points *C* and *D* of the measured thing stand in the same relation, then the thing is one yard long. This Euclidean space is analogous to the logical space that Wittgenstein is invoking. In comparing the represented situation with a real situation, we have to read off the internal relations within both situations and compare them.

Wittgenstein finds this overall analogy problematic in his later philosophy. It needs to be clear that the represented situation is an imaginary one that has to be compared with a real situation. It is as if we had an imaginary yardstick that we laid down when measuring. The comparison takes place in Euclidean space where we compare two vectors. This is a case of a private comparison. In §16 'The standard meter,' I am going to argue that this analogy can be rectified by getting rid of the abstract Euclidean space.

9.3 Frege's objection

Frege, without having available the text of the *Tractatus*, but with Wittgenstein in mind,[52] raised the objection to the picture theory of meaning that it is unable to give a satisfactory account of the correspondence of a picture with reality:

> It would only be possible to compare a picture [Vorstellung] with a thing if the thing were a picture too. And then, if the first did correspond perfectly with the second, they would coincide. But this is not at all what is wanted when truth is defined as the correspondence of a picture with something real. For it is absolutely essential that the reality be distinct from the picture. But then there can be no complete correspondence, no complete truth. So nothing at all would be true; for what is only half true is untrue. Truth cannot tolerate a more or less. But yet? Can it not be laid down that truth exists when there is correspondence in a certain respect? But in which? For what would we then have to do to decide whether something were true? We should have to inquire whether it were true that a picture and a reality, perhaps, corresponded in the laid-down respect. And then we should be confronted by a question of the same kind and the game could begin again. So the attempt to explain truth as correspondence collapses. And every other attempt to define truth collapses too. For in a definition certain characteristics would have to be stated. And in application to any particular case the question would always arise whether it were true that the characteristics

> were present. So one goes round in a circle. Consequently, it is probable that the content of the word 'true' is unique and indefinable.[53]

In Wittgenstein's terms, this objection focuses on the comparison of a picture representing a situation with a real situation. Frege's argument proceeds in two steps: (1) A real situation, in order to be comparable with a picture, has to be a picture too; (2) These two pictures cannot be identical. They have to coincide only in a certain respect. To specify such a respect, one needs to apply the picture theory again. Therefore, any picture theory of meaning is circular in defining the correspondence between language and the world.

Frege's first point leads to the question as to what is actually compared. Two mental pictures or two facts? Wittgenstein says explicitly that a 'picture is a fact.'[54] But what we have to compare with reality is thoughts, i.e., propositions with sense, not mere propositional signs. Only 'a thought contains the possibility of the situation of which it is the thought.'[55] By this we can understand that a represented situation must be something imaginary.[56] What Frege is insisting on is that if we want to compare two entities, they have to be in the same space. This is something that Wittgenstein fully realized in the early 1930s.[57] I think, however, that Frege's requirement is met even within the Tractarian framework. The pictorial relationship which is embodied in the method of projection transforms a sign into a represented situation. Because this relationship is internal, the represented situation is already there. It is in *a certain respect* identical with the picture, i.e., with the propositional sign.[58] If the relation were external, some further account of bringing the represented and the real situation into the same space would be needed.

The second point is much more serious and in the end fatal for the Tractarian picture theory of meaning. The problem is this: how do we define what is significant in a picture? In other words, how do we determine what makes up the logical form of a picture—or of a sign? Employing again the analogy with the yardstick, one could ask how we recognize its graduating lines. The method of projection cannot be presupposed at this stage because it is a part of the sense of the proposition that we are seeking to define.[59] The present problem of giving meaning to a sign is an instance of the more general problem of introducing the internal/external distinction.

Frege considers and right away dismisses the alternative of perfect correspondence. Perfect correspondence would mean that the picture and the situation it represents would be identical. Everything in the picture would make up its logical form. The picture would only represent itself. This is the case of a *reflexive* internal relation, which is something inherently nonsensical. As Frege puts it, 'it is absolutely essential that the [represented] reality be distinct from the picture.'[60]

Let me illustrate the point at issue with the map-territory relationship. The expression 'The map is not the territory' is ascribed to the Polish philosopher Alfred Korzybski. We can try to imagine a map (which is a kind of picture) that is identical with the territory it is supposed to represent. Lewis Carroll, in his book *Sylvie and Bruno Concluded*, makes this point in a humorous dialogue. 'So we now use the country itself, as its own map, and I assure you it does nearly as well.'[61] Jorge Luis Borges, in his very short story *On Exactitude in Science*, depicts the unfortunate fate of a one-to-one map:

> In that Empire, the Art of Cartography attained such Perfection that the map of a single Province occupied the entirety of a City, and the map of the Empire, the entirety of a Province. In time, those Unconscionable Maps no longer satisfied, and the Cartographers Guilds struck a Map of the Empire whose size was that of the Empire, and which coincided point for point with it. The following Generations, who were not so fond of the Study of Cartography as their Forebears had been, saw that that vast map was Useless, and not without some Pitilessness was it, that they delivered it up to the Inclemencies of Sun and Winters. In the Deserts of the West, still today, there are Tattered Ruins of that Map, inhabited by Animals and Beggars; in all the Land there is no other Relic of the Disciplines of Geography.[62]

Maps or pictures in general are always pictures of something. A picture identical with the represented thing is no picture at all. Reflexive cases of the internal relation of representing make no sense. The *maxim of no reflexive uses of internal relations* will be further addressed in subsequent chapters.[63]

Let us move on now to Frege's second alternative. A picture has to coincide with the represented situation only in a certain respect. This means that some features of the picture represent and some do not. The features that represent make up the logical form of the picture. Wittgenstein gives an account of how to determine a logical form in the *Tractatus* at 3.31s where he introduces the notion of a *propositional variable*. A proposition (which is a picture) represents a class of situations. An expression (Ausdruck) 'is the common characteristic mark of a class of propositions.'[64] To get an expression we need to turn all the representing parts[65] of the proposition into variables 'whose values are the propositions that contain the expression.'[66] Then we can say that an expression is represented by means of a propositional variable. Such a propositional variable represents a class of propositions which in turn represents a class of situations. What remains in the propositional variable is the *logical form* of the proposition[67] which is identical with the logical form of the represented situations. These representing relations (from an expression to a class of propositions and then to a class of situations), thus preserve the logical form of the proposition and of the situations it represents.

What remains to be specified is the range of values that a propositional variable may take. These values have to be stipulated. It is, however, important that they have to be stipulated *a priori*, and not derived from any particular case:

> We portray the thing, the relation, the property, by means of variables and so shew that we do not derive these ideas from particular cases that occur to us, but possess them somehow *a priori*.[68]

But when it comes to the exact specification of how such a stipulation should be carried out, Wittgenstein says merely that 'To stipulate values for a propositional variable is to *give the propositions* whose common characteristic the variable is.'[69] It seems therefore that the stipulation amounts to an enumeration of the represented situations. Wittgenstein's account of how to specify the situations that are represented by a proposition comes thus to this: these situations must simply be enumerated one by one. They cannot be specified by any general form, because this would make the whole procedure circular.

This account does face several problems though. The most striking one is that propositions would be able to represent only a finite number of situations that have been given *a priori*. However, this is not how language works. Wittgenstein became unsatisfied with this in his later philosophy. His reflections about the ostensive definition can be seen as a response to this problem. Frege's worry is that the expression determining the respect in which a picture and a situation coincide has to have a meaning assigned in advance. Wittgenstein's worry about the ostensive definition is that the expressions determining a genus (e.g., 'number,' 'color,' 'length,' and so on) need to be defined in advance as well.[70]
The analogy goes as follows: let us take a complex *P* that we want to use as a picture. But *P* cannot coincide with represented things perfectly, but only in a certain respect.—In which respect?—In *color*. Hence *P* represents or is a picture of all other objects that have the same color. In other words, there is an internal

relation between the colors of *P* and all other objects of the same color. One may ask further, however: what do you mean by the *same color*? Do you demand pinpoint accuracy?—Yes, I demand the highest distinguishable accuracy.—One may go on asking endlessly. An ostensive definition faces an analogous problem. Suppose one says: 'That is called "sepia".'—'In which respect?'—'I mean this color is called "sepia".'—'Do you mean this color exactly or is there any degree of fuzziness?'—And so on …

It seems that giving meaning to a picture is a hopelessly never-ending process, like ostensive definition. It is difficult to imagine how this problem can be tackled in the *Tractatus*. There is, however, a solution available in Wittgenstein's later thinking. As he puts it: 'Explanations come to an end somewhere.'[71] 'The chain of reasons has an end.'[72] There is a last definition like there is a last house in this road.[73] The last definition or the last respect that has to be specified is when agreement is reached. It is not, however, any prior agreement in definitions but, in the end, in practice and in form of life.[74] A definition or an act of giving meaning to a picture is successful only when subsequent praxis shows that there is public agreement here. Only subsequent praxis can show that people use the same method of projection. It is obvious that this explanation by means of public agreement is not available in the Tractarian framework.

IV

Wittgenstein's later writings

10

Definitions of the internal/external distinction in the later writings

In his later writings (from 1929 onwards), what Wittgenstein says is for the most part consistent with his earlier account of internal relations. What changes is his focus. Internal relations can be exhibited not only in tautologies, but also in grammatical propositions in general. Internal relations are relations that hold in virtue of grammar.[1] Grammatical propositions are either explicit statements of the grammar of a language-game or also—in Wittgenstein's final texts—implicit descriptions of our human form of life. The criterion of (un)thinkability is very soon replaced by the criterion of temporality: internal relations are expressed in propositions that are timeless as opposed to temporal propositions which express external relations. Wittgenstein now insists resolutely that internal relations hold only between concepts and any talk of internal relations between objects has to be understood as referring to internal relations between concepts describing these objects.[2]

10.1 Disappearance of the saying/showing distinction

In Wittgenstein's later writings, we can find only a few remarks mentioning the saying/showing distinction in connection with the external/internal distinction. The main idea is that internal relations hold between complexes. They cannot be described, but only *shown* in descriptions between these complexes.[3] The reason why the relata of internal relations must be complexes is that they must be capable of being described. These complex relata do not need to be restricted to facts; they can also be complex acts, practices, or types of behavior. Let us consider two complexes: one is described by 'There are three white circles,' whereas the other is described by 'There are two black circles.' These descriptions show several internal relations: between the colors (white is lighter than black), the numbers (three is more than two) and the identity of the shapes. These relations are internal because when these two complexes (with their descriptions) are given, their internal relations are also given. If one fails to see these internal relations in the complexes, one would see, in a sense, different complexes. And the sense here is that in such a case they would not be able to describe the complexes by these descriptions, but only by other ones. These complexes would be different yet unchanged at the same time. This paradoxical appearance will later be developed in Wittgenstein's account of aspect-perception: 'The expression of a change of aspect is the expression of a *new* perception and at the same time of the perception's being unchanged.'[4]

It would, however, be a mistake to believe that Wittgenstein rejected or repudiated the saying/showing distinction. Rather, it has been transformed into the difference between what language expresses and what is shown by grammar.[5] Accordingly, internal relations are relations within grammar or grammatical relations. This characteristic is thus turned into the essential feature of internal relations: 'Internal relations (internal properties) are nothing other than what is described in grammar.'[6] This definition of internal relations can be taken as a generalization of the pre-Tractarian definition that Wittgenstein dictated to Moore.[7] Internal relations are still shown in the notation and can be expressed not only in tautologies, but also in grammatical propositions generally. Undoubtedly, logical tautologies are grammatical propositions.

We have the following recording of a conversation between Wittgenstein and Thouless: the claim that a grammatical proposition states an internal relationship is further explained by this subsequent definition: 'an internal property is one without which the X possessing it would no longer be called X, that is, it is one which seems to state the essence of X.'[8] Here I see an echo of the Tractarian definition in terms of unthinkability.[9] For an object *X* and its internal property *p*, it is unthinkable that it could not possess the property *p*. It is unthinkable to call an object *X* and, at the same time, refuse it the property *p*. This means that there is a grammatical proposition (a grammatical rule) stating that *X* implies *p*. This grammatical proposition also states that there is an internal relation between the concepts *X* and *p*. Any mention of an essence of things is, thus, understood as internal relations being expressed by grammatical propositions. In short: '*Essence* is expressed by grammar.'[10] Internal relations are thereby not reified as independent things.

The Tractarian definition of an internal relation in terms of unthinkability[11] is thus altered into a mere consequence of the new definition: if an internal relation is expressed in a grammatical proposition, it is unthinkable that its relata would not be related by this relation, i.e., it is unthinkable that a grammatical proposition could not be true. However, this conception of unthinkability later becomes relativized to a language-game. It is possible to conceive of a grammatical proposition becoming a genuine empirical proposition in another language-game.[12] This conception of unthinkability becomes, at the very least, ambiguous in Wittgenstein's later texts, which might be the reason why he ceased to define internal relations in terms of unthinkability.

This ambiguity of the notion of unthinkability can be characterized as follows: for a given true proposition *p* (*p* is for instance '1 + 1 = 2') we can ask whether it is thinkable that *p* is not true. We are invited to imagine a situation in which *p* does not hold. Clearly, we have to come up with some non-actual situation, for in the actual situation *p* is true. But then it is unclear to what extent we are allowed to change (in imagination) the actual situation. It is plausible that we can change everything factual, but we have to preserve conceptual matters. In other words, we cannot change the meaning of *p*. If we nevertheless could think that *p* means something different from what it actually means, the criterion of (un)thinkability would break down. We could always imagine that *p* means 'It is raining' together with the fact that it is actually not raining. Hence we can think that *p* is not true for every *p*.

The criterion of thinkability therefore rests on the distinction between conceptual and factual facts. But the distinction between the conceptual and the factual is obscured in ordinary language and in the distinction between internal and external relations.[13] However, Wittgenstein also offers the following consideration:

> It might be imagined that some propositions, of the form of empirical propositions, were hardened and functioned as channels for such empirical propositions as were not hardened but fluid; and that this relation altered with time, in that fluid propositions hardened, and hard ones became fluid. [...] [T]he same proposition may get treated at one time as something to test by experience, at another as a rule of testing.[14]

The criterion of thinkability is of no help here. Wittgenstein eventually came up with another criterion that can help us to distinguish between sentences that express internal and external relations. This is the criterion of temporality, which is going to be addressed in §10.4.

10.2 Concepts and objects

What is going to be discussed in this section is the central characteristic of the distinction between internal and external relations in Wittgenstein's later writings. Its centrality is backed up by numerous remarks from Wittgenstein's manuscripts spread over his entire later philosophical career.

As already elaborated in the chapter on the internal/external distinction in Wittgenstein's early texts (§6), internal relations hold between concepts (or properties, qualities, universals) while external relations hold between objects (or particulars). The problem is, however, that the same verbal manifestation can be used for describing one and the same state of affairs, which at times can express an internal relation, but at other times express an external relation. One of the tasks of philosophical analysis is to make clear whether an internal relation or an external relation is involved. Moreover, for the sake of this book, the uncovering of this distinction is regarded as the leading methodological principle of Wittgenstein's thinking.

Wittgenstein repeatedly presents various clusters of examples in order to illustrate how this confusion comes about and how it can be eliminated. The examples which Wittgenstein used most frequently are the relations *longer than* and *darker than.*

Let us turn first to the relation of being longer than.[15] The state of affairs (or simply: the situation) is as follows: we have two line segments drawn on a piece of paper.[16]

The line segment *a* is 3 m long and the line segment *b* is 2 m long. We can describe this situation as follows:

(23) Line *a* is 3 m long.
(24) Line *b* is 2 m long.

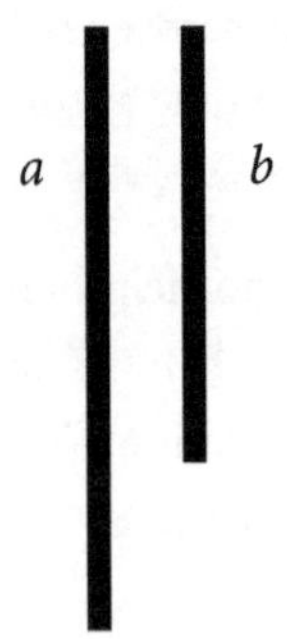

Figure 10.1 Two lines

These propositions express the external properties of these two line segments. In addition to that, they also express an internal relation of being longer than between these two propositions. This relation can be expressed as

(25) *a* is longer than *b*.

But this expression is ambiguous. It might mean that

(26) Line segment *a* is longer than line segment *b*.

or

(27) The length 3 m is longer than the length 2 m.

The former proposition expresses an external relation holding between two line segments. The latter proposition expresses an internal relation holding between two numbers. This proposition expresses that 3 > 2. It might be used as a (partial) definition of the relation longer than. Thus, here, it is a grammatical proposition.

This example is in accord with what has been expounded so far. It is thinkable/possible that the line segment *a* could become smaller and cease to be longer than the line segment *b*. It is, however, unthinkable/impossible that 3 could not be greater than 2.

We can now, in turn, proceed to the relation of being darker than.[17] As we have already seen, in the *Tractatus* Wittgenstein uses this relation as an example of an internal relation.[18] A certain shade of blue is darker than some other shade of blue. This is an internal relation. A linguistic expression of this relation may, however, be confusing. Suppose we have two material objects (suits, bodies, plates, rectangles, etc.) *a* and *b*. Body *a* is black and body *b* is white. Now consider the following expression:

(28) *a* is darker than *b*.

By this sentence we can express an external relation between these two objects on the one hand. It might be used in the sense that

(29) Suit *a* is darker than suit *b*.

By (28) one can also express, on the other hand, an internal relation between the two colors:

(30) The color of *a* is darker than the color of *b*.

This proposition is, in the context of our example, tantamount to

(31) Black is darker than white.

At this point, I have to refer back to our discussion of the Tractarian example of an internal relation between two shades of blue:

(32) Midnight-blue is darker than sky-blue.

I then argued that this proposition is true because of the fact that sky-blue has a brightness of 92 per cent and midnight-blue has a brightness of 44 per cent in the HSV color space. Within this color space (32) expresses, thus, an internal relation which may be put as 44 < 92. In the same color space, black has a brightness of 0 per cent and white one of 100 per cent. Hence the propositions (30) and (31) both express the internal relation 0 < 100. These grammatical propositions are, however, not eternal truths. One could imagine a color space (albeit an uncanny one) in which sky-blue would be darker than midnight-blue or even white darker than black.

These two relations are by far the most extensively discussed examples in connection with the external/internal distinction in Wittgenstein's writings. The next three examples appear far less often. The relation of being earlier can relate two events or two dates. Wittgenstein uses the following sentence:

(33) Caesar [was born] before Augustus.[19]

If two persons or their dates of birth were related here, the relation of being earlier than would be external. But a relation of being earlier than between two historical dates (here 100 BC and 63 BC) is internal.

The penultimate example is the relation of having the same number of elements. We can say, for instance, that

(34) This sack has the same number of potatoes as that sack.[20]

This sentence may express an external relation between these two sacks or an internal relation between the numbers of potatoes in these sacks. Wittgenstein compares this sentence with the following one:

(35) The hand has the same number of strokes as the pentagram has points.[21]

This sentence is not ambiguous between expressing an internal and an external relation. It expresses an internal relation between the (human) hand and the pentagram. The fact that the pentagram has five points lies in the definition of the pentagram. One could argue that a human hand does not necessarily have five strokes, because one of its fingers may be cut off. In this case, four strokes

Figure 10.2 Pentagram

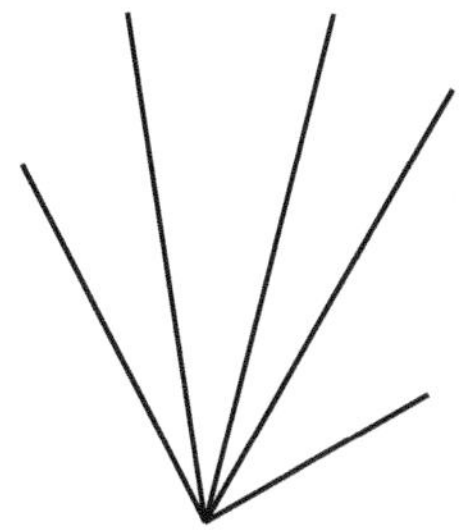

Figure 10.3 Hand

would not depict a human hand, but a human hand without one finger. The internal relation expressed in (35) holds not between actual depictions, but between abstract geometrical figures: between the pentagram and the schema figure of the human hand.

The relation of having the same number of elements makes sense even if it were a unary relation, i.e., the property of having a certain number of elements. Here is Wittgenstein's example:

> Exercises: Number of notes–the internal property of a tune; number of leaves–the external property of a tree.[22]

For the sake of this example let us concentrate on a single musical motif as a part of a tune. The central opening motif in Beethoven's Fifth Symphony is a four-note figure:

Figure 10.4 The opening motif in Beethoven's *Fifth Symphony*[23]

It is essential to this motif that it consists of four notes. If it had a different number of notes, it would not be the opening motif of Beethoven's *Fifth Symphony*.

For a particular tree though, it is not essential that it has a definite number of leaves. A tree can lose some or all of its leaves or new leaves can grow but the tree still remains the same in the sense of numerical identity. If the matter that concerns us is the concept of a tree, it is not essential either how many leaves have objects (i.e., particular trees) that fall under this concept.

The last example that I am going to discuss in this section is the difference between external and internal similarity[24] which is prominent in Wittgenstein's writings on the philosophy of psychology. And here again, there is an ambiguous sentence at the outset:

(36) The two faces are similar.

Using this sentence, one may mean 'the faces of *those men* that interest me, or it may be these facial *forms*, wherever I encounter them.'[25] The similarity between those men is external, while the similarity between their facial forms is internal. A similarity between two men is external because they may change their appearances and cease to be similar. A similarity between two facial forms is an internal one, if and to the extent to which these forms can be characterized by similar descriptions. So, for example, a round form is similar to an elliptical form but dissimilar to an angular form. The question of whether the two forms are similar is a geometrical one.[26] One may say, for example, that the round form and the elliptical form are both continuous curves while the rectangular form is not.

10.3 Crossing different language-games

What all these examples have in common is that a sentence can be used to describe one and the same state of affairs in two different ways. On the one hand, one may be interested in particular objects in the state of affairs, in their properties, and in the relations between them. Or one may be interested, on the other hand, in the properties of and the relation between the concepts used to describe the state of affairs. In the former, external relations are involved, while in the latter internal relations are involved.

But why does this distinction matter? Why and in which cases is it important to distinguish whether one intends to speak about objects and their relations, or about concepts and their relations?[27] Why is it sometimes important to be clear about whether one is using a proper proposition or a grammatical proposition? Consider the following sentences mentioning two objects, labeled *a* and *b*:

(37) *a* has the same length as *b*.

(38) *a* has the same color as *b*.

(39) *a* was created at the same time as *b*.
(40) *a* has the same number of parts as *b*.
(41) *a* is similar to *b*.
(42) *a* and *b* are similarly beautiful.

These sentences may all be used in order to assert this or that similarity between the objects in question. That these two objects are the same or similar in this or that way is an accidental fact. Object *a* can have the same length or color or number of parts as object *b*, but it does not need to. In this sense these sentences express the external relations between the objects *a* and *b*.

One may intend by (37)–(39) to point out the identity of two lengths, two colors, or two points in time. The objects *a* and *b* serve only as examples here. One may use (37) to explain what is meant by two objects having the same length (and in the case of any doubts, they would have to be placed alongside one another and compared).[28] Sentence (38) may be used to illustrate what counts as the same color (e.g., that tiny subtleties do not matter and, hence, do not disturb their identity[29]). 'At the same time' can mean at the same second or in the same century. Sentence (39) may be helpful in clarifying this ambiguity. Things can usually be decomposed into their parts in many different ways. Sentence (40) can be used to explain what counts as a part here. Sentence (41) can be used to focus on the similarity in question. And finally, (42) may be used to elucidate some aesthetic feature or rule.[30] The important thing here is that in the case of confusion, other objects could be used for the same purpose, which is to express the same internal relation.

The point of all these examples is to show that these sentences could 'fall "between several games,"'[31] where they can be used to serve different purposes. They can be used factually for expressing external relations, or conceptually for expressing internal relations.[32]

The notion of falling between different language-games deserves more of an in-depth scrutiny. Wittgenstein delimits the role of language-games by claiming that they 'are rather set up as objects of comparison which are meant to throw light on the facts of our language by way not only of similarities, but also of dissimilarities.'[33] Accordingly, language-games are objects which are compared with (some parts of) our language.[34] Language-games are invented or fictional, which means that it is not important whether such an activity actually takes place. What kind of objects are they? In most of the examples Wittgenstein gives us they are simplified or, rather, schematized descriptions of language use together with other relevant extra-linguistic activities. Such schemata are compared with (the descriptions of) actual language use.

What language and language-games have in common is that they are rule-guided activities. Provided that we are interested in the rules of grammar, then language-games can be individuated by their rules. Here is how this individuation works: provided that we are able to split a given description of a linguistic activity into two parts so that (at least partly) different grammatical rules are active in these parts, then we can take these two parts as different language-games. One can also, however, take these two language-games as one game if one has a reason to do so.

Language-games are also primarily (although not exclusively) the conceptual tools employed in philosophical analysis for surmounting philosophical confusions.[35] I would like now to focus on one form such confusions can take which is central to Wittgenstein's later writings. A philosophical confusion (but also a simple problem of understanding) may arise if we are not able to assign to a given linguistic expression its appropriate context of use. If the meaning of a word is its use in language, we have to be able to put this word into its context in order to understand the word at all. It is obvious that we do not need to imagine the whole context in all its details; a schematic description of an appropriate language-game is usually enough. Thus, a philosophical confusion may now arise if we do not provide a language-game, or if we provide the wrong one. Wittgenstein labels such a diagnosis as the 'crossing of different language-games' or 'fall[ing] between several games.'

We shall now consider some sentences that are prone to such a confusion—sentences that may express a genuine proposition in one language-game and a grammatical proposition in another. If language-games were individuated by their rules, such sentences would also fall within multiple language-games. The risk of confusion would be bolstered if these two different language-games differed only in this one sentence. I will focus precisely on such sentences (sometimes called *Doppelgänger*[36]) and on language-games. Suppose the following general scenario: one has to teach or learn a certain rule in order to apply it afterwards. We can distinguish between two stages of this process: the *language-game of teaching* and the *language-game of applying* the rule. These language-games are different, for what is a rule in the latter is not a rule. Although it is not necessary to mention the would-be rule explicitly during the process of training, in many cases it is anyway. Such mentioning would have a declarative character (using Searle's terminology) and we can treat such sentences then as *imperatives*. Hence, one can easy imagine that one and the same sentence expresses a genuine proposition in the *language-game of teaching* and a grammatical proposition in the subsequent *language-game of applying* a rule.[37] In other words: the form of the sentence is the same, but it expresses an external property in the former language-game and an internal property in the latter one. The language-game of applying a rule logically presupposes the language-game of teaching. There is, thus, a *vertical* relation[38] between these two language-games.[39]

10.4 The criterion of temporality

We know from the previous section that internal relations only hold between concepts while external relations can hold between concepts, between concepts and objects, or between objects. This difference might be confused in the surface grammar, for an internal as well as an external relation can be expressed by one and the same sentence in different language-games. So, given the context of a language-game, one could wonder how to find out whether an internal or an external relation is being expressed.

For this purpose Wittgenstein developed what I shall call the *criterion of temporality*. The main idea behind this is that external relations are expressed by temporal sentences while internal relations are expressed by timeless sentences.[40] The temporal character of sentences is something that was of particular interest to Wittgenstein throughout his later philosophical writings. One of the leading questions he poses in the *Philosophical Grammar* reads: 'Is time essential to sentences?'[41]

Temporal sentences are such that their truth or falsity depends on time. More exactly, their truth or falsity depends on accidental circumstances which are, of course, time-dependent. Timeless (or non-temporal) sentences are, by contrast, independent of external circumstances. Whether a sentence is temporal or timeless does not need to be manifested in its mere appearance. Not all temporal sentences contain an explicit adverbial of time. A deeper reflection on the sentence's use is now required.[42]

The reflection is this: a use of a sentence is regarded as temporal if this is indicated grammatically or if it would be *plausible* to insert an explicit adverbial of time or a time clause into the sentence in the same context of the language-game. In other words, this criterion consists in considering making the grammatical form of the sentence temporal. At this point we must clarify what counts as a plausible modification. Wittgenstein has left us with numerous examples here as well. For example:

> 'The 100 apples in this box consist of 50 and 50'—here the non-temporal character of 'consist' is important. For it doesn't mean that now, or just for a time, they consist of 50 and 50.[43]

We are asked to consider whether it would be plausible to insert 'now' into (43):

> (43) The 100 apples in this box consist of 50 and 50 *now*.

Although such a variant of the sentence is syntactically correct, it does not contribute to its meaning. Let us take the arithmetical statement:

> (44) 100 is equal to 50 + 50.

The grammar of English does not prevent us from inserting an adverbial of time into this sentence:

> (45) 100 is equal to 50 + 50 *now*.

Or other modifications:

> (46) 100 has been equal to 50 + 50 since arithmetic was invented.
> (47) Every time I try to count it 100 is equal to 50 + 50 at that point in time.

Sentences (45)–(47) are not meaningless; they even follow from (44). But they do not contribute to the meaning of (44); they do not make (44) more accurate. This is why it is not plausible to explicitly impose temporality on the sentence.[44]

Let us proceed to some less trivial cases. The sentence

> (48) 'Dædalus' contains seven sounds.[45]

could be taken phonetically as a report of an experiment in counting. In this case, it would be more accurate to say

> (49) *As pronounced now* 'Dædalus' contains seven phones.

This is an empirical proposition. The word 'Dædalus' could be pronounced differently. Then it is *thinkable* or *possible* that the result could have been different from what it was. Sentence (48) could be understood *phonologically*, however, as a grammatical proposition in the sense

> (50) The sound-pattern 'Dædalus' has seven phonemes.

In this case, it is not possible to insert any adverbial of time in (48). To be clear, (50) may be a result of a *particular* method of counting the sounds given *particular* rules of pronunciation, but what is expressed here is that one must have decided on *this particular* method of counting. We could also have decided on another method: for example, we could have taken into account the consonants or vowels. Then the sound-pattern 'Dædalus' would have contained four consonants or three vowels. Other methods are also *thinkable* or even *possible*. These considerations do not detract from the timeless character of (48) and (50). What is expressed here is the grammatical proposition attributing to the word 'Dædalus' the internal property of having seven sounds.

Let us apply the criterion of temporality to the sentences (37)–(42) discussed in the previous section. One may argue that the internal/external distinction does not exhaust the ambiguity of these sentences. We can reformulate (37) as claiming the equivalence of two definite descriptions:

(51) The length of *a* is equal to the length of *b*.

Then we can adopt Keith Donnellan's distinction between *attributive* and *referential* uses of definite descriptions.[46] These definite descriptions can be used either attributively:

(52) The lengths of *a* and *b*, whatever they are, are equivalent.

Or, we can use these definite descriptions referentially:

(53) The length of *a* is *A*, and the length of *b* is *B*, and *A*=*B*.

I claim now that on both these readings, these sentences express external relations. (52) expresses an external relation because it makes sense to say that

(54) The lengths of *a* and *b*, whatever they are, are equivalent *now*.

Objects *a* and *b* may have the same length, but it is conceivable that they do not. Object *a* can shrink, for example. It makes sense to add 'now' into (52). (53) also expresses an external relation because we can insert a temporal adverb into the first and the second clause:

(55) The length of *a* is *now* *A*, and the length of *b* is *now* *B*, and *A*=*B*.

I am going to argue in §16.4 below that we cannot separate the description 'the length of *a*' from the actual length of object *a*. This means that we cannot take the description 'the length of *a*' to *rigidly* refer to *A* (which is a numerical value).

If we could rigidly refer to the lengths of *a* and *b*, inserting a time clause into (37) and (53) would make no sense. Then these sentences might express an internal relation that is, however, empirical, which would undermine Wittgenstein's analysis. But adding a time clause does make sense here.[47]

The criterion of temporality is thus that if a sentence is or can be made temporal, then it expresses an external relation. In short, temporality implies externality. The reverse claim—that is, if a sentence expresses an external relation, then it is temporal—is less plausible. Laws of nature may be counterexamples here. They are contingent and express external relations.[48] But they are expressed by timeless sentences and it makes no sense to insert any adverbial of time or a time clause into them. Let us take, for example, Newton's Second law:

(56) The relationship between an object's mass m, its acceleration a, and the applied force F is $F = ma$.

This sentence is timeless and it makes no sense to convert it into a temporal one. Laws of nature are those laws which apply everywhere and at all times throughout the universe. Laws of nature are external relations expressed by timeless sentences.[49]

Returning now to the discussion of the Tractarian definition of the internal relation in terms of *unthinkability* in §10.1, it becomes clear what is wrong with this notion. There are two kinds of thinkability mentioned in the last example. For an empirical proposition like (49) it is *thinkable* that it does not hold in *this* language-game. For a grammatical proposition like (50) it is *unthinkable* that it does not hold in *that* language-game, but it is *thinkable* that it does not hold in some other language-game. The notion of thinkability is or may be confused.

The criterion of temporality is at hand to deal with this confusion. The temporality of a sentence is always being considered within a language-game where the sentence is used. This criterion gives us a tool or method for determining whether a given sentence expresses an internal or an external relation in a given language-game.

10.5 Tertium quid

The last characteristic is that the terms of an internal relation are related *directly*, without any mediation, to each other. Internal relations relate their terms through the terms, and not through other things or rules. This characteristic was already present in the early Tractarian account of internal relations: the identification of the one term of an internal relation is, *eo ipso*, the identification of the other term.

The existence of terms, which as we know now are concepts, is the necessary condition of the holding of an internal relation between them. 'An internal relation [...] exists only if its components are present.'[50] If one of the terms did not exist, there would be no internal relation. This means that there is no internal relation that does not actually relate its terms. There could not be the relation of being darker without there being entities that are supposed to be related, namely its color shades.[51]

That the terms are related by an internal relation lies within these very terms. 'An internal relation holds by virtue of the terms being what they are.'[52] There are, of course, concepts that are not internally related. But if the concepts are related, their mere existence guarantees their internal relatedness. There is, thus, no third thing[53] that would relate the concepts. Internal relations, so to say, emerge when concepts are given. In other words, internal relations are *supervenient* to its terms or 'supervenience is written into our understanding of the concepts.'[54]

Having said that, I now want to expound two interrelated points about this characteristic of internal relations. The first one is that from knowing one term and knowing that this concept is internally related to another concept (or concepts), it is possible to infer (logically) what the other concept is (or the other concepts are). As in the Tractarian account, we can conceive of internal relations as sorts of operations which can be applied to a term in order to compute the other term. This analogy between internal relations and mathematical operations is, however, not very close: the outcome of a mathematical operation is always unique, but applying an internal relation to a concept can lead to a multiplicity of other concepts that are related in this way. By applying the relation of being darker to sky-blue, we get as an outcome not only midnight-blue, but all the other color shades that have lower brightness than sky-blue, e.g., sapphire-blue. One can make the outcome unique if one makes the relation more precise.

For instance, by applying the relation of being 40 percent darker to sky-blue, one gets as the outcome midnight-blue exactly.

To make this clear, I would like to add a mathematical example. Consider the numbers 1597, 2584, and 4181. Although these numbers do not seem to be related at first sight, they are in fact a succession of the seventeenth, eighteenth, and nineteenth Fibonacci numbers. They are internally related by the *ternary* relation of being in the Fibonacci sequence. There is a unique way of computing the next element out of the previous ones. The next element is such that

(57) $F_n = F_{n-1} + F_{n-2}$

One might now have the impression that these three numbers are internally related *because* they make up a Fibonacci sequence. So there is a third thing after all: the rule of how to compute the next member of the series out of the previous ones. The numbers 1597, 2584, and 4181 are, in fact, internally related in infinitely many ways, because there are an infinite number of series that have these numbers as their members. It would be a deep misunderstanding to think that the rule of computing the next member of a series is a third item relating the preceding members to the next one. This is something which I am going to focus on now.[55]

The second point is that the internal relations hold only in virtue of their terms. It would be misleading or even false to say that they hold in virtue of other rules or other grammatical propositions. It seems now that grammatical rules are precisely those that internally relate the terms. For instance, one might assume that midnight-blue and sky-blue are internally related *because* of the rules in the HSV color space. Or that 'Dædalus' has seven sound patterns *because* of the rule that assigns the number of sounds in a given word.

These concepts are individuated by their roles in language-games. If two (or more) concepts are internally related, they are so in virtue of the rules that define these very concepts. Accordingly, the internal properties of a concept are made up by the rules defining the concept. The relation that is not constitutive of its terms is an external relation. If we say that an internal relation does not hold in virtue of a third thing, it means that it does hold exclusively in virtue of the grammatical rules that define or govern its terms. The holding of an internal relation can be deduced or computed out of these rules; so that no other rules are necessary.

Let me illustrate this point with one of our familiar examples. That midnight-blue and sky-blue are internally related by the relation of 'being darker' can be read off from the definitions that give their internal properties: midnight-blue has a brightness of 44 percent and sky-blue one of 92 percent. No other rule is required here. I can imagine, for instance, the relation of being more important (for me) and say that sky-blue is more important for me than midnight-blue. This is an external relation because such a rule is a third thing that cannot be deduced from the internal properties of the related terms. That the sound-pattern 'Dædalus' has seven sounds must be evident from the pattern itself and from the rule or method for counting sounds.

The example with the Fibonacci numbers is slightly more complicated, but only at first sight. The matter of concern here is, in fact, a simple equation like 3 + 2 = 5. Wittgenstein asks himself 'How can one calculate that 3 + 2 = 5?!'[56] There is no internal relation between '5' and '3 + 2,' one (here, a Kantian philosopher) would have to say. Wittgenstein wants us to imagine a fact like this: '| | | | |' correlates with '| | + | | |.'[57] It is evident now that there is a one-to-one correlation between these complexes. Hence the relation must be internal. No other rule is necessary except the rules for numbers and the rule for addition. The rule for a number is simply to make a certain number of strokes and the rule for addition is to put the strokes together.

10.6 No exceptions

The point that internal relations do not allow for any exceptions has often been neglected among commentators. Wittgenstein writes that internal relation are exact[58] or that

> they persist always, unalterably, in the whole that they constitute; as it were independently of any outside happenings. As the construction of a machine on paper does not break when the machine itself succumbs to external forces.—Or again, I should like to say that they are not subject to wind and weather like physical things; rather [they are] unassailable, like schemas.[59]

Since internal relations are the expressions of grammar in a language-game, they hold whatever happens. The only way to change them is to change the grammar, which is tantamount to changing the language-game. There is no possibility of any failure with respect to the holding of an internal relation as opposed to the ever-present possibility of a real machine failing. An internal relation holds exclusively between concepts and in virtue only of these very concepts. In this sense, internal relations can be expressed only by analytic truths.

Several commentators have already advanced the view that Wittgenstein, in his later philosophy, allowed that internal relations could be expressed not only by analytic truths, but also by synthetic ones. In their influential interpretation, Baker and Hacker write: 'Wittgenstein repudiated the implication that any expression of an internal relation must be a necessary truth or tautology.'[60] Baker and Hacker argue that internal relations that are not expressed by analytical sentences are, inter alia, relations between psychological concepts and their criteria. There is, for instance, an internal relation between the concept of pain and instances of pain-behavior (such as whining or moaning). This relation is internal, because it is formulated in grammar. But the sentence 'If someone is moaning, they are in pain' is not a tautology. The criteria for some words are defeasible. Someone may fake pain-behavior without really being in pain, and they may suppress pain-behavior despite being in pain. The inner state (of pain) is not necessarily related to its outward criteria since there are exceptions to the rule. From this fact, Baker and Hacker conclude that 'Though not tautology, the relation of pain-behavior to pain is an internal relation.'[61]

Internal relations hold solely among concepts. A sentence asserting an internal relation between objects (or events) has to be read as a sentence expressing an internal relation between concepts.[62] The relation of pain-behavior to pain is in fact the relation between the *concept* of pain and the *descriptions* of pain-behavior. The relation is, however, not that pain-behavior is pain. This meaning would be a behavioristic diminution of the concept of pain. The relation is that pain-behavior is a *criterion* of being in pain.

The concept of a criterion carries the (albeit rare) possibility of deception on its shoulders. To be a criterion of something is a different kind of internal relation than, for instance, in 'thunder and lightning mean a thunderstorm.' There can be more distinct criteria of psychological states. That only one of these criteria actually holds does not imply that the other ones have ceased being criteria for now. There is no exception or temporary suspension of validity.

The criterial definition of a psychological concept can eventually be replaced by a more rigid definition. The scientist may define pain as a stimulation of nociceptors. This is, however, a conceptual change. This new concept of pain is not identical with the old one based on criteria. These criteria thus turn into symptoms of the new concept.[63] So we have the following relations:

(58) Pain-behavior is a criterion of $pain_{old}$.
(59) A stimulation of nociceptors means $pain_{new}$.
(60) Pain-behavior is a symptom of $pain_{new}$.

The first two sentences express internal relations; the last one expresses an external relation. Pain-behavior is only a concomitant phenomenon of pain if pain is defined by (59).[64]

The conceptual stipulation is a very rare phenomenon; it is in a sense 'a trivial way'[65] of introducing conceptual change. Our conceptual usage may naturally evolve through time. It may be that such a change rests on 'imponderable evidence' that cannot be predicted *a priori*:

> And now the question remains whether we would give up our language-game which rests on 'imponderable evidence' and frequently leads to uncertainty, if it were possible to exchange it for a more exact one which by and large would have similar consequences.[66]

In his final writings, Wittgenstein thus seems to concede that language-games with their grammar may evolve due to empirical evidence.[67] This would in effect undermine the distinction between grammatical propositions and empirical propositions and by implication undermine the distinction between internal relations and external relations.

I think that we can keep the distinction between internal and external relations valid if we consistently insist that this distinction is relative to a given language-game. Nobody will deny that our concepts evolve through time. If a change of a concept is small, we tend to think that it is the same concept. If a change is bigger or more substantial, we tend to the view that one concept has evolved into another one, though these two concepts may have the same verbal expression. It is of little importance what the *cause* of the conceptual change was. It is also of little importance whether the change was due to a one-off stipulation or a gradual evolution. But if this change leads to conceptual confusion, we should conceive it as a case of the crossing of different language-games.

10.7 Summary

In Wittgenstein's later texts, we can therefore find the following characteristics of internal and external relations:

1 Internal relations hold only between concepts while external relations hold between objects and concepts.
2 Internal relations can be exhibited in grammatical propositions which express either rules of a language-game or general facts of our human form of life.
3 Propositions that express internal relations are timeless, whereas propositions that express external relations are temporal.
4 Internal relations relate their terms only in virtue of these very terms, not in virtue of other things or rules.
5 Internal relations allow no exceptions.

11

Intentionality

Wittgenstein's account of intentionality is a good example of his method of analysis based on the distinction between internal and external relations. The metaphysical mystery of human intentionality is dissolved by making clear the grammar of language.

Apart from a few exceptions, Wittgenstein does not discuss intentionality under this precise name, but he does discuss various kinds of intentionality. The most common kind is the nature of expectation and how an expectation is related to its fulfillment. Other kinds of intentionality Wittgenstein touches on are wishes, fears, hopes, desires, orders, beliefs, hypotheses, and other intentional states. An intentional state is always related to something that does not or might not exist. It may refer to a state of affairs in the past or in the future, or it may be unknown or uncertain whether the state of affairs is realized. Although an intentional state may refer to the past, its fulfillment (satisfaction, verification, falsification, etc.) is possible only in the future. In short, the intended state is not available at the moment of intending.[1]

If something is to be expected, that expectation is directed to the future. The expected state of affairs may or may not be realized. The same is valid for a wish or a desire. A hypothesis, a belief, or a fear may refer to the past; but they are also directed to the future because of their future verification or falsification. Intentionality also includes a family of allied phenomena which do not need to have any common feature. Two states of affairs are usually related to intentional states: the present intentional act and a state of affairs that satisfies the intention. These two states are separated in time. The mystery of intentionality consists in the way in which an intentional act is supposed to reach its satisfaction.

The main problem concerning intentionality that Wittgenstein faces is an epistemological one. How does an agent come to recognize that a present state of affairs satisfies their previous intention? How does one know that this is what they wanted? How does one know that the present state of affairs verifies or falsifies their previous hypothesis? Or to restate the problem in a more Wittgensteinian fashion: how does one know that the present act is in accord with a rule that was previously stated? In spite its own peculiarities (further discussed in this chapter), the problem of the recognition of a previous intention belongs to the family of rule-following problems.[2]

11.1 Russell's causal theory

At the beginning of the 1930s, Wittgenstein approaches intentionality against the background of the causal accounts of intentionality given by Russell and by Ogden and Richards in the 1920s. The difference between these approaches and Wittgenstein's *picture conception* of intention is the same as that between external and internal relations. Wittgenstein writes accordingly:

> But the essential difference between the picture conception and the conception of Russell, Ogden and Richards, is that it regards recognition as seeing an internal relation, whereas in their view this is an external relation.[3]

Before turning to Wittgenstein's own conception I shall sketch Russell's account of intention from *The Analysis of Mind*[4] and the way in which this is based on external relations.

For Russell, a prototypical type of intentional act is *desire*. The thing that is distinctive about desire is that it is accompanied by a feeling of discomfort. This feeling causes an action which should likely bring about quiescence. If this action is successful, it will bring pleasure. The intentional object (of a desire) is the final state of affairs which removes the discomfort and brings pleasure. Russell calls the whole process from desire to pleasure a '*behaviour cycle*.'

The ontological status of a behavior cycle is now clear: the connection between desire and fulfillment is causal. But there are two epistemological problems or questions which emerge here. First, when one has a particular desire, how does one know what exactly will satisfy it so that one can choose a suitable action to achieve this satisfaction? Second, when one experiences a particular pleasure, how does one know that the present state of affairs is exactly that which one has desired? The first question arises at the beginning of a behavior cycle, the second at its end.

As to the first question, one could infer from past experience (from the fact that similar desires have been satisfied by certain states of affairs) that the actual desire will most *likely* be satisfied by a certain state of affairs. As to the second question, the end of a behavior cycle is recognized by the end of the dissatisfaction following the pleasure. These mental events are dependent on the desire and on the action that is supposed to satisfy this desire. If one knows that the actual pleasure is exactly that which they desired by recognition, then the pleasure is causally related to the previous desire. This epistemological problem nevertheless remains when one behavior cycle is interrupted by another, as Russell agreed.[5] If so, when one experiences the pleasure, it is difficult to decide which cycle is to be terminated.

The relation between desire and its object is an *external* one because there must be a third element, namely the feeling of pleasure. The desire is not matched with its satisfaction until there is a feeling of pleasure.[6] An analogous external relation holds between an expectation and the thing that has been expected:

> We have first an expectation, then a sensation with the feeling of expectedness related to memory of the expectation. This whole experience, when it occurs, may be defined as verification, and as constituting the truth of the expectation.[7]

The relation between an expectation and the expected state becomes external, since the truth of its realization depends on the feeling of confirmation. One has to remember and confirm that the actual state of affairs is exactly that which one has expected.

Wittgenstein's objections to Russell are focused on the second epistemological problem, as discussed above. How do we get to know that the present state of affairs is exactly that which we have desired? Wittgenstein wrote that:

> I believe Russell's theory amounts to the following: if I give someone an order and I am happy with what he then does, then he has carried out my order.
> (If I wanted to eat an apple, and someone punched me in the stomach, taking away my appetite, then it was this punch that I originally wanted.)[8]

Wittgenstein's objection to Russell's account is that whatever brings pleasure during the course of a behavior cycle is that which was originally intended (desired, ordered). This fact makes intentional acts indeterminate, for one cannot know in advance all the things that might bring satisfaction. Although there may be some kinds of intentional acts that are indeterminate in this way, most of them are determinate. An order is a determinate affair. Its objective may happen to be irrelevant before the order has been carried out or it may be accomplished by some unexpected event. But if this happens, the original intention of the order remains unaffected.

The example with the apple seems to be unfair to Russell. A punch in the stomach usually does not cause any pleasure. The behavior cycle is only interrupted or overlaid by another behavior cycle. Then, however, subsequent pleasure may terminate one of these cycles, or maybe both. This empirical indeterminacy is brought about by the conceptual indeterminacy in Russell's theory, which does not make clear what counts as a behavior cycle and what counts as an interruption or termination of a cycle. In any case, by introducing additional behavior cycles, the indeterminacy cannot be avoided.[9]

The crux of the matter lies in the fact that one cannot directly compare a supposed satisfaction with the original intention. 'I cannot confront the previous expectation with what happens.'[10] The intentional act lies in the past; that is why such a comparison in Russell's theory can be made only indirectly, based on a possibly unreliable memory. If the causal chain within a behavior cycle were broken, we would have no criterion for recognizing the original intention at all.

11.2 Internal relation between expectation and fulfillment

According to Wittgenstein, this indeterminacy can be overcome if we take the relation between an (expression of) expectation and its satisfaction as an internal one: 'The causal connection between speech and action is an external relation, whereas we need an internal one.'[11]

Wittgenstein's account of intentionality can be summed up by the note: 'It is in language that an expectation and its fulfillment make contact.'[12] This note on intentionality is, however, like all of the discussion of intentionality in the *Philosophical Investigations*, extremely compressed. Wittgenstein's earlier texts from the beginning of the 1930s present (save for minor exceptions) the same theory in a more intelligible way.

Wittgenstein calls his early 1930s account of intentionality the 'picture conception.' This, of course, echoes his Tractarian picture theory of meaning. The picture conception of intentionality can now be summed up as follows: 'What is essential to intention is the picture: the picture of what is intended.'[13] This claim must not be interpreted in a literal sense. Since the Tractarian proposition is a picture of a fact, so an expectation is (or contains) a picture of what is expected. The picture view of meaning amounts to an internal relation between a proposition and a fact. This view is now analogous to the picture conception of intention: there must be an internal relation between an intention and its fulfillment. Or: the relation between an expectation and its fulfillment is internal. Although Wittgenstein does not subsequently use the label 'picture conception,' this conception of intentionality is to be found in the *Philosophical Investigations* as well.[14]

We know from §10.2 that internal relations are realized among concepts only. The terms of such internal relations are, thus, not mental acts but descriptions or expressions of these acts. Given that expectation is, *prima facie*, an expression of expectation, and its fulfillment is an expression of fulfillment,[15] to describe an expectation means to describe the conditions of its fulfillment. A description of an expectation can differ from a description of its fulfillment. There must be a grammatical internal relation that transforms the former description into the latter. The relation between an expectation and its fulfillment is essentially a grammatical relation. Here are some examples:[16]

(61) 'The expectation that *p*' = 'The expectation which will be fulfilled if *p*'
(62) 'The wish for it to be the case that *p*' = 'The wish that is satisfied by the event *p*'
(63) 'The hypothesis *p*' = 'The hypothesis that is verified by the fact *p*'
(64) 'The proposition *p*' = 'The proposition that the fact *p* makes true'

The proposition on the left-hand side does not need to have the same form as the proposition on the right-hand side. Consider, for instance, the order 'Would you like to close the window?' and its fulfillment 'The window is closed.'[17] The descriptions may differ in their grammatical forms, mood, or tense. This consideration only underlines the fact that the relation between an intention and its fulfillment has a grammatical nature.

Wittgenstein likens this internal relation to an arithmetical calculation: 'From expectation to fulfilment is a step in a calculation.'[18] Consider the process of the calculation $25 \times 25 = 625$. There are certain formal steps that must be carried out in order to calculate the result from the input. The conclusion is that the same is valid for the relation between an expectation and its fulfillment. Moreover, both relations can be calculated with the same degree of certainty.

Now we can return to the two epistemological problems which we discussed above. On having a particular expectation, how does one know what its satisfaction will be? How does one know whether the actual state of affairs satisfies the previous expectation? If we admit that there is an internal relation between the descriptions of these events, then the problems will disappear. Either a single description will hold for both events; or one description can be *computed* from the other one. The trouble lies in the questions themselves, because they suggest an external view of intentionality: 'And if expectation is the thought "I am expecting it to happen that p" it is senseless to say that I won't perhaps know until later what I expected.'[19]

In order to recognize a past intention, we do not need to remember our mental state at that moment of intention. The only thing that is remembered is the description of the intention. If we expect rain, we have to remember this description and apply it in the actual situation. The problem of recognition of my past intention is, hence, the problem of applying the description in a future situation. To put it in other terms: in order to recognize my past intention *p*, I have to apply the rule for *p*. The internal relationship between expectation and its fulfillment is a special case of the internal relationship between a rule and its application (further argued in §13).

As argued in §10.5, the terms of internal relations are connected directly without any need for any mediation by a third thing. If one term is present, the other one must be too. Now, the fact that there is an internal relation between an expectation and its fulfillment might suggest that if there is an expectation, there must also be its fulfillment. This claim implies that expectations are not automatically fulfilled, which is obviously absurd.

The internal relation in question is, of course, between the descriptions of these events. If there is a description of an expectation, there will be a description of its fulfillment. No mediating thing is acting that could be described independently of the expression 'the fulfillment of the expectation':

> The fulfilment of expectation doesn't consist in the occurrence of some third thing that, in addition to being described as 'the fulfilment of the expectation', could also be described as something else, i.e. as a feeling of satisfaction, for instance, or of joy or whatever.[20]

This account does not rule out that there may be some feeling of satisfaction. This feeling is, however, not a necessary part of expectation. We have to distinguish between knowing what the possible fulfillment of an expectation would be, and knowing that the expectation has, in fact, been fulfilled. This is analogous to the distinction between knowing the meaning of a proposition and knowing that a proposition is true or false. There might be a feeling of satisfaction, if a certain proposition is true, but this feeling is not regarded as essential to the proposition.

This account of intentionality was rejected in T. Crane's 'Wittgenstein on Intentionality and Mental Representation.' Crane agrees with Wittgenstein that there must be a grammatical rule that 'the expectation that *p*' is 'the expectation that is fulfilled by the fact that *p*.' But for Crane, this observation cannot suffice to cover the entire account of how intentionality works. The expectation is that *p* can be fulfilled in addition by an event *e* that is not grammatically related to *p*.[21] Crane's example is the following story: I expect that the postman will bring my mail in the morning. There are, unknown to me, two postmen: Mr. Jones and Mr. Smith. My expectation is fulfilled by the postman's bringing my mail. It is only true on Monday that my expectation that the postman will bring my mail is the expectation that is fulfilled by Mr. Jones' bringing my mail. But I have not expected this, because I did not know that Mr. Jones is the postman. Hence, my expectation was fulfilled by a fact that I had not expected. Crane concludes:

> What this shows is that you can describe what actually fulfills your expectation [...] in a way that is independent of the description of the expectation itself. Wittgenstein's point, by contrast, is that you can only describe the object of the expectation in the way it is specified in the description of the expectation itself.[22]

It seems that Crane is wrong. Wittgenstein's point is not that every description of the fulfillment of the expectation *p* has to be internally related to *p*. The fact that fulfills the expectation that *p* (like all facts) can be described in many different ways. Some of these descriptions (or 'actions under a description' to borrow Anscombe's term) are internally related to *p*, some are not (they are related externally to *p*). In order to understand the expression 'the expectation that *p*,' it is not necessary to know that *p* is (or apparently is) *e*. This may be an accidental fact.[23] Curiously enough, Wittgenstein anticipated this objection in *The Big Typescript*:

> 'I'm looking for my cane. – Here it is!' The latter is not an explanation of the expression 'my cane' that's essential to understanding the first sentence, and that therefore I couldn't have given before my cane had been found. Rather, the

> sentence 'Here it is', if it isn't a repetition of a verbal explanation that could (also) have been given earlier, must be a new synthetic proposition.[24]

By the same token: 'I expect that the postman will bring my mail in the morning.—There he goes, it's Mr. Smith!' As argued in §10.6, internal relations can be expressed only by analytic truths. The proposition that today's postman is Mr. Smith is synthetic and thus cannot express an internal property or relation. Wittgenstein's account, based on internal relations, aims at explaining the meaning of the expression 'the expectation that *p*' regardless of whether the expectation has been fulfilled. This story must be not confused 'with a proposition that asserts the existence, the being, of an object.'[25]

11.3 Yardstick and fitting

The inquiries about intentionality focus on two related metaphors or analogies that Wittgenstein used. The first analogy is that expectation is like a yardstick or a measuring rod (Maßstab) for measuring subsequent events and to judge whether they satisfy the expectation. Expectation and its fulfillment come together like a yardstick measures an object. The second analogy is that expectation and its fulfillment fit (passen) together in pieces like a cylinder and a piston do. These analogies aim to propose the same view, the aim of which is in the end to explain the relation between language and reality:

> You cannot compare a picture with reality, unless you can set it against it as a yardstick.
> You must be able to fit the proposition on to reality.[26]

We must not forget that these remarks belong to the early 1930s context of the picture conception of meaning and intentionality. An expectation is a picture of its fulfillment. 'Picture' is used metaphorically here. This pictorial relationship can also be likened to the relation between a yardstick and the object measured. The core of the analogy is obviously the idea of comparing two things. A yardstick is compared with an object in order to find out its length. Both the yardstick and the measured objects are material things; expectation and its fulfillment do not need to be.

The internal relation between expectation and fulfillment, or between a description of an expectation and a description of its fulfillment, is analogous to the internal relation between a yardstick and a measured object. And once again, this relation holds between descriptions of these objects. In this sense, there is the internal relation of having the same length between the length of the standard meter and the length of all other objects that are one meter long. Wittgenstein concludes from these considerations that a yardstick and the object measured must have something in common. This implies that a single description holds for both.[27]

The same can be true of expectation and its fulfillment. Let an expression of an expectation be 'I expect that *p* occurs' and an expression of its fulfillment be '*p* has occurred.' Then '*p* is—in the strictest sense—what is common with a yardstick and the object measured.'[28] This statement should not be understood in the sense that there lies some third thing *between* an expectation and its fulfillment. All that this analogy suggests is that the same expression *p* is involved in both descriptions of these two events.

I would like to point out a lingering possibility of misunderstanding here. If a single description (like 'to be one meter long') held for the standard meter and also for an object that is indeed one meter long, we could then say of the standard meter that it is one meter long. This is something that Wittgenstein clearly denies later in the *Philosophical Investigations*, §50. Although the same expression ('to be one meter long') is involved in descriptions of these objects, it cannot be applied to them in the same sense. 'My table is one meter long' is an empirical proposition. 'The standard meter is one meter long' is the expression of a rule. The confusion would be complete if one says

(65) My table and the standard meter are both one meter long.

Is this an empirical proposition, or an expression of a rule, or a muddle?[29]

Now we shall turn to the other term of the analogy: *p* is contained both in a description of expectation and in a description of its fulfillment. One might think that the fulfillment has to be somehow *contained* in the expectation, like a shadow.[30] Then, however, an expectation would be its own fulfillment; an expectation would be fulfilled by the very act of expecting.[31] This is absurd. We cannot say that 'the expectation that *p*' is *p*. We can, however, say that 'the fulfillment of the expectation that *p*' is *p*. This is an important asymmetry in the internal relation between expectation and its fulfillment—or between an intention and its object.

Wittgenstein says that this is the point at which the simile of a yardstick breaks down.[32] English grammar does not rule out sentences like (65). This sentence is not *prima facie* meaningless, and one may imagine a context in which it could be used without misunderstanding. But it is absurd to say that an expectation already contains its fulfillment, and hence, it is fulfilled straight away. This may be the reason why the analogy with the yardstick virtually vanished from Wittgenstein's writings after *The Big Typescript*, and why he afterwards spoke of intentional phenomena mostly in terms of fitting.

Let me attempt to generalize this point. Wittgenstein's argumentative strategy in analyzing intentionality is, first, to make clear the difference between conceptions based on external relations and those based on internal relations and, second, to assess the possible reflexive cases of internal relations. If an expectation already contained its fulfillment and we could refer to both events by a single description, it would be a case of the reflexive use of an internal relation. Such reflexive cases are often nonsensical and indicate a wrong analysis of the phenomena in question. Wittgenstein eventually realized this. His treatment of such cases is the focus of §11.4.

The other analogy Wittgenstein employs in explaining intentionality is that an expectation and its fulfillment *fit* together somehow. Unlike the previous one, this analogy survived up until the *Philosophical Investigations* in almost the same formulations.[33] The initial consideration is that one might say that intentional thoughts are something unsatisfied:

> 'A plan as such is something unsatisfied.' (Like a wish, an expectation, a suspicion, and so on.)
> By this I mean: expectation is unsatisfied, because it is the expectation of something; belief, opinion, is unsatisfied, because it is the opinion that something is the case, something real, something outside the process of believing.[34]

This metaphor of (non-)satisfaction resembles Frege's account of functions as being *unsaturated*. In what sense, then, might expectation be unsatisfied? Wittgenstein considers two answers: the first one is based on external relations. Hunger is a feeling of non-satisfaction which can be satisfied by providing some food.[35] Satisfaction of hunger brings quiescence or even pleasure. This closes the behavior cycle. This view of satisfaction thus implies a causal, i.e., an external account of intentionality. Wittgenstein is, thus, after some other sense in which expectation is unsatisfied. The metaphor is not a causal or temporal one. It is a spatial one:

> What is our prototype of nonsatisfaction? Is it a hollow space? [...] For example, if we lay it down that we call a hollow cylinder an 'unsatisfied cylinder' and the solid cylinder that fills it 'its satisfaction'.[36]

We can also have two cylinders, or a cylinder and a piston (which is, in fact, a solid cylinder). We can speak of satisfaction if the piston *fits* into the cylinder. Now we can restate the analogy: the expectation and its fulfillment fit together like a cylinder and a corresponding piston.

There is, however, a certain danger of taking this analogy too literally. Cylinders and pistons are material objects. The relation of fitting between them is an external relation. Consider the following investigation into the grammar of 'to fit':

> Exercises: (1) When is a cylinder C said to fit into a hollow cylinder H? Only while C is stuck into H? (2) Sometimes we say that C ceased to fit into H at such-and-such a time. What criteria are used in such a case for its having happened at that time?[37]

Does the sentence '*C* fits into *H*' express an internal relation or an external relation? We can employ the criterion of temporality from §10.4. If we can say that *C* ceased to fit into *H*, then the sentence '*C* fits into *H*' expresses an external relation. And as we already know, internal relations only hold between concepts. Accordingly, we have to look for the appropriate descriptions of the objects, if their fitting is supposed to be an internal relation. Obviously, if two cylinders fit together, they must have—at least partially—the same shape. This leads to the idea that 'when one wants to describe these two one sees that, to the extent that they fit, a *single* description holds for both.'[38] Our analogy yields, thus, that expectation and its fulfillment fit together insofar as a single description holds for both. This is, however, misleading, for the distinction between expectation and its fulfillment must also be preserved.

It is actually not quite correct that a single mathematical description holds for both a cylinder and a piston with respect to whether they fit. If the cylinder can be described by the *convex* function p, then the piston is described by the corresponding *concave* function $-p$. Now we can apply this consideration to both expectation and fulfillment:

> The expectation of p and the occurrence of p correspond perhaps to the hollow shape of a body and the solid shape. Here p corresponds to the shape of the volume, and the different ways in which this shape is given correspond to the distinction between expectation and occurrence.[39]

This remark restates the point made earlier: although the same expression p is involved in the descriptions of both objects, it is not exactly the same description. The expectation p is not the same state of affairs as p itself, which is its fulfillment.

We can conclude this section by saying that both analogies aim to explain the same insights into the nature of intentionality: expectation and its fulfillment come together in language, by which we understand that a single expression is employed in their descriptions. In this sense, they are internally related. They are, however, not identical. It is important to point out that Wittgenstein employs both these analogies in highlighting the internal relationships between various other phenomena.

11.4 Intransitive intentionality

Wittgenstein offers a different, or rather a more complex, analysis of intentionality in *The Blue Book*. As we saw in the previous sections, the picture conception of intentionality was motivated by the Tractarian picture theory of meaning, and further driven by epistemological questions concerning knowledge of the intentional object. Wittgenstein's focus shifted further in *The Blue Book* in 1934. Now he takes into consideration the use of words like 'expecting,' 'wishing,' 'longing,' 'fearing,' etc. It turns out that a single analysis would not be sufficient for 'These cases of expectation form a family; they have family likenesses which are not clearly defined.'[40]

Wittgenstein distinguishes between two kinds of use of expressions for intentional phenomena here in *The Blue Book*. The analysis from the previous sections suggests *transitive* uses, because intentional verbs are used transitively here, i.e., they take a direct object: one expects *something*, is afraid of *something*, wishes *something*, is longing for *something*, etc. In addition to this, Wittgenstein considers the possibility that some of these verbs can be used *intransitively*, i.e., without any direct object. Some cases are straightforward. One can be afraid of something but one can also just have a feeling of fear without being afraid of something in particular. The intransitive use of some of the other verbs is harder to conceive of.[41] Let us have a look at Wittgenstein's most prominent case of intentionality, namely: expectation.

Are there also cases of intransitive expectation? There are indeed: 'There is a totally different use of the word "expectation" if we use it to mean a particular sensation.'[42] We can use the word 'expectation' to refer to a feeling of tension or exultation without referring to what is expected. Such use can be made explicit by the expression 'the sensation of expectation.' Moreover, Wittgenstein also considers the case of 'the sensation [of] the expectation that *B* will come.'[43] Does this expression refer to the sensation of the expectation or to the state of affairs that *B* will come? In this case, *B* is not an *argument* of the function 'expecting that *x* will come.' It is rather an *index*[44] that alludes to a certain kind of expectation. The subordinate clause is a much closer specification of the sensation. The 'expectation that *B* will come' is, thus, a characteristic of certain sensations (e.g., expecting someone is associated with positive feelings). So although the surface grammar suggests the transitive use, the expression 'the sensation of the expectation that *B* will come' can be used intransitively.

This is clearly a concession to Russell's analysis. If the phrase the 'expectation that *B* will come' is used intransitively, then we cannot be sure what its fulfillment is until the behavior cycle has been closed. Wittgenstein adds, however, that such intransitive uses of the word 'expectation' are not very common.[45] I want to point out here one important difference between Russell's analysis of intentionality and Wittgenstein's intransitive cases. Russell's account of desire is based on external (or more exactly, on causal) relations. Wittgenstein's analysis of the intransitive uses of intentional expressions does not invoke any relation at all. There is no semantic reference to anything in the future mediated by a causal chain.

There might be a temptation to explain intransitive cases in a transitive way with an unknown (or unconscious) intentional object. 'Whenever before we said "I have a sensation of fear" (intransitively) we will now say "I am afraid of something, but I don't know of what."'[46] There are indeed such cases of ignorance. What Wittgenstein is opposed to is accepting such postulating of an unknown object for a general explanation for intransitive uses of intentional idioms. The problem is actually that the verb 'to know' is used in a non-standard way in expressions like 'an unknown/unconscious object of fear.' It is difficult to explain how one gets to know what the intentional object was. Suppose I had an undirected feeling of fear and later on, I get to know what I was afraid of. Then we are facing the second epistemological problem from §11.1: how does one get to know that the present state of affairs is exactly that which one was afraid of? This suggests that the postulation of an unknown intentional object does not explain the cases of intransitive intentionality, because 'the difference which [we have] tried to explain away reappears when we carefully consider the use of the word "to know" in the two cases.'[47] To make the point clear, the relation between an intentional state and its unknown intentional object is external. In order to establish the connection, there must be some third thing, namely the recognition ('getting to know'[48]) of a previously unknown object.

Wittgenstein's analysis of intentionality from *The Blue Book* is, in the sense described above, more complex than his later 'official' account from the *Philosophical Investigations*. Although he mentions intransitive or undirected uses of intentional expressions in the *Philosophical Investigations*,[49] there is a more detailed discussion that appears in the *Remarks on the Philosophy of Psychology*: here '"expect" can mean: to believe that this or that will happen—but also: to occupy one's time with thoughts and activities of expectation, i.e. [to] *wait for*.'[50] Undirected expressions are analyzed there in terms of *experiencing meaning*.[51]

To recapitulate: Wittgenstein's analysis consists of two main steps: The first step is to distinguish between internal and external relations. Most of the cases of intentional idioms can be analyzed by an internal relation between the intentional act and its fulfillment. In the second step, we have to consider certain singular cases where the intentional object is missing or unknown: First, we have to resist the temptation to posit the intentional object in the intentional act (that is, to say that expectation contains its fulfillment), for it would be a case of a reflexive use of an internal relation. Second, there are cases in which intentional idioms directly express a sensation. The intentional object is not the main focus here. We have to be careful about explaining such cases by postulating an unconscious intentional object. Such an analysis faces similar epistemological problems to the one based on external relations.

12

Reason, motive, and cause

In the previous chapter, Russell's causal conception of intentionality was confronted with Wittgenstein's conception based on internal relations between an intentional action and its object. We can now slightly modify the terminology which allows us to put the problem discussed above into a broader context. We can say of an intentional action that it has a *reason* or a *motive*; and in the same vein, such an action must have a *cause*. Let us assume that I am about to perform an action *p* in order to achieve *q*; that is to say, *q* was my *reason* for doing *p*. Therefore, I am about to do *p* because of *q*; thus here, *q* was my *motive* for doing *p*. So, for instance, an order to do *p* can be a *reason* for doing *p*; or my fear of *q* is a *motive* for taking action in order to avoid *q*, etc. Independently of this, one may ask whether *q* was the cause of *p*—or in fact what sort of causality is operating in this example.

It is thus only a matter of terminology whether all species of intentionality can be restated in this way—as a relation between an action and its motive.[1] To be on safer ground, one could say that the relation of being a reason for doing or a motive for doing belongs to the family of intentional relations which Wittgenstein aims to conceive as internal relations. As he stresses, the words 'reason,' 'motive,' or 'cause' can be used in very many different ways.[2] The same is valid for the related expressions 'because' or 'why,' etc. The diagnosis is, then, that the surface grammar of our everyday language confuses us about (or at least does not fully distinguish between) internal and external relations.[3] In what follows I shall argue that the distinction between reasons and causes is another instance of the distinction between internal and external relations.

To begin with, let us consider the following examples from Wittgenstein's *Lectures and Conversations on Aesthetics*:

> 'Cause' is used in very many different ways, e.g.
>
> (1) "What is the cause of unemployment?" "What is the cause of this expression?" [Experiment and statistics]

(2) "What was the cause of your jumping?" "That noise." [Reason]
(3) "What was the cause of that wheel going round?" You trace a mechanism.[4]

In order to avoid a misunderstanding Wittgenstein wants to reserve the expression 'cause' for a (relation of) mechanical causality between two events. A cause in this sense can be found statistically or by tracing the underlying mechanism. This is to say that what is the cause of a certain action is always a hypothesis based on past experience. Such experience may include the knowledge of certain physical processes in one's brain which are typically not known to an agent. An important consequence is that one cannot be absolutely sure what exactly the cause of one's action was. It should therefore be clear that causal relations are external: they are realized between events, not concepts; they are expressed in temporal propositions.[5]

The most striking difference between a cause and a reason/motive for Wittgenstein is that an agent knows without any doubt the motive of their action: 'we can only *conjecture* the cause but we *know* the motive.'[6] Wittgenstein takes this statement to be a grammatical one. The motive for an action or the reason for a belief is something constitutive of the very action or belief:

> The causes of our belief in a proposition are indeed irrelevant to the question [of] what we believe. Not so the grounds, which are grammatically related to the proposition, and tell us what proposition it is.[7]

Now, I want to address two interrelated points: The first one concerns what counts as a motive, or as a reason. A rational motive or a reason cannot be just anything that an agent avows. The second point is the objection that a motive can be unconscious, i.e., unknown to an agent. One may later forget the original motive for one's action or be self-deceived or insincere about it. Both these points threaten my claim that the relation of being a motive or a reason is internal.

Now to the first point: a motive for an action or a reason for a belief is not arbitrary. If the *relation* between an action and its motive is not obvious, the agent has then to indicate a *rule* that has led them—step by step[8]—from the motive to the action. The motive can itself be an expression of this rule. In the 1930s, Wittgenstein pondered the idea that this rule must be a kind a calculation: 'Giving a reason is like giving a calculation by which you have arrived at a certain result.'[9] This statement means that between an action and its motive there is the same kind of relation as between a mathematical equation and its result. Note that the same kind of relation holds between both expectation and fulfillment.[10] As argued in §10.5[11] this relation is internal.

A slightly different account of this relation is to be found in the second part of the *Philosophical Investigations*, and in subsequent writings.[12] The relation between an action and its motive is established here in the language-game of the judging of motives. All that is needed is a technique for the judging of a motive. A judgment within this language-game may resemble a calculation, but it does not need to. We can think of some simple instances of judgments and take these as sorts of measuring rods in order to judge cases that are more complicated.[13] This later account of the relation of being a motive is, thus, the generalization of the calculation-model from the 1930s. What is important here is that the relation between a motive and an action that an agent performed is an instance of the relation between a rule and its application. This relation must be internal as I shall argue in §13.

As to the second point: an agent might avow a different motive for their action from the real one (it may be a case of ignorance or self-deception or a lie). As argued above, knowledge of a cause is always *hypothetical*—as opposed to a motive/reason. But it seems now that a motive can also be hypothetical in the sense that it is determined by the agent's sincere avowal.[14] There is a certain confusion lurking here, for 'motive' or 'reason' can be ambiguous here. A reason may mean the actual reason or may mean any possible, hypothetical reason:

> sometimes what we say acts as a justification, not as a report of what was done, e.g. I *remember* the answer to a question; when asked why I give this answer, I gave a process leading to it, though I didn't go through this process.[15]

We have to distinguish between a *report* of an actual or past motive and a *justification* of the action. The point of a report is that it should be sincere. When someone is asked for their actual motive, they should report their motive truthfully and the answer depends on their sincerity (and on their memory). But something different goes on when the agent is asked for a justification. Then it does not matter what the past motive was. All they need to give is a rule of which the present action is an instance. It does not matter whether the agent had really followed this rule.[16]

In §§10.2 and 10.4, there are several examples of sentences that are ambiguous between expressing internal or external relations. The same is true of the following kind of sentences:

(66) p is the motive for doing q.
(67) p is the reason for believing q.

If these sentences are reports of an actual motive or reason, they can be restated as being explicitly temporal:

(68) *p was* my motive for doing *q*.
(69) *p* is *the* reason why I *now* believe that *q*.

According the criterion of temporality (§10.4), these sentences express external relations. Asking for a justification is something different. In this case, (66) and (67) are timeless and could be restated as:

(70) *p* is *a possible* motive for doing *q*.
(71) *p* is *a possible* reason for believing *q*.

Again, following the criterion of temporality, these sentences express internal relations. I would like to elucidate this matter further by Wittgenstein's analogy with a route:

> The question 'Why do you believe that?' can be compared with the question 'How do you come to be here?'.[17]

Wittgenstein says that this question allows two answers. There are, in fact, however three answers to be found in Wittgenstein's lecture notes. (1) The first answer consists in giving the physical or psychological cause of one's being located here. This answer will have to describe various phenomena (e.g., stimuli, reflexes, connections of pathways in one's nervous system, etc.), the circumstances in which they occurred, and the causal laws operating here. (2) The second answer would be specifying the way I actually went here. (3) The third answer is by giving any route that I could have got here by.[18] The first answer corresponds to giving the actual cause, the second one to a report of the actual reason, and the third to a justification by giving a possible reason. The first answer expresses an external relation and the last one expresses an internal relation. In the second answer, there is expressed an external relation by means of an internal one.

12.1 The Principle of Sufficient Reason

In this and in the following section, I am going to investigate the various philosophical implications or applications of the method outlined above. One, and for Wittgenstein maybe the most important implication, has already been discussed in §11.1; namely, the implication for Russell's causal theory of intentionality and of meaning in general.[19] I will, in turn, therefore discuss Wittgenstein's denial of the Principle of Sufficient Reason and his (if not actual denial then at least) doubts about the psycho-physical parallelism of mind. Finally, I will look at Donald Davidson's influential and explicitly anti-Wittgensteinian account of subsuming rational relations under causal relations.

Wittgenstein mentioned the Principle of Sufficient Reason in his early manuscripts and in a letter to Russell from 1914.[20] Curiously enough, in this letter, he equates the principle with the law of causality. In *The Blue Book*, Wittgenstein considers the idea that there must be 'a chain of reasons reaching back to infinity.'[21] This is, I claim, a formulation of the principle which is traditionally conceived of in the following wording:

(72) For every fact *F*, there must be a reason why *F* is the case.[22]

The history of the principle goes back to pre-Socratic philosophy. Its time of glory came, however, in the seventeenth century. The principle became one of the central ideas driving the metaphysical systems of Spinoza and Leibniz, who actually coined the term 'Principle of Sufficient Reason.' It is relevant to present concerns that both these philosophers used the expression 'causa sive ratio' [cause or reason] in formulating their main principles, marking the fact that they did not distinguish between cause and reason. Here are Spinoza's formulations of the principle:

(73) Nothing exists of which it cannot be asked what is the cause (or reason) why it exists.
(74) For each thing there must be assigned a cause, *or* reason, both for its existence and for its non-existence.[23]

These formulations explicitly do not distinguish between cause and reason. This is deliberately so in Spinoza: because causal and rational relations have the same root in substance, they are coextensive. Schopenhauer, who might have inspired Wittgenstein here, in his dissertation *On the Fourfold Root of the Principle of Sufficient Reason* accuses the philosophical tradition of confusing different kinds of reasons.[24]

Before going into the details of Wittgenstein's critique of the principle, I want to pause now to extend this route analogy. The principle could amount to the following claims:

(75) 'Wherever you are, you must have got there from somewhere else, and to that previous place from another place; and so on *ad infinitum*.'

(76) 'Wherever you are, you *could* have got there from another place ten yards away; and to that other place from a third, ten yards further away, and so on *ad infinitum*.'[25]

(75) is analogous to the claim that the chain of *actual* reasons of an agent is infinite. A chain of actual reasons is based on external relations. (75) is obviously false. Nobody has gone on an infinite route. By the same token, (76) is analogous to the claim that the chain of *possible* reasons is infinite. Even this claim is problematic for Wittgenstein and in the end untenable.

Wittgenstein is also strongly opposed to the principle. Not all actions or beliefs need to have a reason, but all events do have causes. The principle is the conclusion of the following fallacious argument:

(P1) Causal chains are infinite.
(P2) Chains of reasons are causal chains.
(C) Chains of reasons are infinite.

Wittgenstein takes the first premise, i.e., the principle of causality, to be a grammatical rule of the language-game of mechanics.[26] The second premise is just an expression of the confusion of cause and reason. The language-game of giving reasons is different from that of mechanics. 'A reason can only be given within a game. The links of the chain of reasons come to an end, at the boundary of the game. (Reason and cause.)'[27] There are propositions that cannot (or do not need to) be justified within a given language-game: 'And this again joins on to the confusion between cause and reason. We need have no reason to follow the rule as we do. The chain of reasons has an end.'[28] The expressions of rules belong to the propositions that we do not need to give reasons for—in a given language-game. This is connected to the central question of the rule-following discussion:

'How am I able to obey a rule?'—if this is not a question about causes, then it is about the justification for my following the rule in the way I do. If I have exhausted the justifications I have reached bedrock, and my spade is turned. Then I am inclined to say: 'This is simply what I do.'[29]

The main substance of this remark is the justification for following a rule. If one aims to justify one's rule-following, one has to give a reason for it. But following a rule is constitutive for this very rule.[30] In other words: a rule is constituted by the praxis of its following. The reason why you follow this rule in *this* way and not in *that* way is internally related to the reason why you follow *this* rule and not *that* rule.

If a rule is the reason for an action or a belief, there is no reason for the rule itself. Language-games with their rules are expressions of human praxis. This is the bedrock; this is simply what we do. There is, nevertheless, a temptation to transgress the praxis and ask further for a reason for the language-game itself. Why exactly this or that language-game?

There are several ways to confront this temptation or answer this question. It would be too easy to say that beyond the boundary of a language-game, i.e., beyond the bounds of sense, there is simply *nonsense*. This attitude amounts to a refutation of any answer to the question of why. I would like to offer three possible answers.

First, there is always a causal explanation for why we employ this or that language-game. I have in mind historical, etymological, or evolutionary explanations, etc. This kind of answer is based, of course, on an external relation with all its disadvantages over an answer that is internally related to the language-game in question.

Second, by attempting to answer the question, i.e., by attempting to justify a rule, one could step into another language-game. What is an expression of a rule in one language-game can be an empirical proposition in another game. A certain sentence can express an empirical proposition in the language-game of rule-teaching; the same sentence will then express a rule as soon as the application of the sentence has been mastered. Between these games there is a *vertical relation*.[31] It may happen that there is no other language-game where a rule can be justified. If so, one can just invent or construct one. What else are metaphysical systems if not invented attempts to justify our everyday praxis? The chain of reasons may then only be infinite if we keep constructing additional language-games in which the chain can continue.

The third way to justify a rule is in fact Wittgenstein's own proposed answer given in the quotation above: 'This is simply what I do.' This is a reflexive construction 'which masks the beginning of the chain of reasons.'[32] Similar constructions are not uncommon in philosophy: consider, e.g., the Spinozian concept of *causa sui*, or the biblical description of God: 'I am that I am.'[33] To pick up on the general threads of this book, we have here again the reflexive use of an internal relation. Such uses are not necessarily nonsensical. But we have to be aware that they mark the end of a chain of reasons, i.e., a *terminus ad quem* of a justification.

12.2 Psycho-physical parallelism, super-mechanism and the mind

There are various kinds of relationships between mental and physical phenomena. We can speak of their isomorphism (*viz.* they have the same structural properties), parallelism (*viz.* they occur in tandem). or even identity (*viz.* the mind and body are one and the same thing as claimed by Spinoza[34]). Wittgenstein offers no knockdown argument against these metaphysical conceptions of mind, though. His aim is rather to show that these conceptions are unnatural and ultimately unjustified, and that our inclination for their validity results from a primitive conception of grammar which confuses cause and reason.

The language-games of giving reasons/motives (reasoning) and of giving causes (mechanics) are distinct activities. It may, however, seem that they share the same realm. This is to say that they are different ways of referring to the same phenomena, which here are mental states. One difference might be the one between the first-person and the third-person perspectives on mental states. Wittgenstein is opposed to this idea:

> A motive is not a cause 'seen from within'! Here the simile of 'inside and outside' is totally misleading – as it so often is. – It is taken from the idea of the soul (of a living being) in one's head (imagined as a hollow space). But this idea has been mixed with other incompatible ideas, like the mixed metaphors in the sentence: 'The tooth of time that heals all wounds, etc.'[35]

Let me try to unravel this from the end. This metaphorical talk of time contains, in fact, two metaphors: 'time has teeth'[36] and 'time heals all wounds.' Now Wittgenstein claims that these metaphorical ideas are incompatible. Time's teeth leave marks of disintegration and thus collapse. We can see such marks at castle ruins. The metaphor of healing wounds suggests, however, that something broken will be put back together again. The whole metaphor thus implies both integration and disintegration. The view that a motive *is* a cause seen from within also contains two incompatible ideas: the mind is a mechanism and the mind is something inside the head. The former idea is of a mind that is a mechanism consisting of one's brain (or the head or the whole body). The latter takes the mind as hovering in a hollow space and perceiving the mechanism from within. The mind cannot be, then, both a mechanism and located inside this same mechanism. This, therefore, is how these ideas are incompatible with each other, which completes the argument for the claim that a motive is also not a cause as seen from within.

However, Wittgenstein gives us some independent arguments against these two conceptions of mind. My present concern here is with Wittgenstein's argument against the mechanistic model of the mind. He has, in fact, a lot of arguments in this respect and so I will focus on the one related to the main subject of this book, namely the difference between internal and external relations.

Taking the mind as a mechanism or as a machine means conceiving of the language-game of mechanics as superior to other language-games. The mechanistic model does not need to imply directly any kind of identity theory as discussed above. One has to explain, however, the way in which other language-games are based on (or grow out of) the language-game of mechanics. All these language-games are expressions of human practices. We have to explain in particular how it is possible that we are able to be involved in the practices or techniques of reasoning, inferring, intending something, or calculating, all of which are based on internal relations. In short, how is it possible to achieve the *super-rigidity* of internal relations out of the underlying causal, i.e., external relations?

Internal relations hold with logical necessity or super-rigidity, whereas external relations do not. Moreover, internal relations hold only in virtue of their precise terms.[37] To know one term amounts to knowledge of the other terms of an internal relation. If the mind were a mechanism, we would necessarily know at least some future states of this mechanism:

> The machine as symbolizing its action: the action of a machine—I might say at first—seems to be there in it from the start. What does that mean?—If we know the machine, everything else, that is its movement, seems to be already completely determined.[38]

A present state of the machine and its future state are related externally by the causal relation. We assume, however, that the machine could *compute* internal relations. Then, however, its consecutive states have to be related internally as well. We can denote these states of the machine M as s_1 and s_2 and consider the following conditional description of M:

(77) If M is in state s_1, then its next state *must* be s_2.

As established in §10.6, internal relations hold without exceptions. Does (77) hold without any exception? It is obvious that (77) holds unless the machine malfunctions:

(78) If M is in state s_1, then its next state *must* be s_2, if M is working correctly.

If (77) has to be understood as (78), then no internal relation is expressed. But the saving clause would not be necessary if the machine could not have a malfunction. We have arrived, thus, at the idea of a machine that cannot have a malfunction—the idea of a perfectly rigid mechanism,[39] of a super-mechanism.[40] If such a machine could not break down, it would have to contain all of its future movements and states, i.e., they would have to 'be really—in a mysterious sense—already *present*.'[41] Wittgenstein also argues that the idea of a super-mechanism is confused: '"People say there is a super-mechanism, but there isn't." But no one knows what a super-mechanism is.'[42] The upshot of this argument is thus: we wanted to explain the mind by using something that we are familiar with, but the picture has been mixed up by something unknown or even mysterious.

We have to distinguish here between an actual machine (which is able to perform a computation) and an ideal machine, e.g., a Turing machine computing a recursive function. Actual machines are liable to malfunction, but so too are human minds. But if the mind were a machine, the notion of malfunction would not make any sense. There would not be any authority that could detect a malfunction and correct the actual machine. The correct way of functioning would be defined by the actual working of the machine. The actual machine therefore lacks *normative* force.[43] If the mind were such a machine, it would lack normative force too.

There is a close connection here to the problem of rule-following which is going to be discussed in the next chapter. Suppose that a machine has to compute the plus function, but the machine computes that '68 + 57' is 5. What then? Or who could be the judge here? How could we decide whether the machine is computing the plus function, but malfunctioning, or computing another function, say *quus*? Or it could be another machine that does the judging. But other machines are liable to malfunction in the same way. Or is it agreement among several machines? This question is analogous to the one of whether an appeal to communal agreement can decide the correct application of a rule in a novel situation.

These problems lead us to a very simple question: what internal relation is exhibited in a given machine and how do we know it? Frege pointed out that it is impossible to ascribe a unique number to a pile of playing cards.[44] This means in our terms here that material objects such as a pile of cards have no internal properties. Frege's strategy of escaping from Russell's paradox was to ascribe numbers to concepts. Wittgenstein's insistence that internal properties can only be ascribed to concepts and that internal relations hold between concepts also draws on this Fregean idea.

Now we can pursue this idea a little bit further. The so-called *triviality arguments* against functionalism in the philosophy of mind argue that every physical machine (of a certain complexity) implements every possible computation.[45] Every series of movements of a machine can be interpreted as an implementation of any internal relation. This means, however, that a machine on its own cannot implement every internal relation unless 'we can already *presuppose* a distinction between the correct and incorrect functioning of the machine.'[46] Either the mind-machine is a super-machine which cannot break down, or we have to provide an independent account to explain its normativity. Thus, the idea of the mind as a mechanism cannot be the whole account of the human mind.

In the remaining part of this section I shall briefly focus on a very weak version of psycho-physical parallelism. It is based on the idea that the actual processes of reasoning must make a physical difference in the agent's brain. Wittgenstein is, however, not willing to accept this form of parallelism either:

> 903. No supposition seems to me more natural than that there is no process in the brain correlated with associating or with thinking; so that it would be impossible to read off thought-processes from brain-processes. I mean this: if I talk or write there is, I assume, a system of impulses going out from my brain and correlated with my spoken or written thoughts. [...] The case would be like the following—certain kinds of plants multiply by seed, so that a seed always produces a plant of the same kind as that from which it was produced—but *nothing* in the seed corresponds to the plant which comes from it; so that it is impossible to infer the properties or structure of the plant from those of the seed that it comes out of—this can only be done from the *history* of the seed. So an organism might come into being even out of something quite amorphous, as it were causelessly; and there is no reason why this should not really hold for our thoughts, and hence for our talking and writing.
> 904. It is thus perfectly possible that certain psychological phenomena *cannot* be investigated physiologically, because physiologically nothing corresponds to them.[47]

What is Wittgenstein's argument here and how is this argument related to the distinction between cause and reason? Several commentators have pointed out that Wittgenstein is arguing here *inter alia* against Wolfgang Köhler's trace theory of memory.[48] I think we can take Wittgenstein to be arguing against the more radical view which Klagge calls the denial of *supervenience*, i.e., the view that 'there could be a difference in memories, or resulting plants, without *any* difference in brains, or seeds.'[49] Let me first analyze the following claim about plants:

(79) If two plants are different, there *must* be a difference in their seeds.

It is, however, perfectly possible that different plants grew up from the same seeds. Their growth is influenced by their environment and these influences may be responsible for their difference. Wittgenstein is considering here, in fact, a stronger claim:

(80) If two plants are different, there *must* be a difference in their histories.

I take the history of a plant to be its growth from a seed to its present form. Now, (80) seems to be analogous to:

(81) If two memories are different, there *must* be a difference in the underlying brain states.

What kind of compulsory force is expressed by the 'must' in these sentences? Is it a logical compulsion? These sentences are timeless and thus, according to the criterion of temporality, they should express internal relations. As noted above,[50] Wittgenstein takes the law of causality to be a grammatical rule. Something like this must be true of (80) and (81) too. The compulsion of the 'must' is also the compulsion of a grammatical rule. If (81) were a rule, then which language-game would it belong to? Wittgenstein is reported to have made the following statement which might be helpful here: '*Now* (today) we have every reason to say there must be a difference.'[51] We can thus take (81) to mean:

(82) If two memories are different, there is a *reason* to say there *must* be a difference in the underlying brain states.

Let me call this the *principle of causal mediation*. This wording suggests that the rule belongs to the language-game of reasoning. On the other hand, the rule states that causality between psychological phenomena *must* be mediated physiologically. This is to say that the rule must belong to the language-game of mechanics. There is an obvious conclusion: (82) is crossing over different language-games. If so, if (82) were a rule of both these language-games (that is, those of reasoning and of mechanics), we would have to give up the principle that internal relations hold between concepts only.

The true status of the principle of causal mediation is that of an ideal: 'There is an ideal—a direction in which investigations are constantly pushed. "There *must* be" corresponds to this ideal.'[52] This declaration has a certain Kantian flavor and I would like to argue that Wittgenstein follows—maybe unknowingly—in Kant's footsteps. Wittgenstein sees the source of the temptation to follow the principle of causal mediation in a primitive conception of grammar:

> The prejudice in favour of psycho-physical parallelism is also a fruit of the primitive conception of grammar. For when one admits a causality between psychological phenomena, which is not mediated physiologically, one fancies that in doing so one is making an admission of the existence of a soul *alongside* the body, a ghostly mental nature.[53]

What is the primitive conception of grammar that leads to an admission of the existence of a Cartesian soul detached from the body?[54] I think that the primitive conception of grammar amounts to taking grammar for something other than a conceptual scheme expressing human practices, activities, and techniques. It amounts to mistaking grammatical rules for metaphysical statements answerable to the essence of reality. In short, the primitive conception of grammar is such that it is not autonomous. Only if we took the grammatical rules of the language-games of reasoning and mechanics for metaphysical principles would we be tempted to postulate any unifying principles (like the principle of causal mediation) underpinning these games and hence unifying the realms of reality which correspond to them.

This line of argument finds its predecessor in Kant's *Antinomy of the Judgment*.[55] Kant considers this antinomy in the context of explaining living organisms by purely mechanical laws. Can living organisms, and human beings especially, be explained by causal laws only? Or do we need another kind of explanation? He states this antinomy in two variants. The first variant is presented by the following two maxims:

> *Thesis:* All production of material things is possible in terms of merely mechanical laws.

> *Antithesis:* Some production of material things is not possible in terms of merely mechanical laws.[56]

These theses obviously contradict each other, because the antithesis is a negation of the thesis. They are irreconcilable because they are 'constitutive principles concerning the possibility of objects.'[57] A principle is constitutive in this sense if it is an *a priori* presupposition of our experience. It is a necessary condition of possible experience. For the antinomy to be resolved, we have to convert these principles into *regulative* maxims which then would read:

> *The first maxim* of judgment is this *thesis*: All production of material things and their forms must be judged to be possible in terms of merely mechanical laws.
> *The second maxim* is this *antithesis:* Some products of material nature cannot be judged to be possible in terms of merely mechanical laws. (Judging them requires a quite different causal law – *viz.*, that of final causes.)[58]

Taking the principles as regulative maxims of judgment does not solve this antinomy; it is rather the first and preliminary step towards its resolution. As regulative principles, these maxims do not discredit any mechanical explanation of living organisms; they actually help us in our search for genuine mechanical explanations.[59] There *must* be, in the end, a mechanistic explanation of nature (living organisms included) which can be called knowledge. Kant's method in his dialectics can be summed up as the process of converting metaphysical principles into constitutive transcendental principles (which is done mostly in the *Critique of the Pure Reason*) and converting these, in turn, into regulative maxims in order to resolve the antinomy of judgment (in the *Critique of Judgment*). This process is driven by our striving for the unity of all knowledge.

I think that Wittgenstein goes even further in questioning this striving for unity. He clearly recognized the regulative character of the principle of causal mediation. In addition to this, he does not see any need to provide a unification of causal explanations and explanations based on reasons and motives. That there *must* be a causal explanation is only an ideal that we *may* (but do not need to) pursue.[60]

12.3 Davidson's causal theory of action

I am going to conclude my discussion of the distinction between cause and reason by looking at an influential critique of it by Donald Davidson. I will argue that Davidson's critique does not pose any serious problem for

Wittgenstein's position and that Davidson is guilty of several confusions that Wittgenstein was combating. This discussion will, I hope, provide us with some deeper assessment of the distinction between cause and reason.

Before going into the details of Davidson's argument, let me reiterate the crux of Wittgenstein's position. The question 'Why did you do action *X*?' allows for basically three kinds of answers: (1) an actual cause of *X*, (2) *the* actual reason for doing *X*, and (3) *a* possible reason for doing *X*. These answers express, successively, an external relation, an external relation by means of an internal one, and an internal relation. Moreover, as argued in §12.2, it is not necessary that the relation of being *the* actual reason is accompanied by a causal relation.

Davidson's position is that rationalization, i.e., the explanation of an action by giving *the* agent's reason, 'is a species of causal explanation.'[61] What Davidson is after is also not merely a justification of the action (*a possible* reason for it), but *the actual* reason why it was performed.

> But then something essential has certainly been left out, for a person can have a reason for an action, and perform the action, and yet this reason not be the reason why he did it. Central to the relation between a reason and an action it explains is the idea that the agent performed the action *because* he had the reason. Of course, we can include this idea too in justification; but then the notion of justification becomes as dark as the notion of reason until we can account for the force of that 'because'.[62]

What makes a possible reason for the action into the real reason? Davidson claims now—'failing a satisfactory alternative'[63]—that the actual reason for the action is such that there is a causal connection between the reason and the action. Davidson's (unlike Wittgenstein's) linguistic intuition is that 'because' suggests a causal connection. But even if Davidson were right about the meaning of 'because,' it would not imply that the real reason for the action is also its cause.

If the existence of a causal connection is not, according to Wittgenstein, the distinguishing feature of the actual reason over a merely possible reason, how can Wittgenstein then account for this distinction? The easiest way to find out the agent's actual reason for their action is to ask them: 'The reason may be nothing more than just the one he gives when asked.'[64] There does not need to be any further reason,[65] because the chain of actual reasons always has an end (§12.1). Such an avowal may be disturbed by the possibility of ignorance, self-deception, or a lie as already argued above.[66] But then, if there is a suspicion, we have to look at the context of the action. Sometimes there is evidence that there is a reason to believe that the agent's avowal did not reveal the actual reason. Sometimes we can use the methods of psychoanalysis to reveal the agent's reason for their action. In such cases, however, a different language-game is being played.[67] This means that what counts as a reason is defined by the praxis and techniques of asking for reasons. We can, but do not need to, include psychoanalytic methods in this praxis.

To sum up: if Davidson's claim is that an explanation of an action by giving *the* agent's reason is a species of causal explanation, then this claim is based on an unfounded assumption which I have called the principle of causal mediation. If Davidson's argument is that the existence of a causal connection is the only account for the distinction between an actual reason and a merely possible reason, then we can find another account in Wittgenstein. And finally, if Davidson's claim is that *the* agent's reason is perhaps (or even often is) causally connected with their action, then there is no disagreement between Davidson and Wittgenstein at all here.

13

Rules and their applications

Language is internally related to the world. This is the core of the Tractarian picture theory of meaning. Wittgenstein abandoned this view at the beginning of the 1930s. However, we must not understand this to mean that the relation between language and the world then became external. The internal relation between language and the world had instead been transformed into the internal relation between a rule and its applications.

The problem is that Wittgenstein was never wholly explicit on this matter. The claim that rules are internally related to their applications is for the most part an exegetical construction advanced primarily by Baker and Hacker in their response to Kripke's rule-following paradox.[1]

Wittgenstein's most explicit statement concerning the relation between a rule and its applications is his remark from 1931:

> One thing is clear, if I have (correctly) followed a rule, the result will stand in an internal relation to the source fact and to the expression of the rule. I cannot express this internal relation except by restating those three complexes because [...] everything is already settled in this restatement.[2]

In the context of this remark, Wittgenstein argues that an application of a rule to a certain source fact (Vorlage) that leads to a certain result is not a causal process. Wittgenstein talks about three complexes, but we can take the expression of the rule together with the source fact (Vorlage) as one complex and the result of the application as another complex. The rule has to match the source fact in order to transform it into the result. Thus understood, we can then say that there is an internal relation between a rule and its application.

Put this way, however, this statement becomes rather misleading. We must not forget that, strictly speaking, the expression of the rule applied in a certain situation stands in an internal relation to the result of this application. An example may help here. Suppose we have a rule which orders us to do *B*, if *A*.

The expression of this rule (if *A*, do *B*) applied in the situation *A* stands in an internal relation to *B*.

We know from §10.2 that internal relations hold solely between concepts. Accordingly, then, the internal relation is not between a rule and an act that is in accord with it but between the expression of the rule (applied in a situation) and a description of the result. We have to insist here on the distinction between a rule and an *expression* of this rule.

Taking the internal relation in question in this way, we can infer from knowing a rule what its application is in a given case. In short: knowing a rule amounts to knowing its application. Wittgenstein expresses this idea in a negative context: 'It seems so clear here: it is one thing "to *understand* a word" and another "to *apply* it."'[3] Wittgenstein speaks here of knowing a word, but we take him to be speaking about rules in general, for words are what they are due to their grammatical rules.

13.1 The rule-following paradox

Baker and Hacker are generally right that 'the concept of a rule and the concept of what accords with it (what is a correct application of it) are internally related'[4] and that this view is implicit in Wittgenstein's treatment of rules and rule-following. Their argument (or one of their arguments) against Kripke and his rule-skepticism is that they take this relation to be external. This means that 'the identity of the rule is divorced from its applications; what the rule is is one thing, what its applications are is another, and only an agent's independent interpretation links the two.'[5] This claim means, however, that from an expression of a rule we cannot infer what a description of its application would be, let us say, in a novel situation. This creates a paradox. One has mastered a rule through a finite set of its applications; thus, one might be unable to apply it in a novel situation.

Let us take the following series: 2, 4, 6, 8, 10… Suppose that I have mastered the rule of this series for numbers less than 1000. I am now asked to continue the series above 1000. Ought I to continue the series in this way: 1000, 1002, 1004… or this way: 1000, 1020, 1040…? The point is that there is a rule for every continuation of the series. Or Kripke's most famous example: suppose that I have never computed '68 + 57.' The correct result of this computation is, of course, '125.' But there is also a non-standard interpretation of the sign '+' according to which the result of this computation is then '5.' And Wittgenstein now admits this general point: 'This was our paradox: no course of action could be determined by a rule, because every course of action can be made out to accord with the rule.'[6]

Kripke distinguishes between a *straight* solution and a *skeptical* solution to this paradox. A solution is straight 'if it shows that on closer examination the scepticism proves to be unwarranted'[7] by rejecting one or more of the premises of the paradox. A skeptical solution, however, accepts the paradox and tries to argue that it does not disturb any of our ordinary practices or beliefs. First to skeptical solutions: the paradox can be surmounted by an appeal to some kind of third step that mediates between a rule and its applications.

This third step could be (i) an interpretation or a mental image. But, as Baker and Hacker argue, an expression of the interpretation is, in fact, another formulation of the rule. If it had been impossible to apply the rule in the former formulation, it would also be impossible to do so in the latter formulation. Hence, an interpretation of a rule is not a third step that could mediate between a rule and its application. Another skeptical solution may appeal to (ii) human biological nature (to the human form of life as it is understood biologically). It is obvious that our language is conditioned by human nature or in Wittgenstein's terms by the 'general facts of nature.' Such facts, being the basis of grammar, lie outside grammar. They may cause us to have this or that rule, but they cannot justify it or be a reason for it;[8] (ii) Kripke's solution to the paradox is to appeal to community agreement. 'The situation is very different if we widen our gaze from consideration of the rule follower alone and allow ourselves to consider him as interacting with a wider community.'[9] Kripke's solution is based, thus, on what he calls the 'public checkability' of applications of the rule. If someone applied a rule wrongly, the community is then able to check and possibly correct their action.

Internal relations do not allow for any third mediating term between its terms as argued in §10.5. In order not to disturb the internal relation between a rule and its applications, one would have to argue that the third term is internally related both to the rule and to its applications. We saw that an interpretation of a rule is internally related to a rule, but there is no independent reason why such an interpretation should be internally related to an application of a rule.

Kripke's solution is based on the idea that community agreement is an internal property both of a rule and of its applications. In fact, agreement about a rule would amount to agreement about its applications. The crucial question is: is the agreement of the community an internal property of a rule? Kripke's critics like Baker and Hacker argue that community agreement is external to a rule:

> Community agreement yields a sense of objectivity (or assertion-conditions for correctness) only by severing the internal relation between the rule and what accords with it. In place of that internal relation the community view substitutes the notion of community *agreement*, which is not an *internal property* of the rule.[10]

A community can agree on a rule at time t_0, which means agreeing on its future applications. What guarantees, however, that agreement about the rule's application at time t_1 matches the previous agreement at time t_0? The majority of the community may be mistaken about it. Baker and Hacker thus conclude:

> There is no possibility of building consensus in behavior (or shared dispositions) into the explanation of what 'correct' means except at the price of abandoning the insight that a rule is internally connected to acts in accord with it.[11]

An agreement of the community or a communal agreement, to sum things up, cannot then be the desired mediator between a rule and its applications. But following a rule has an essentially social character; it is a practice, a habit, a custom, an institution—to use Wittgenstein's attributes. A kind of communal agreement is, of course, among these practices. Using language presupposes communal agreement about this or that language.[12] Communal agreement is, like the 'general facts of nature,' a part of the framework which makes rule-following possible.

At this point, Kripke or a rule-skeptic may admit that there has to be an internal relation between a rule and its applications[13] without having a communal agreement as its internal part. They may insist, however, that the problem is an epistemological one. The problem is: 'How do I know that "plus", as I use it, denotes a function that, when applied to 68 and 57, yields 125?'[14] In other words, how do I know that, thus far, I have followed this or that rule under the expression 'plus'? How do I know which internal relation is the right one? The role of communal agreement might be to decide about this epistemological problem. Hence, an appeal to the internal relation between a rule and its applications is void if one strives for a skeptical solution of the paradox.

A straight solution of the skeptical paradox will consist in showing that no third mediating term between a rule and its application is necessary, because there is neither an ontological nor an epistemological gap between a rule and its applications. All the preceding attempts to give a skeptical solution miss out the fact that internal relations are held among concepts. They focus on the application of a rule as an act, as an event. What we have to focus on is, however, a description of the application. In what follows, I am going to reiterate the argument from §10.5 and adjust it to the present problem.

We have to show that there is an internal relation between an expression of a rule applied in a given situation and an expression of the result of this application. In Kripke's case, we need to show that there is an internal relation between '68 + 57' and '125.' These concepts (the plus sign and the signs for the natural numbers) are individuated by grammatical rules that define these concepts. All we have to *prove* now is that these rules are not independent.[15] Ironically, this idea is formulated by Kripke himself:

> One might even observe that, on the natural numbers, addition is the only function that satisfies certain laws that I accept – the 'recursion equations' for +: $(x)\ (x+0=x)$ and $(x)\ (y)\ (x+y'=(x+y)')$ where the stroke or dash indicates successor; these equations are sometimes called a 'definition' of addition.[16]

Kripke, however, rejects this idea on the following grounds:

> The problem is that the other signs used in these laws (the universal quantifiers, the equality sign) have been applied in only a finite number of instances, and they can be given non-standard interpretations that will fit non-standard interpretations of '+'. Thus for example '(*x*)' might mean for every x<h, where h is some upper bound to the instances where universal instantiation has hitherto been applied, and similarly for equality.[17]

To cast skeptical doubt upon the rule for addition would involve doubting other rules too. Kripke mentions the rule for the universal quantifier and for the equality sign. Most importantly, these skeptical doubts would involve rules for natural numbers too. We can recursively define addition as the only function on natural numbers which satisfies the conditions mentioned above. On the other hand we can define natural numbers by their algebraic properties with respect to addition, e.g., associativity, commutativity, existence of the identify element, etc. It is not important what defines what; whether addition is defined by employing natural numbers or *vice versa*.

The skeptic cannot then question the rule for addition while leaving all the other grammatical rules (and especially those for natural numbers) untouched. The rule for addition is not left hanging in the air. It is grammatically (internally) connected to a myriad of other rules, e.g., to the rule for subtraction and, most importantly, to the grammatical rules for natural numbers. If someone applied the rule for addition wrongly, a community might be able to correct them. However, this cannot be an arbitrary decision; the community has to point out the other rules that are internally related to this rule. The community (or even a single person) has to give a *reason* why the application of the rule was wrong.

To conclude: in order to give a straight solution to Kripke's paradox, one has to stress the internal relation between an expression of a rule applied in a certain situation and an expression of the result of this application. What determines an application of a rule in a novel situation is the rule itself together with the grammatical rules for the description of this situation. These rules themselves are then sufficient to compute the result.

13.2 Inexplicability of rules and the determinacy of sense

Towards the end of §12.1, I mentioned a possible way of explaining or justifying a rule by the use of the reflexive constructions 'This is simply what I do' or 'I do what I do.'[18] This means that there is no independent reason for this rule available. If there is an explanation, it must be internally related to this very rule, which implies that the (expression of this) rule must already contain its explanation. Wittgenstein writes in the early 1930s:

> What I want to say is that a sign in some sense cannot be explained. It must speak for itself in the rules for its use. It has to say everything, by giving every possible (clear) explanation.[19]

Wittgenstein demands that rules, which explain or govern the meaning of signs, have to speak for themselves. In the end, 'the whole language must speak for itself.'[20] But neither signs nor rules are pictures or pictorial representations. The determinacy of sense cannot be presupposed so easily. There must be the possibility of misunderstanding, because language, in fact, sometimes fails to speak for itself. We are now facing the following dilemma. On the one hand, signs are being used in accordance with rules and rules aim to explain the meaning of signs. They are hence already explanations. On the other hand, we cannot determine rules by means of any expressions, i.e., by means of any signs, because these signs have to be explained by other rules. In short: rules determine signs and signs determine rules. [21]

The problem stems from the fact that language is for the Wittgenstein of the early 1930s a *calculus*, an internally related system of rules. All external relations are forbidden here.[22] Language as a calculus falls short of its practical dimension. Language users play no role in this system.

Wittgenstein eventually realized that rules (or at least some rules) could be determined by human practices and behavior. The question as to how to follow a rule is pointless, because it suggests that there must be an answer, an explanation of the rule. Some rules, however, cannot be explained by signs in certain situations. If someone does not understand a rule, they may call for further explanations. There must be, however, a *final* explanation. They follow this expression of a rule without any further explanations. This consideration explains why Wittgenstein says: 'When I obey a rule, I do not choose. I obey the rule *blindly*.'[23] We are tempted to cut off any need for further explanations by the reflexive construction 'This is simply what I do.' To say that I obey the rule blindly or 'This is what I do' is, in fact, not a reply at all to the question concerning the following of the rule.

If human praxis is constitutive for the rules of our language, then language users must agree in this praxis. This agreement, however, does not encompass anything factual. Language users do not need to agree about what is true and what is false. Rather, they must agree in the language they use:

> 'So you are saying that human agreement decides what is true and what is false?'—It is what human beings say that is true and false; and they agree in the *language* they use. That is not agreement in opinions but in form of life.[24]

Here, we have to look at language from an outside perspective which Wittgenstein also calls 'the ethnological approach.'[25] This perspective is in contrast to an inner perspective on language, which is a closed, internally interrelated system here. What is important here is that these perspectives do not exclude each other. Rules, on the one hand, make up a system; they are not independent of each other. The rule for addition is not independent of the rules for natural numbers. Each of these rules, on the other hand, is an expression of the actions about which language users agree. The rules for natural numbers and for addition are expressions of our practices of counting which do not need any further justification. This is simply how we count, or—to mention other practices addressed in this book—this is simply how we measure things, ascribe colors, produce works of art, etc.

Internal relations are embodied in the rules of our language. We can look at internal relations from the inner perspective and conceive of them as a system or rather as systems. Complex algebraic structures like lattices, rings, monoids, groups, groupoids, loops, or categories are examples of such systems where the inner perspective is more important. Human practices with such formalized systems are rather conservative.[26] The outside perspective is, thus, less important. This is not to say that human practices are of no relevance in mathematics. The nature of its praxis is just such that the outside perspective does not reveal many important insights in this field.

Internal relations are, however, also constituted by human practices. Shared human practices are models or vehicles for conveying internal relations.[27] The internal relations between the paradigmatic samples for numbers, colors, or units of length are constituted by our practices of counting, ascribing colors, or measuring. It matters how we check that two sets have the same number of elements. We have to pair their elements off. It matters how we ascribe color to a thing. We look at its surface (not the inside) and if we are uncertain about the exact color, we have to compare it with a sample in a sample book. Finally, it matters how we measure the length of an object. We can use another object of a known length and place them alongside each other. People used to use their hands or feet as the objects of comparison. Not all hands or feet are, however, the same length; and moreover, the lengths of hands and feet change as people grow. It is better to use a uniform object of comparison whose length is more or less constant. This includes using rulers and yardsticks. There has to be agreement about these methods of counting, ascribing colors, or measuring things, and not about the color or the length of a certain thing. All of these practices and the internal relations that they constitute shall be addressed in the next chapters.[28]

The tendency in Wittgenstein's thinking to view internal relations as constituted by our praxis culminates in his final writings, which were collected in the book *On Certainty*. At least some internal relations are rooted not in this or that language-game; they are rooted deeper in our pre-linguistic behavior such 'that a language-game is based on it, that it is the prototype of a way of thinking and not the result of thought.'[29] This behavior is not the result of any decision, any training, or any act of baptizing. These internal relations are also not learned, at least not explicitly: 'I do not explicitly learn the propositions that stand fast for me.'[30] In conclusion, internal relations may be expressions of our human form of life, of general facts about our human nature.

14

Mathematics

We have seen in some of the previous chapters that mathematical statements are paradigmatic cases of internal relations.[1] And indeed, the core of Wittgenstein's conception of mathematics can be summed up in the motto that 'arithmetical rules are statements of internal relations.'[2] This is not to say that this taking of arithmetic (and in fact of all mathematics) as based on internal relations is all Wittgenstein has to say about the philosophy of mathematics. On the contrary, his contribution to the philosophy of mathematics is extremely diverse. This is why in this chapter I have to restrict myself to the discussion of topics directly related to the distinction between internal and external relations.

In particular, I am going to focus on Wittgenstein's insistence on the pictorial aspect of mathematical notation, which is, of course, his Tractarian heritage. Mathematical notation must always be capable of depicting a state of affairs. Here is a clear expression of this attitude:

> There must always remain a clear way back to a picture-like representation of numbers leading through all arithmetical symbols, abbreviations, signs for operations, etc.[3]

Wittgenstein identifies numbers with numerals and this strategy also applies to mathematical proofs: 'A proof must of course have the character of a model.'[4] Numbers and proofs are for Wittgenstein kinds of *prototypes* of certain activities—especially the activities of counting and performing experiments. Numbers or proofs are the *yardsticks* or *measures* of reality. Like in the *Tractatus*, the pictorial relationship is based here on internal relations.

This finitistic conception of mathematics is threatened, however, by general arithmetical propositions. Do they picture some general characteristics of numbers? There is an analogous question within the Tractarian framework. If a proposition were a picture of reality,[5] what would a generalized proposition depict? Wittgenstein realized that his Tractarian account of generality was deficient. In this chapter, I am going to argue that the Tractarian account of generality fails because it confuses internal generality with external generality. Then I will proceed, in turn, to Wittgenstein's conceptions of numbers and proofs.

14.1 Generality

First let me turn to Wittgenstein's conception of generality (or of general propositions) from 1929. Here he criticized his Tractarian view that quantified propositions are infinite conjunctions or disjunctions.[6] The problem lies in an attempt at quantifying over infinite domains. We can never capture such quantification by enumeration. In order to understand a generalized proposition one has to know all elements from the infinite domain, which is, of course, impossible.[7]

This shows that the word 'all' is ambiguous here. 'There are as many different "alls" as there are different "ones."'[8] And indeed, general propositions can sometimes be analyzed as finite conjunctions. But then we have to provide an account of quantifications over seemingly infinite domains. In order to provide such an account Wittgenstein distinguishes between an *internal generality* and *external generality*.[9] Consider the following arithmetical statement:

(83) $(x)\ ((x + 1)^2 = x^2 + 2x + 1)$

This statement is supposed to quantify over the infinite domain of (let us assume) natural numbers in order to express something general. The Tractarian account yields the following analysis of (83):

(84) $((0 + 1)^2 = 0^2 + 2{\times}0 + 1) \wedge$
$((1 + 1)^2 = 1^2 + 2{\times}1 + 1) \wedge$
$((2 + 1)^2 = 2^2 + 2{\times}2 + 1) \wedge$
...

However, according to the later Wittgenstein this would be an inappropriate analysis. The notation for generality[10] (x)—as well as the notation for existence $(\exists x)$—indicates that an internal relation is expressed between the two sides of the equation.[11] The notation for generality, then, expresses that there is an arithmetical operation transforming the one side of the equation into the other one. This is a case of an internal (or provable) generality which is, in fact, no generality at all. (83) is thus not about *all* numbers (natural, real, or whichever); but it is about two expressions and their structural relation.

Internal generality is opposed to the external generality of non-arithmetical language. Consider the following non-arithmetical general proposition:

(85) All men die before they are 200 years old.[12]

This is an empirical proposition expressing an external property of all men. The generality of this proposition is based on induction. If there were a man over 200, this proposition would be falsified. No evidence could, by contrast, falsify (83). If one found a number that did not comply with (83), (83) would be evidence of a miscalculation. Wittgenstein further argues that not even all cases of external generality can be analyzed into a logical product. This is, however, not our present concern. We are concerned with mathematical notation in this chapter.

14.2 Numbers

There are different kinds of numbers in mathematics, e.g., the cardinal numbers, the rational numbers, the real numbers, the complex numbers, etc. We are tempted to think that there is some essential feature which all numbers have in common. There is no such thing according to Wittgenstein. It would also be wrong to say that they make up a family resemblance class. We have to distinguish sharply between numbers that have a finite representation and numbers that have a potentially infinite representation. Only numbers that are capable of a finite expression are for Wittgenstein numbers in a proper sense; they are *mathematical extensions*. Clearly, only finite numerals can be identified with numbers. He calls such numbers *cardinal numbers*, which was in conformity with usage at the time. Numbers with a potentially infinite expansion—like irrational, real, or complex numbers—are, in fact, not concepts but rules which generate their infinite expansions.[13]

Wittgenstein also had problems with what was then the received definition of cardinal numbers. Drawing on Cantor, Frege and Russell defined cardinal numbers as cardinalities of equinumerous (gleichzahlig) sets. Cardinalities of finite sets are *natural numbers*. There are, in addition to these, so-called transfinite cardinal numbers, which describe the cardinalities of infinite sets. Wittgenstein, however, rejected the view that there are different infinite cardinalities in his finitistic conception of mathematics. But if we deprive cardinal numbers of the hierarchy of transfinite numbers, what we get is precisely the natural numbers. We can, thus, take Wittgenstein's claims about cardinal numbers as claims about natural numbers.

Now to Wittgenstein's key definition of a cardinal number: 'A cardinal number is an internal property of a list.'[14] Or more extensively:

> The sign for the extension of a concept is a list. We might say, as an approximation, that a number is an external property of a concept and an internal property of its extension (the list of objects that fall under it).[15]

A number is an external property of a concept, for a concept does not determine the number of elements of its extension.[16] The concept of a book, for instance, does not determine how many books there are or must be. In other words, if a concept is given by a defining property (by an intension), the number of elements falling under this concept is not determined a *priori*.[17]

On the contrary, if we have a concrete extension of a concept, its number is its internal property. The following list of strokes | | | has three elements and this is its internal property. If we added one stroke to it, it would be a different list. Lists of strokes like | | | are for Wittgenstein prototypes of (natural) numbers:

> If 3 strokes on the paper are the sign for the number 3, then you can say the number 3 is to be applied in our language in the way in which the 3 strokes can be applied.[18]

There is, however, further clarification needed here. The list of strokes is not an abstract list. It is a concrete list written down on the paper. We can write down three strokes on a piece of paper and use this sheet of paper as a paradigm for the number 3. We can furthermore store this sheet of paper in a mathematical archive and use it whenever someone might be uncertain about the meaning of the numeral 3. The list | | | serves in this sense as a yardstick. The numeral 3 is a substitution or rather an abbreviation for the list | | |. Numerals are, thus, picture-like representations of numbers.

We should not conceive of the list | | | as a set with three members or even as any set of cardinality 3: 'Here the strokes function as a *symbol*, not as a *class*. Russell's argument rests on a confusion of sign and symbol.'[19] Wittgenstein's concrete and finitistic approach takes numerals as concrete objects as opposed to Frege-Russell's approach that is based on abstract sets. The decisive advantage of Wittgenstein's conception of numbers over Frege and Russell's is that numbers are rooted in our primitive activities[20] like children's finger-counting or counting on an abacus. Moreover, Russell's definition of numbers is based on an actual correlation between equinumerous sets:

> In Russell's theory only an *actual* correlation can show the 'similarity' of two classes. Not the *possibility* of correlation, for this consists precisely in the numerical equality. Indeed, the possibility must be an *internal* relation between the extensions of the concepts, but this internal relation is only given through the equality of the 2 numbers.[21]

This argument is, however, a little bit tricky. An actual one-to-one correlation between two classes of things is an external relation. This correlation presupposes that the two classes are numerically equivalent. Then, however, 'the numerical equivalence is not determined by the correspondence, but the numerical equivalence makes the correspondence possible.'[22] Two classes are equinumerous if it is *possible* to correlate their elements one-to-one. The possibility of correlation is an internal relation. We can say that

(86) There are three books lying on the table

if it is possible to correlate them with the paradigmatic list | | |. We can reformulate (86) by inserting the paradigm into it:

(87) There are | | | books lying on the table.

This means that there is an internal relation of possible correlation between the paradigmatic list and those books lying on the table. And more appropriately: there is an internal relation of a possible correlation between the number of strokes on the paradigmatic list and the number of books.

Now, we have to make explicit the distinction between statements of numbers *in* mathematics and statements of numbers *outside* mathematics:

> Statements of number *in* mathematics (e.g. 'The equation $x^2 = 1$ has 2 roots') are therefore quite different in kind from statements of number outside mathematics ('There are 2 apples lying on the table').[23]

Consider the following equation (which is a statement in mathematics):

(88) 2 + 2 = 4

Inserting the paradigmatic lists into this statement yields:

(89) | | + | | = | | | |

There is possibly a one-to-one correlation between both sides of the equation, which means that there is an internal relation (of a possible correspondence).

The analysis of statements *outside* mathematics like (86) is a different one. First of all, (86) is an experiential statement. The meaning of the numeral 3 here is defined by a reference to the paradigmatic list. This internal relation holds between the number of books and the number of strokes. It is not a relation within the sentence like in (88) or (89), but is a relation to something else, namely to the paradigmatic list.

Confusing these two uses of numerals would result in possibly nonsensical reflexive uses of internal relations. Consider the following statement:

(90) There are 3 strokes in | | |.

What is the meaning of the numeral 3 in this sentence? Its meaning must be derived from the very same paradigmatic list. If so, we get:

(91) There are | | | strokes in | | |.

This is, however, a very peculiar statement of identity aiming to express a reflexive internal relation between | | | and | | |. (90) cannot be a definition either, because 'The form 3 can only be transposed, it cannot be defined.'[24] Hence we can take (90) as a substitution rule transposing the form | | | into the form 3. The number 3 is an internal property of the list | | |. 'It is nonsense to say of an extension that it has such and such a number, since the number is an *internal* property of the extension.'[25]

To sum up: numerals outside mathematics are being used transitively, deriving their meaning from paradigmatic samples (paradigmatic lists). Numerals within mathematics express internal relations between different samples. But we cannot ascribe a number to the very same paradigmatic list which defines this number. This would then be a nonsensical reflexive use of an internal relation.

14.3 Proofs

The concept of a mathematical proof is—as one would expect in the Wittgensteinian spirit—a family resemblance concept. There are logical differences among different kinds of proofs. A recursive proof, for instance, is, in fact, a guide to the construction of special proofs. Wittgenstein was critical of the notions of an inductive, a logical (Russellian), or an existence proof *inter alia*. After excluding these suspicious kinds of proofs, he nevertheless then tries to capture something like the *nature* of proof.[26]

We can proceed from the assumption that mathematical propositions are statements of internal relations. In this respect they are like grammatical propositions.[27] A proof of a mathematical proposition aims to *show* or rather *lay down* its internal relatedness to a system of other mathematical rules:

> What is proved by a mathematical proof is set up as an internal relation and withdrawn from doubt.[28]
>
> Proof must shew the existence of an internal relation.[29]
>
> A mathematical proof connects a proposition with a system.[30]

Consider again the proposition '68 + 57 = 125' as discussed in §13. Its proof must show that this proposition is compatible with the rule for addition and with paradigmatic samples of the natural numbers.[31] To prove a mathematical proposition amounts to showing how to arrive at it from other (primitive) propositions by means of formal operations. For Wittgenstein, mathematical proofs must be constructive (hence his aversion to existence proofs that are not constructive).

A mathematical proposition which is proved is thus an internal part of the proof. We may say that 'the completely analysed mathematical proposition is its own proof.'[32] In other words, mathematical propositions get their meanings from their proofs.[33] This account threatens the existence of mathematical problems, i.e., mathematical propositions that have not been proven yet. Proven and unproven mathematical propositions are, however, not at the same level:

> The proposition with its proof doesn't belong to the same category as the proposition without the proof. (Unproved mathematical propositions—signposts for mathematical investigation, stimuli to mathematical constructions.)[34]

The very notion of an 'unproven mathematical proposition' is misleading, for it suggests that they are also statements of internal relations that are not apparent for the time being. The expression 'mathematical conjecture' would be more appropriate here. The crucial question is whether a mathematical conjecture expresses an internal relation or an external relation. Let us consider the famous Goldbach Conjecture (an example Wittgenstein himself employed):

(92) Every even number greater than 2 can be expressed as a sum of two primes.

Although we still do not possess any rigorous proof of Goldbach's Conjecture,[35] we can understand it. We just do not know whether the conjecture is true or false. Would this undermine Wittgenstein's position that mathematical propositions get their meaning from their proofs? Wittgenstein, however, calls our understanding of this conjecture into question:

> To *believe* Goldbach's Conjecture, means to believe you have a proof of it, since I can't, as it were, believe it *in extenso*, because that doesn't mean anything, and you cannot imagine an induction corresponding to it until you have one.[36]

What we understand here is that for a given number *n*, we are able to find out whether *n* can be expressed as the sum of two primes. But if (92) is supposed to be a mathematical proposition, the general quantifier must express an internal relation.[37] We cannot, however, imagine such an internal relation until we know it or are able to construct it. We can employ brute force techniques or statistical considerations in order to give a heuristic justification of Goldbach's Conjecture. If so justified, we can hardly treat Goldbach's Conjecture as expressing an internal relation. Goldbach's Conjecture justified heuristically has, thus, a different meaning from (92) than if it were rigorously proven.[38] We can understand Goldbach's Conjecture in a *compositional way*, i.e., we understand all the concepts involved and the way in which they are combined. If Goldbach's Conjecture were rigorously proven, we would understand it by virtue of its proof, i.e., by virtue of its internal relations to other mathematical propositions.

We can conclude from the previous discussion that a mathematical proposition gets its meaning from its proof, which lays down an internal relation to other mathematical propositions. We cannot understand a mathematical proposition until we possess its proof.[39] On the other hand, a mathematical conjecture is not meaningless.[40] Although it could have the same surface form as the corresponding mathematical proposition, it expresses an external relation and thus has a different meaning from the mathematical proposition. The proof of a mathematical conjecture 'alters the grammar of a proposition.'[41] The proof changes a proposition that expresses an external relation into a proposition that expresses an internal relation.

What now needs to be examined further is the pictorial aspect of mathematical proofs. Wittgenstein is quite explicit in this respect:

> When I say 'a proof is a picture'—it can be thought of as a cinematographic picture. [...]
> Proof, one might say, must originally be a kind of experiment—but [it] is then taken simply as a picture. [...]
> The proof must be our model, our picture, of how these operations have a result.[42]

A proof is also a picture—or rather a *motion* picture—of an experiment. What kind of experiment? Consider a class of some already-proven mathematical propositions. We can, as it were, experimentally try to transform them by applying mathematical operations in order to yield the desired proposition which has to be proven. The experiment consists in trying to construct the desired proposition (which has the status of a conjecture for the time being) out of already-proven mathematical propositions. There is no systematic way of choosing suitable initial propositions and suitable operations. This may involve constructing ancillary terminology and proving ancillary mathematical propositions, i.e., lemmas. These peculiarities are one of the main reasons why some mathematical conjectures are so hard to prove.

There is, however, another sense in which a proof can be taken as a picture of an experiment. We may transform every mathematical proposition that is contained in a certain proof into a statement *outside* mathematics as demonstrated in the previous section. For instance, we may transform

(93) $1 + 1 = 2$

into

(94) One apple and one apple on my table makes a total of two apples.

Sentence (93) expresses an internal relation, whereas (94) expresses an external relation. If we transform all the steps of a proof in this way, we get a description of a real experiment. We arrive at something like this: if one starts with a certain state of affairs and proceeds according to prescribed rules, then the resulting state of affairs *must* be so-and-so. The 'must' in the preceding sentence is, however, not a logical must. There needs to be a *ceteris paribus* clause added: '... the resulting state of affairs must be so-and-so, *if nothing goes wrong*.' There are thousands of ways that an experiment could go wrong. A description of an experiment based on external relations is not normative here. If we want to insert normativity into it, we have to add the *ceteris paribus* clause or—and this is of the utmost significance—we have to take it as a picture 'of how these operations have a result.'[43] This is how an experiment can be taken as a proof.

I have identified two ways in which a proof can be taken as a picture of an experiment. The first one is an experimental attempt at transforming some mathematical propositions in order to arrive at the proposition that has to be proven. The second one is to take the mathematical propositions involved in a proof as statements outside mathematics expressing external relations. Then a mathematical proof can be taken as a picture of a real experiment. These two ways complement rather than contradict each other.

Having said this, we are now in a position to investigate the next and final twist of Wittgenstein's considerations about mathematical proofs. As noted above, mathematical proofs aim to integrate mathematical conjectures into the system of already-proven mathematical propositions. A conjecture is turned into a proposition by providing its proof, which is a picture of an experiment. But how can we take a proof as a picture? There must be some act that elevates something into a picture so that it will be considered as a picture of some other thing.

Wittgenstein employed the idea of *depositing something in the archives* in order to explain how we can handle standards of colors like color swatches or standards of length like the standard meter.[44] These are particular objects that are deposited into some prominent place and considered as paradigmatic cases (as samples as opposed to examples) of particular properties. Wittgenstein now imagines that we can also put some significant calculations and proofs into the archives:

> A calculation could always be laid down in the archive of measurements. It can be regarded as a picture of an experiment. We deposit the picture in the archives, and say, 'This is now regarded as a standard of comparison by means of which we describe future experiments.' It is now the paradigm with which we compare.[45]

A proof—not an abstract proof, but rather its visual shape impressed on a piece of paper—is deposited in the (mathematical) archives and regarded as a paradigm of future experiments. A proof on a piece of paper is a particular object like the standard meter or standard sepia. There must be an internal relation between the proof and an experiment. Although internal relations do not hold between objects, they do hold between concepts. There is, however, no genuine contradiction here. We have to focus on the visual shape of a proof.

Some of its features have to correspond to some features of an experiment. We can see this as a generalization of Wittgenstein's account of numbers which was discussed in §14.2.[46] Numbers are defined by paradigmatic lists. We may, of course, perform experiments regardless of any proofs. But then the experiment would be deprived of any normative force. We could not decide whether the experiment went right or wrong and what its final outcome was.

Hence, in order to be able to read off the result of an experiment we need something like a yardstick. 'The proof is our model for a particular result's being yielded, which serves as an object of comparison (yardstick) for real changes.'[47] An experiment is a concrete process which results into a certain state of affairs. This state has to be *measured* and 'the proof serves as a measure'[48] here.[49]

I opened my discussion of Wittgenstein's thoughts about mathematics with his insistence on the pictorial aspect of mathematical notation. Numerals like | | | are picture-like representations of numbers; proofs and calculations are more complicated cases of such picture-like representations. There is no fundamental difference between them in this respect.

The final point I would like to discuss concerns the applicability of a picture-like representation. Let us begin with some easy cases. How do I apply the list of strokes | | | to a particular state of affairs, e.g., to apples on my table? We have to project the list onto the state of affairs. Wittgenstein insists that arithmetical constructions can guarantee their applicability:

> You could say arithmetic is a kind of geometry; i.e. what in geometry are constructions on paper in arithmetic are calculations (on paper). You could say, it is a more general kind of geometry. [...]
>
> The point of the remark that arithmetic is a kind of geometry is simply that arithmetical constructions are autonomous like geometrical ones and hence so to speak themselves guarantee their applicability.[50]

If arithmetical constructions are like geometrical constructions with respect to their applicability, we have to ask what guarantees the applicability of geometrical constructions. The question can be put in terms of the internal/external distinction as pursued here: what guarantees that there is an internal relation between the list | | | (deposited in the archives) and three apples on my table? A relation between these objects is an external one. The idea of depositing something in the archives makes sense only if the deposited object guarantees its own applicability, i.e., its own projection. This is essential to all mathematics: 'But I see the "mathematically essential" thing about the process in the projection too!'[51]

We can only deposit in the archives an object we know how to project. The object has had to play some role in our activities and techniques before. We have to know in advance that it is essential to the list | | | that it is a paradigm of a number and not a paradigm of color or length. That is to say: in order to define or rather transpose the number 3 using the list | | | we have to presuppose the concept of number. This is a well-known idea from the beginning of the *Philosophical Investigations* where Wittgenstein focuses on ostensive definition:

> So one might say: the ostensive definition explains the use—the meaning—of the word when the overall role of the word in language is clear. Thus if I know that someone means to explain a colour-word to me the ostensive definition 'That is called "sepia"' will help me to understand the word.[52]

The list | | | (written down on a piece of paper and deposited in the archives) is an instrument of language like the standard meter.[53] The same is valid for calculations and proofs as well. They do not have their meanings in isolation, but rather within our practices.

15

Colors

The theme of colors pervades Wittgenstein's writings and this book as well. The very first remark on colors in connection with internal relations is to be found in an entry from the pre-Tractarian Notebooks from 1916:

> That the colours are not properties is shewn by the analysis of physics, by the internal relations in which physics displays the colours.[1]

I think that the point of this rather cryptic remark is to express a certain preference for grammatical investigations over physical investigations of colors. What the analysis of physics shows us is that colors are, at best, secondary properties, i.e., they are not the (primary) properties of objects. What is distinctive—and philosophically relevant—about colors is their mutual relations. What colors are from the viewpoint of physics[2] plays an inferior role in Wittgenstein's inquiries, or more precisely the physical viewpoint gradually fades away. What he is after here is rather the logic, grammar, or geometry of colors (these characteristics can be used here interchangeably). This is to say: Wittgenstein investigates colors as they appear to us and as we speak about them.

This idea can be further developed by noting a certain analogy between color systems and number systems:

> We have a colour system as we have a number system.
> Do the systems reside in *our* nature or in the nature of things? How are we to put it?—*Not* in the nature of numbers or colours.[3]

Colors are neither properties of objects, nor Platonic qualities. Colors are nodes in our color systems (the plural is important here). The relationship between colors and mathematics is very close: mathematics has a certain pictorial aspect; colors must be, in Wittgenstein's view, connected to the way they appear—let me call this the phenomenological aspect of colors. Furthermore, basic colors as well as natural numbers can be defined by paradigmatic samples, i.e., by internal relations to these samples. Like the fact that not all numbers are of the same sort,[4] 'not all colour concepts are logically of the same sort.'[5] This means that what we call 'color' in our everyday language may belong to different color systems, to different language-games.

15.1 Lightness and darkness

For Wittgenstein, the most prominent example of drawing the distinction between internal and external relations is the *lightness* relation. This example appears throughout Wittgenstein's works from the *Notebooks* to the last *Remarks on Colour*. Here is the very first remark:

> From the fact that [...] one colour is darker than another, it seems to follow that it *is* so; and if so, this can only be if there is an *internal* relation between the two; and we might express this by saying that the *form* of the latter is part of the *form* of the former.[6]

The already quoted remark from the *Tractatus* reads: 'This shade of blue and that one stand, *eo ipso*, in the internal relation of lighter to darker.'[7] This thread is again picked up in Wittgenstein's conversations at the beginning of the 1930s:

> I can \certainly\ say: the one suit is lighter than the other one, but not: this grey is lighter than that grey/ (if the word 'grey' is specified differently in both cases)/. That is to say, 'lighter' and 'darker' are external properties of the materials but internal ones of the colours.[8]

The theme recurs again in the *Remarks on the Foundations of Mathematics*[9] and culminates in the very first paragraph of the *Remarks on Colour*:

> A language-game: Report whether a certain body is lighter or darker than another.—But now there's a related one: State the relationship between the lightness of certain shades of colour. [...] The form of the propositions in both language-games is the same: 'X is lighter than Y'. But in the first it is an external relation and the proposition is temporal, in the second it is an internal relation and the proposition is timeless.[10]

In previous sections of this book[11] I have expressed an internal relation between two color shades as an arithmetical statement within the HSV color space. I chose exactly this color space (which was designed a long time after Wittgenstein's death) because it has brightness as one of its dimensions and, thus, there is an easy way of expressing the lightness relation in a mathematical statement. Most important here is the whole idea of color spaces as abstract mathematical models which represent colors (and other visual properties) as tuples of numbers and allow the translating of statements about colors into arithmetical statements. In addition to this, they provide a surveyable representation of the color space in two- or three-dimensional space.[12] That is why we can speak of the geometry of colors. Wittgenstein is one of the progenitors of the idea of color spaces, which is now indispensable in computer graphics or image processing.

The common point of the remarks quoted above is that the lightness relation is an internal relation between color shades and an external relation between objects. Internal relations hold within a color space. They constitute 'the logic of colour concepts'[13] or rather a part of it. The lightness relation is not the only relation that can be captured in a color model; one can think of other relations such as saturation or colorfulness.

15.2 Paradigmatic samples

We can think about color spaces on an abstract level without any reference to actual colors as they are perceived. This may be useful in applied sciences, but Wittgenstein insisted on the close connection between color spaces and the way we perceive colors. We may ask the following question: how do we define color concepts? Wittgenstein's way of answering this question is to ask another question: how could children learn to use color concepts? A reasonable answer may be that we can give meaning to a color concept by giving an ostensive definition by pointing at a paradigmatic sample. Wittgenstein initially considers a very simple case:

> The word 'blue', for example, is correlated with a certain colored patch which is a sample.[14]
>
> Suppose I pointed to a piece of paper and said to someone: 'this colour I call "red"'. Afterwards I give him the order: 'now paint me a red patch'. I then ask him: 'why, in carrying out my order, did you paint just this colour?' His answer could then be: 'This colour (pointing to the sample which I have given him) was called red; and the patch I have painted has, as you see, the colour of the sample'.[15]

According to these remarks, we can think of color concepts as substitutes for samples. If someone is uncertain about the actual application of a color concept, they can then *compare* the actual case with the sample. Color concepts are analogous to the concepts for numbers which are also substitutes for paradigmatic lists. And just as there is an analogous internal relation between a yardstick and a measured object,[16] so too is there an internal relation between the sample for red and any red object. More precisely, there is an internal relation between the color of the sample and the color of any red object.

Having said this, we now have to address several points that may complicate this simple picture. First, it is not self-explanatory how a comparison of a sample with an object should be carried out.

> There are even many different kinds of comparing and copying. There is rough and exact copying, comparison of this green with other greens, comparison of two colors by means of a color wheel with respect to the amount of yellow they contain.[17]

The sample and the object that is compared have to be of the same color. It is, however, not clear what counts as the same color. Sometimes we rely on perceptual evidence, at other times more precise methods are needed. Sometimes we need exact agreement, while at other times we are satisfied with approximate agreement. Sometimes we take environmental influences into account, and at other times we do not. And so on. In a nutshell: 'Everything depends on the method of comparison.'[18] Dealing with color samples and the comparing of colored objects have to have their place in our practices before we define any particular color concept. This means that we must know how to project the sample onto other objects or use it in our practice.[19]

A second point is that children usually do not use a single paradigmatic sample in order to apply color concepts. The schema above is to be taken as an idealization. Children are usually taught or rather trained to use color concepts via a series of examples (as opposed to samples).[20] The normative aspect of the practice is warranted in the first place by an authority, e.g., by their parents. But if their parents were uncertain or in disagreement about the application, a reference to a paradigmatic sample might be helpful. A child needs to be trained using series of examples until they are able to apply the color concept in a novel situation alone. This means that the child has to grasp a *rule* for the color concept. What interests us here is, in fact, only the application of the rule.[21] What a child has to learn using a series of examples is the method of projection of the sample, i.e., the method of comparison.

Suppose now that we have succeeded in defining some color concepts by paradigmatic samples. The problem is, however, that the linguistic expressions for these colors may be ambiguous with respect to the distinction between internal and external properties. They may *fall between several language-games* as addressed in §10.3. Let us focus on a simple language-game here (as introduced at §§48–9 of the *Philosophical Investigations*). We have four colors: white, black, red, and green. The syntax of this language-game is very simple. A sentence is only a series of the initial letters of these colors. So for instance, the sentence 'RRG' means that there are two red squares followed by one green square. We may, however, hesitate here regarding what a sentence consisting of one single letter, e.g., 'R,' actually means. This expression could *describe* a complex consisting of only one square on the one hand, or it could also be a *name* for that very square on the other hand.

Wittgenstein considers, then, the possibility that the naming (of a square) is a limiting case of the describing (of a complex of squares). This would, in effect, dismiss the difference between describing and naming. To say that there is a complex consisting of one red square would be tantamount to saying that the square is red. This stance, though, could easily lead to confusion. We can use the expression 'R' or the sentence 'There is a red square' in the course of ostensive teaching to explain the meaning of 'R' or 'red.' In short: we could use the sentence 'R' either as a genuine proposition or as a rule (that is, as a grammatical proposition). This situation fits exactly within our general scenario as presented in §10.3.

To avoid any misunderstanding we are invited to take naming and describing as different activities. In Wittgenstein's words: 'For naming and describing do not stand on the *same* level: naming is a preparation for description. Naming is so far not a move in the language-game.'[22] Naming is thus not a move in the language-game of describing colored squares. It is, however, a move in the *language-game of teaching the rule*. In this preparatory language-game, one has to learn what 'R' or rather 'This is red' means. It is crucial that in this language-game, the demonstrative 'this' refers to the color of the square, not to the square itself. 'This is red' actually means 'This color is called red.'

Mastering a paradigm changes the nature of the language-game: 'By bringing in a paradigm we have altered the game.'[23] Hence, after the rule has been mastered, we can go over to the *language-game of applying the rule*, i.e., of describing colored squares. Red is an internal property of the color shade that one was pointing at in the preparatory language-game. 'R' or 'This is red' now means that there is a complex consisting of one red square. 'This' refers now to the complex one is pointing at, and 'R' or 'This is red' ascribes the external property of containing a red square to this complex.[24]

The next point that needs to be addressed is whether we can meaningfully assert that the paradigmatic sample of a color has this very color. Can we, for instance, meaningfully assert the following sentence?

(95) The paradigmatic sample of blue is blue.

Wittgenstein gives a straightforward answer. We cannot assert sentences like (95). 'Samples such as this are part of our language; the patch is not one of the applications of the word "blue."'[25] There is a more detailed discussion of this issue in the *Philosophical Investigations*:

> Let us imagine samples of colour being preserved in Paris like the standard metre. We define: 'sepia' means the colour of the standard sepia which is there kept hermetically sealed. Then it will make no sense to say of this sample either that it is of this colour or that it is not.[26]

There is, however, no *prima facie* reason why we could not assert that the sample of blue is blue and the standard sepia is sepia-colored. Why could we never assert sentences like (95)? Maybe we cannot compare the paradigmatic sample with itself. But Wittgenstein does not use this argument. The remark quoted above continues, however:

> We can put it like this: This sample is an instrument of the language used in ascriptions of colour. *In this language-game* it is not something that is represented, but is a means of representation.[27]

It makes no sense to assert (95), but only with the reservation 'in this language-game.' Now we have to ask which language-game is meant and what Wittgenstein's argument is here. In the language-game of teaching the rule, we can assert

(96) This is blue,

while pointing to the paradigmatic sample (which we are attempting to define), because this sentence in fact means:

(97) Let this color be called blue.

We cannot assert (95) or (96) in the language-game of applying the rule, because the sample 'is a means of representation.' We can take this idea quite literally and imagine a language without any color concepts. When one wants to say that an object has a certain color, one will have to take a paradigmatic sample and put it in front of the object. To express (96), one would then have to take the paradigmatic sample of blue and attach it to the object like we attach labels to exhibits in museums. In order to apply the sample to another object, one would have to remove it from the previous object and attach it to the new one. In this scenario, it would be impossible to express the assertion that the paradigmatic sample of blue is blue, because we cannot attach this sample to itself.

We can understand the claim that samples are means of representation in the sense that they are, or at least can be, involved in grammatical rules governing color concepts. In my previous discussion of colored squares, I pointed out that 'R' or 'This is red' can be used as a genuine proposition or as a rule (that is, as a grammatical proposition). Hence, (95) and (96) are genuine propositions in the language-game of teaching, but they are grammatical propositions in the language-game of applying. This is why they cannot be asserted. This is, however, not the reason why they are possibly nonsensical. We can use these sentences to report a rule of an actual language-game. (96) is a typical example of a sentence that is ambiguous as regards the distinction between internal and external relations.

The reason why they are possibly nonsensical lies deeper. As stated at the beginning of §15.2, sentences like (96) express an internal relation between the paradigmatic sample and the object pointed at. In the language-game of applying the rule, sentence (96) expresses an external property of this object. But if this object were the paradigmatic sample itself, (96) would express an internal relation of the sample to itself. At the same time, it should express its external property (that is, its color). This is therefore flawed, since blue is an internal property of the paradigmatic sample of blue. The same surface form

(98) x is blue

is used to express an internal property of the paradigmatic sample (employing a reflexive construction) and an external property of other objects *within the same language-game*.

We have here another instance of Wittgenstein's general argumentative schema, which is the main focus of this book. The first step consists in drawing a clear distinction between conceptions based on external and internal relations. The second step is to assess possible reflexive cases of internal relations. First, we have to consider whether sentences of the form (98) are used to express the internal relation of color identity or an external property of an object. If the former is the case, we have to look at possible reflexive cases of this internal relation, i.e., an internal relation of the paradigmatic sample to itself.

15.3 Relations between colors

Definitions of colors by reference to paradigmatic samples do not take into account the mutual relations between colors. Each color and each color shade has its own paradigmatic sample which is entirely independent of the other samples. There are human practices that use colors in this way. We have color sample tools in graphics software; or we use a color sample if we want to instruct the person painting our house. We just pick whichever shade of color we want and later we can compare the result with the sample. These practices are in fact an exception. In a great deal of human practices, relations between colors are important and useful. Color samplers usually consist of a great number of paradigmatic samples. If we take into account relations between colors, we can significantly reduce the number of samples to a few basic ones. These are the so-called basic (or simple, or pure) colors. Other shades of color, the so-called intermediate or mixed colors, can be defined by internal relations to basic colors.

Realizing that ascriptions of colors are not mutually independent led Wittgenstein to abandon the program of logical atomism. I am not going to focus on the *color exclusion problem*, but on the related problem of the status of the proposition ascribing intermediate colors. Consider the following statement:

> A mixed colour (or better, an intermediate colour) made up of blue and red is a mixed (intermediate) colour via an internal relationship to the structures of blue and red. Expressed more precisely: What we call 'an intermediate colour between blue and red' (or 'bluish-red') is so called because of a relationship that shows in the grammar of the words 'blue', 'red' and 'bluish-red'.[28]

This formulation suggests that an intermediate color like 'bluish-red'[29] shares a part of the structure of red and a part of the structure of blue. We can think here of surface structures that reflect light of certain wavelengths. The structure of red (and of blue too) is that such a surface reflects light of 620–740 nm (450–495 nm for blue). 'Bluish-red' would then be a mixture of small pigments reflecting light of these wavelengths. However, according to Wittgenstein himself, this analysis is wrong. The quotation from *The Big Typescript* continues:

(The very proposition that talks about an internal relationship between the structures originates in an incorrect idea – in that idea that sees complicated structures in the concepts 'red', 'blue', etc., structures whose inner construction must be shown by analysis.)[30]

Wittgenstein repudiates the idea that simple color concepts have structures, and not the idea that an intermediate color is defined by internal relations to simple colors. In Wittgenstein's earliest manuscripts, internal relations were defined in terms of structures.[31] Here we can now notice a certain shift in Wittgenstein's thinking. The incorrect idea mentioned above is that internal relations are *exclusively* relations between structures. Wittgenstein is thus heading towards a more general account of internal relations as rules of grammar. Here is the final part of the quotation from *The Big Typescript*:

But the relationship of pure colours to their intermediate colour is of an elementary kind. That is to say, it doesn't require that the proposition that ascribes the colour bluish-red to an object is made up of the propositions that ascribe the colours blue and red to it. And in a like manner the relationship among various shades of a reddishblue, for instance, is an elementary relationship.[32]

Consider a proposition ascribing bluish-red to an object:

(99) *A* is bluish-red.

We cannot eliminate the expression 'bluish-red' by equating (99) with the product of the following propositions:

(100) *A* is partly red.
(101) *A* is partly blue.

(99) implies neither (100), nor (101), nor their product. The relationship between blue, red, and bluish-red is of a grammatical nature. In the HSV color space, color shades are defined by their hue in terms of grades ranking from 0° to 360°. Red has a hue of 0° or 360°, blue 240°, and bluish-red (or purple) 300°. That bluish-red is an intermediate color between blue and red is expressed by the following mathematical statement:

(102) $240° < 300° < 360°$

In the same manner, an internal relationship between various shades of reddish-blue, e.g., that violet is bluer that magenta, can be expressed as:

(103) $274° < 300°$

Internal relations between color shades are not relations between the structures of colors. They are grammatical relations within a color space meaning that they are relations within structures used for a surveyable representation of colors.[33] 'Here we have a sort of mathematics of colour.'[34]

In the previous discussion, I took blue and red to be simple colors. But let me pause to look more closely at the issue of simplicity of colors. That red is simple is a fact about our grammar. This is to say that *to be simple* is an internal property of red, blue, or white *inter alia*. Here is a confirmation of this idea in Geach's lecture notes:

> *Jackson*: 'White is simple' is timeless.
> *Wittgenstein*: 'White is simple' is to 'the room's colour is simple' as '7 is prime' is to 'the number of papers in my pocket is prime'. It makes no sense to ask what white would be like if it weren't simple.[35]

As we know from §10.4, timeless sentences express internal properties and relations. Now if grammar is autonomous, i.e., not answerable to extra-linguistic reality, then what counts as a simple color is arbitrary. One community may count green as a simple color, but another as an intermediate one. Furthermore, is the question of simplicity of colors only a matter of choosing this or that color space? The answer is obviously no, because we have to take into consideration our experience of colors. We can therefore ask: is green/red/yellow a simple color, or an intermediate color? Why is orange or violet an intermediate color? What experience would be decisive in this matter?

The point of introducing simple or primary colors is to describe all other color shades as combinations (mixtures) of these simples. What we are after, therefore, is an experience of color mixtures as combinations of certain simple colors. We have to select simple colors in such a way that given any color shade we will be able to recognize what it is a mixture of. Let us begin with an unproblematic example: 'In any case, orange is a mixture of red and yellow in a sense in which yellow isn't a mixture of red and green.'[36] Perceiving an orange spot, one can experience the *resemblance* between orange red and yellow. This experience is not available in the case of yellow if one tries to see it as a mixture of red and green. This kind of evidence should convince us that orange is an intermediate color between yellow and red and that yellow is not an intermediate color between red and green. The same is valid of green. We cannot describe it as bluish yellow or yellowish blue and hence green is a simple color.[37] Here is another kind of experience:

> It makes sense to say of a colour that it is not pure red, but contains a yellowish, or bluish, whitish or blackish tinge; and it makes sense to say that it contains none of these tinges but is pure red. In this sense one can speak of a pure blue, yellow, green, white, black, but not of a pure orange, grey or reddish-blue. [...] That is to say, the colour circle has four special points. For it does make sense to say 'This orange is situated closer to red than that one (not on the plane of the colour circle, but within colour space)'; but it's not an equivalent expression to say 'This orange is situated closer to bluish-red than that one' or 'This orange is situated closer to blue than that one'.[38]

Of intermediate colors like orange or violet, it makes no sense to say that they contain a reddish tinge. Simple colors are also those that can be experienced in a pure as well as a tinged form. This is to say that the difference between pure and tinged makes sense only when applied to simple colors. Intermediate colors are, in contrast to simple colors, those (i) where the distinction between pure and tinged makes no sense, *and* (ii) where we are able to recognize which simple colors they are mixtures of. Employing these criteria, Wittgenstein identified four simple colors in accordance with the classic color theory of Ewald Hering (1872): red, green, blue, and yellow (white and black are also simple colors that affect the lightness and darkness dimension).

In addition to the relations of being a mixture of and resemblance, there is an opposite relation of the impossibility of mixture. Wittgenstein's most discussed example is the impossibility of mixing red and green:

> 'There is no such thing as a reddish green' is akin to the sentences that we use as axioms in mathematics.[39]
>
> It is obvious at a glance that we aren't willing to acknowledge anything as a colour intermediate between red and green. (Nor does it matter whether this is always obvious, or whether it takes experience and education to make it so.)[40]

The topology of our color space should also mark out the set of simple colors and make explicit which simple colors can be mixed together and which cannot. The point I am driving at is that internal relations within a color space are not totally independent of our experience. Although these internal relations are not answerable to any single fact or any single piece of experience, they must comply with the whole of our experience and the way in which experience is interwoven into our practices. With regard to color concepts, we can say that 'It is as if our concepts involved a scaffolding of facts.'[41]

Next, I shall connect the theme of internal relations within a color space with themes in the later Wittgenstein, namely with aspect-seeing[42] and rule-following. Experiencing orange as a mixture of red and yellow amounts to *seeing* orange *as* reddish yellow or *as* yellowish red. The simple colors that an intermediate color consists of are, as it were, its *aspects*. To see that a color shade is reddish is a case of *seeing* it *as* red. As already stated, not all combinations of simple colors are possible. It is impossible, for example, to mix red and green. This means that we do not have the ability to see red as greenish—or we cannot imagine what a greenish red would look like.

An important point in this discussion is that we do not need to experience an intermediate color as a mixture of simple ones *all the time*. In the same vein, an aspect may change and we can experience a change or dawning of an aspect. Wittgenstein describes such an experience in the following words: 'what I perceive in the dawning of an aspect is not a property of the object, but an internal relation between it and other objects.'[43] What this cryptic remark could mean is discussed in Chapter 17. It is clear, however, from this remark that an aspect may change; an aspect may remain unnoticed, or it may dawn suddenly, etc. We can make analogous claims about colors and their tinges: a tinge may remain unnoticed, or it may suddenly occur to us. Let us consider a colored object, e.g., an apple. One may describe the apple as having a red color. Later on, one may notice that the color of the apple has a yellowish tinge. This experience can be described as a dawning of an aspect and the perceiving of an internal relation between the color of the apple and yellow. Hence, Wittgenstein can say that:

> 'internal properties' of a colour gradually occur to us, which we hadn't thought of at the outset. And that can show us the course of a philosophical investigation. We must always be prepared to come across a new one, one that has not occurred to us earlier.[44]

The idea is that at the outset, we learn color concepts by reference to examples and paradigmatic samples, and later on, in the course of language acquisition, realize that our color concepts are interconnected in various ways. The perception of these internal relations is, however, conditioned by the experience of the dawning of an aspect. Such an experience does not need to occur or there might be people incapable of it. This kind of incapability Wittgenstein calls 'aspect-blindness.'[45] However, aspect-blindness is not *achromacy*, i.e., the inability to distinguish any color from grey. Aspect-blind people are naturally able to distinguish between different color shades. What they are lacking is the ability to experience certain relations between different color shades. They may, for instance, fail to observe that orange is yellowish red. What they are able to do, however, is use color concepts defined by reference to paradigmatic samples. For aspect-blind people, the set of simple colors must be greater. If someone were incapable of experiencing orange as yellowish red, for them orange would be a simple color.

We can now think of our incapacity to see reddish green as a kind of deficiency, and we can imagine people that lack this ability. Wittgenstein was preoccupied with such cases in his *Remarks on Colour*:

> There could be people who didn't understand our way of saying that orange is a rather reddish-yellow, and who would only be inclined to say something like that in cases where a transition from yellow through orange to red took place before their eyes. And for such people the expression 'reddish-green' need present no difficulties.[46]

The idea is that there might be people with a certain kind of aspect-blindness, but are able to experience aspects that we cannot.[47] Is this idea coherent? How do we recognize such people? Wittgenstein suggests the following thought-experiment:

> Someone who is familiar with reddish-green should be in a position to produce a colour series which starts with red and ends with green and which perhaps even for us constitutes a continuous transition between the two. We would then discover that at the point where we always see the same shade, e.g. of brown, this person sometimes sees brown and sometimes reddish-green. It may be, for example, that he can differentiate between the colours of two chemical compounds that seem to us to be the same colour and he calls one brown and the other reddish-green.[48]

Of course, there are continuous transitions from red to green. However, people with normal eyesight are able to produce such transitions only through another color, e.g., through yellow.[49] People with the ability to recognize reddish green are able to produce this transition directly without referencing to any other simple color. Suppose now there were a single person claiming that they could differentiate between brown and reddish green. Such a case would be an instance of a private language, however. The case would be different if there were a community of people who were able to distinguish between brown and reddish green and they agreed in their judgments on this matter.

This brings us to the problem of rule-following. Consider a rule 'add a slight greenish tinge to a given color shade' or in mathematical notation '+G.' As established in Chapter 13, there must be an internal relation between a rule and its application. Accordingly, there must be an internal relation between this rule applied to a red sample and a sample of greenish red. Does this consideration force us to admit that there might be people who 'see colours which we do not see'?[50] The answer is no, for '[t]here is, after all, no *commonly* accepted criterion for what is a colour, unless it is one of our colours.'[51] The ability to distinguish between greenish red and brown does not need to be on a par with the ability to distinguish between yellowish red and pure red. There are other visually discriminable qualities that are not properly called colors.[52] We can speak of something's being 'gold-colored,' but gold is not one of the shades of yellow. 'We speak of the "colour of gold" and do not mean yellow. "Gold-coloured" is the property of a surface that shines or glitters.'[53] Such visual qualities are the subject of the next section.

15.4 Colors in the visual field, transparency

As already noted at the beginning of §15, not all color concepts are logically of the same sort. This is, I think, the main insight pursued in *Remarks on Colour*. Some color concepts stand for simple colors, some for intermediate ones. In this case, we do not need to speak about different logical kinds, because what all these color concepts have in common is that they can be defined by references to paradigmatic samples. Such samples are typically two-dimensional plates and reference is made to their surface colors. This is, however, an idealization, for we perceive colors in our visual space. In this space, we are able to distinguish qualities that cannot be defined by reference to paradigmatic samples. The most salient quality that Wittgenstein discusses is color *transparency* or *opacity*.[54] Some colors (like green) can be transparent, some (like white) cannot.

That white is an opaque color (or that we cannot imagine a white transparent object) seems to be a grammatical rule. We could therefore think of incorporating these characteristics of colors into our color space; we might add an additional dimension into this space. And indeed, Wittgenstein ascribes this suggestion to Philip Otto Runge:

> Runge: 'If we were to think of a bluish-orange, a reddish-green, or a yellowish-violet, we would have the same feeling as in the case of a southwesterly north wind. … Both white and black are opaque or solid. … White water which is pure is as inconceivable as clear milk.'[55]

According to this suggestion, transparency and opacity would be internal properties of colors, because the claim that white is opaque is timeless. Wittgenstein says, however, that '[o]paqueness is not a *property* of the white colour. Any more than transparency is a property of the green.'[56] Why is opacity not an internal property of the color white? Alan Lee considers the explanation that 'opacity and transparency are properties of objects, [but] independent of their colours.'[57] But even then we would be tempted to say that opacity is internal to the concept of white. If opacity were an internal property of white, we would neglect the fact that we have color concepts of different sorts. Opacity is not a property of the color white if this color is defined by reference to a paradigmatic sample. If anything, opacity is an internal property of the concept of white in our visual field: 'Transparency and reflections exist only in the dimension of the depth of a visual image.'[58]

The aim of color spaces is twofold: to define concepts for simple colors by reference to paradigmatic samples and to define internal relations between color concepts. It now seems that if we apply color concepts in our visual field, they acquire additional internal properties and relations. If these relations are internal, there must be grammatical rules vindicating these relations. Wittgenstein considers the kind of rules that may fulfill this function. They are the *rules of appearance* for transparent colored things.[59] Applying such rules[60] we should be able to infer that there cannot be transparent white objects.

In the course of his reflections, Wittgenstein also questions this suggestion: '*Why* can't we imagine transparent-white glass,—even if there isn't any in actuality? Where does the analogy with transparent coloured glass go wrong?'[61] These questions point out the deeper problem of the status of rules for appearance. Are these rules for appearance grammatical rules? Or is our inability to imagine transparent-white glass of a factual nature? This inability might be rooted in our biological nature[62]—similarly to our inability to imagine reddish green. The last sentence quoted above is followed by this general remark:

> Sentences are often used on the borderline between logic and the empirical, so that their meaning changes back and forth and they count now as expressions of norms, now as expressions of experience.[63]

This remark may be taken as Wittgenstein's last word on this, his last methodological hint, which says that one and the same sentence may be used to express both an internal as well as an external relation. What is important, however, is that this ambiguity cannot occur within one language-game. We must strive to split the language-game in order to cope with this ambiguity.[64]

16

The standard meter

The analogy between (the rules of) language and a measuring rod or yardstick (Maßstab) plays an important role throughout Wittgenstein's philosophy. The analogy goes roughly like this: as a measuring rod is laid against an object in order to measure it, so language is laid against reality. It is, however, employed differently in different stages of Wittgenstein's thinking. In the *Tractatus*, a picture, actually a proposition, 'is laid against reality like a measure,'[1] whereas later in the *Philosophical Investigations*, a language-game is an object of comparison, a measuring rod.[2] In this chapter, I am going to examine the most famous case of a measuring rod, namely Wittgenstein's discussion of the standard meter in Paris[3] and his focus on a reflexive case in this analogy, i.e., the case in which the standard meter is supposed to measure itself.

This chapter is framed by the following questions: Is the standard meter one meter long? Can we assert this proposition? Is it an empirical or grammatical proposition? Is this sentence meaningful at all? My investigation is driven by the simple idea that all these claims must be related to a context of a language-game. That a certain sentence can or cannot be asserted or that it is an empirical or grammatical proposition depends on a language-game. One and the same sentence can be an admissible *move* in one language-game, a grammatical proposition in another and even nonsensical in a third. These language-games can be interconnected in various ways. My aim is to reveal these connections. I will focus, in particular, on the relations between the language-game in which the standard meter is defined, and the language-game where it is used as a prototype.

16.1 The definitions

Wittgenstein says that the only thing of which one can say neither that it is one meter long nor that it is not one meter long is the standard meter in Paris.[4]

Kripke says in reply that he must be wrong;[5] the stick which is actually the standard meter is (but might not have been) one meter long as a matter of fact. Most commentators have sided with Wittgenstein.[6] Whether one could meaningfully assert that the standard meter is one meter long depends on how one meter is defined. In this chapter, I would like to suggest three possible definitions. Both Wittgenstein and Kripke would agree that the meter must be defined via an ostensive definition (or an act of baptizing, to use Kripke's term). All the definitions make use of an arbitrary chosen rod which shall play the role of standard meter henceforward. Let us call it S.

(i) The first definition states that everything that has the same length that rod *S* had *at time* t_0 is one meter long.
(ii) The second definition states that any object with end-points coinciding with those of rod *S at any time* (if the object were placed alongside rod *S*) is one meter long.
(iii) The third definition states that—in a literal sense—rod *S* alone is one meter long.[7] Other objects are one meter long—although in a metaphorical (or, rather, a synecdochical) sense—if their end-points coincide with *S* when placed alongside it.

The first definition is to be found in Kripke, for he uses the following wording: 'one meter is to be the length of S at a fixed time t_0.'[8] The second definition has often been attributed to Wittgenstein,[9] while the last definition is the proposal I would like to advocate. I shall argue that the third definition can be attributed to Wittgenstein as well. Moreover, I want to show that Wittgenstein's analysis will be better understood if we employ the third definition.

For Kripke, the statement 'stick *S* is one meter long' is *a priori* but only a contingent proposition. Rod *S* may vary its length over time (and in counterfactual situations as well) and, in this case, will cease to be one meter long. Following the second definition, one cannot say that *S* is (or is not) one meter long, for a measuring instrument cannot be applied to itself. That *S* is one meter long is not an empirical proposition but a grammatical proposition which is actually—in contrast to Kripke's definition—*timeless*.[10] The third definition is the reverse of the second one. It starts by fixing the length of the standard meter and then applies this unit of measurement to all other spatial objects in a derived sense.[11] The second definition starts by defining the length of all objects; however, it cannot proceed to the standard meter, because it is the blind spot of the system.

16.2 The longitudinal variability

The crucial point here is, of course, the longitudinal variability of all spatial objects. The standard meter is no exception. It does not matter what the cause of the variability is (e.g., temperature, pressure, or even human action).[12] How do we detect that an object's length has changed? The answer is simple: by means of measurement using the standard meter (or a measuring instrument, e.g., a ruler which is derived from the standard meter). But how do we detect whether the length of the standard meter has itself changed? Consider the following thought-experiment that is central to my argument. If all objects including all particular measuring instruments except the standard meter were suddenly doubled in size, then we would have a good reason to suppose that the standard meter had been halved. That is, I suggest, the only possible answer if we define the meter along Kripke's lines. This would mean, however, that rod *S* had been deposed from the role of standard meter. This role would no longer be served by rod *S* but by a set of other measuring instruments (provided they all matched) or their average or median length. Who could decide whether rod *S* had been halved or whether the other measuring instruments had doubled in length? All the evidence equally supports both hypotheses. Every situation could be interpreted in such a way that the standard meter had remained unchanged, and to take the role of the standard meter seriously means to accept this interpretation in every case. So this is also the gist of my argument.

Kripke admits the possibility that the standard meter could have changed its length; this possibility, however, cannot be detected in an incontestable way. This is due to the fact that the paradigm of one meter is not a concrete object (rod S) but an abstraction, i.e., the length which it accidentally had at t_0.

We can try to put the point in a more formal way. Consider these formal transcriptions of our three definitions:

(I) $\text{One-meter-long}_t(x) =_{\text{df}} \text{length}_t(x)=\text{length}_{t_0}(\text{S})$
(II) $\text{One-meter-long}_t(x) =_{\text{df}} \text{length}_t(x)=\text{length}_t(\text{S})$
(III) $\text{One-meter-long}_t(x) =_{\text{df}} (\iota x)\ x=\text{S}$
$\text{One-meter-long}'_t(x) =_{\text{df}} (\exists y)\ (\text{One-meter-long}_t(y) \wedge \text{length}_t(x)=\text{length}_t(y))$[13]

One-meter-long is a predicate which applies to spatial objects and is parameterized by time. Length is a primitive function which gives the length of a spatial object (and is parameterized by time too). One may, however, wonder why we are trying to define one meter when we already have what we wanted. If we employ a function which gives the length of an object as a numerical value, then the unit of length must already be defined.[14]

Instead of the function length(x), we can employ a primitive binary predicate of same-length(x,y) which intuitively matches the possible coincidence of x and y in their end-points. Now we can try to restate the formal definitions this way:

(I') $\text{One-meter-long}_t(x) =_{\text{df}} \text{same-length}_t(x, S_{t_0})$
(II') $\text{One-meter-long}_t(x) =_{\text{df}} \text{same-length}_t(x, S)$
(III') $\text{One-meter-long}_t(x) =_{\text{df}} (\iota x)\ x=S$
$\text{One-meter-long}'_t(x) =_{\text{df}} (\exists y)\ (\text{One-meter-long}_t(y) \wedge \text{same-length}_t(x,y))$

We can see that definition (I') is not correct, or we must give up the idea that *S* is a rigid designator, because *S* is not a name or a definite description. *S* is a function here. For the definition (II') a problem arises when we apply the predicate one-meter-long to the rod *S* itself. Then we would have to deal with the expression $\text{same-length}_t(S,S)$. We can simply stipulate that the predicate or, better, the relation *same-length* is reflexive. But then the predicate will no longer correspond to the possibility of the process of placing two objects side-by-side. The third definition avoids such counterintuitive reflexive uses of the predicate *same-length*, leaving it undefined.

If one cannot assert that rod *S* is one meter long, then *a fortiori* one cannot assert that rod *S* has changed its length either, because—as demonstrated by the thought-experiment above—every apparent change in (the length of) the standard meter has to be interpreted as a change in all other objects. Both eventualities (that the standard meter is one meter long and that it has changed its length) are, however, perfectly conceivable and this makes Wittgenstein's account counterintuitive and puzzling. All change, to be sure, has to be conceived of with respect to a stationary background, a *hypokeimenon*. When we recall the dilemma discussed exposed in the previous section, by choosing *S* as the standard meter we stated that all change is to be conceived of relative to *S*. The standard meter is thus an arbitrarily chosen fixed point (or rather: a fixed vector) in our (metric) system of measurement. The background (*hypokeimenon*) here is—and this is Wittgenstein's point—nothing metaphysical, but only a chosen role in this system.[15] That is, I think, a sufficient argument for the claim that the standard meter cannot change its length.

The conjecture that the paradigm of a unit of length cannot change its length does not free us from the effort of keeping the rod, ideally, in a constant environment. The environment where the rod *S* is stored is actually a part of the definition of the standard meter. Once it was the International Bureau of Weights and Measures in Paris; now it is 'a vacuum.'[16] A definition of the standard meter which does not take into account the influence of the environment is, of course, possible; it is, however, as misguided as that of a word which changes its meaning according to the days of the week—an example offered by Wittgenstein. The consequences of this move must be clear: definitions of the standard meter which differ in their references to the environment are distinct from one another. The standard meter defined by the rod which is stored in a vacuum is different from the standard meter defined by the same rod stored in water. Having two such definitions, we can compute the relative contributions of the environment to thermal and volumetric expansion, etc.

16.3 The third definition

Heather Gert has tried, however, to demonstrate that it was not Wittgenstein's intention to assert that one cannot say of the standard meter that it is or is not one meter long. Wittgenstein's later writings actually have a peculiar dialogical structure which implies that not all sentences express Wittgenstein's own view. Focusing on this view, Gert argues that

> the claim that the standard meter cannot be said to be a meter long is introduced as analogous to the claim that elements cannot be said to exist, a Tractarian claim the later Wittgenstein clearly rejects. [...] Wittgenstein does not merely reject his own earlier claim that there are elements to which existence cannot be attributed, he rejects the claim that existence cannot be attributed to an object within the language-game within which it plays the role of element.[17]

In any case, we can take this interpretation as an indication that a straightforward attribution of definition (ii) to Wittgenstein might be problematic. Wittgenstein employs the standard meter above all as an analogy to the more general problem of whether primary elements can be described or named only. But such a question is the wrong one. In order to describe an object, we must be able to name it. So we have to assign a name to it in advance. In Wittgenstein's words: 'For naming and describing do not stand on the *same* level: naming is a preparation for description. Naming is so far not a move in the language-game—any more than putting a piece in its place on the board is a move in chess.'[18] So a game of chess presupposes a preparatory game of the naming of the pieces. In a similar way: a language-game of measuring presupposes a preparatory game of the fixing of a unit of measure, its standard, and the whole method of measurement.

Gert argues, however, that we can use the word as a name and as a description '*even within a given language-game*.'[19] Then, by analogy, we could use the expression 'one meter long' as a name (of the standard meter bar) and as a description (of all other objects that are one meter long) within the same language-game.

I do not find Gert's line of reasoning convincing on this point. The naming of a piece is not a move in chess, although it is a move in the language-game of ostensively teaching the names of the chess pieces. Of course, nothing prevents us from taking both activities as one language-game, for—as Jolley stated recently—'there is [...] no natural unit for the counting of language-games.'[20] The upshot is that we can take the whole of language as one language-game. But Wittgenstein introduces the notion of a language-game *inter alia* in order to separate out language activities that might have the same verbal manifestations. Thus, the word 'R' can stand for the name of an element or for a description of a simple complex consisting solely of precisely this element. This can lead to philosophical confusion. Introducing different language-games—an introductory game of naming and a game of describing—helps us to become aware of what we are doing and therefore to get over this confusion. Here we have a special case of the strategy outlined in §10.3. There I distinguish between the *language-game of teaching* and the *language-game of applying* a rule. Naming is a kind of teaching training and describing is the special case of applying a rule.

Thus, we can distinguish between two language-games in which the words 'R' or 'one meter long' appear in their different meanings, or where they appear in two uses both within a single language-game.[21] The latter option, however, poses the danger that these two uses could be confused. Thus, the sentence 'R (exists)' might stand for 'There is an element called (or named) R', but also 'There is a complex consisting solely of R.' By analogy, '*X* is one meter long' might mean '*X* is the rod that has been stipulated (or named) as being one meter long,' but also that '*X* is as long as the standard meter.'

Definition (iii) is in accord with this analysis. In a preparatory language-game, we have to choose a standard of measurement—specifically, we have to name rod *S* as the standard meter.[22] Such a naming must have a *declarative* character; and as is noted in §10.3 above, it can be taken as an imperative. This is the first step of the definition (iii): saying that rod *S* alone is one meter long.[23] After this is done, we can then *play* the language-game of measurement, which takes the name of the standard meter as assigned and the length of its extension (that is, rod S) as invariable. This means that in this language-game, the (literal) meaning of the term 'standard meter' is borrowed from the preparatory game and applied in a derived sense to all the other objects. There is, thus, a *vertical* relation between these two language-games.

16.4 Internal and external relations

In this section, I want to connect the problem discussed above with the distinction between internal and external relations. This will lead us to a general characterization of language-games in which the sentence 'The standard meter is one meter long' is then found to lack any sense. Lacking sense means here that this sentence is not a move in a language-game, as it cannot be asserted or negated.

In his conversations with Waismann,[24] Wittgenstein says that the relation of being *longer than* between two sticks is external, whereas the relation of being *greater than* between their lengths is internal. Let us slightly modify Wittgenstein's example. Let rod A be as long as the standard meter. This, then, is an external relation. The length of rod A is then the same as the length of the standard meter; this is an internal relation which can be expressed as 1 = 1. Hence all objects that are one meter long are instances of a property that is internally related to the length of the standard meter by the relation of identity. By the same token, all objects that are longer than one meter have a property that is internally related to the length of the standard meter by the relation of being *longer than*.

What sort of relation is expressed by the predicate *same-length*? In definition (I'), the second argument is parameterized by time, which gives us the idea that the whole predicate *same-length* is temporal and according to the *criterion of temporality*[25] it thus expresses an external relation. The temporal parameter, however, does not appear anywhere on the right-hand side of the second (II') or third definition (III'). Thus, the temporal parameter can be canceled out of these definitions and the predicate *same-length*, according to these definitions, can be regarded as timeless, i.e., as expressing an internal relation.

Before turning our attention to the question of whether propositions that express internal relations can be asserted or negated, I am going to discuss a recent account by Doron Avital, who employs the notion of an internal relation in order to defend Wittgenstein's claim about the standard meter against Kripke's criticism. Avital argues—in favor of definition (ii)—that the two end-points (taken as numerical coordinates in Euclidean space) of rod S, which is just the standard meter, exemplify an internal relation of measure. Another object *R* is one meter long if its end-points exemplify the same internal relation as the end-points of *S*. We can put this correspondence in terms of internal properties rather than internal relations. Rod *S* (the standard meter) has the internal property of being one meter long, while rod *R* is one meter long if it has the same property. This is, essentially, the Tractarian model of picturing as examined in §9.2. A picture or 'a proposition describes reality by its internal properties.'[26]

One can also assert that '*R* is one meter long,' because *R* may have other end-points that exemplify another internal relation, e.g., being two meters distant. But we cannot assert sentences like '*S* is one meter in length' or '*S* is one meter in length at t_0' because 'they are true by necessity.'[27] Such sentences cannot be negated and hence they cannot be asserted either. Hence, in order to decide whether a sentence can be asserted or not, Avital employs the *bipolarity* criterion of meaning. If nothing else, this criterion or principle is problematic in Wittgenstein's later work.[28] I have argued that there must be an internal relation between the length of the standard meter and the lengths of all other objects that are one meter long. Avital considers a Euclidean space whose unit vector is marked by the standard meter. The internal relations that Avital has in mind are different ones; they hold true between those points of Euclidean space which are one meter apart. This distance is easy to compute by Pythagoras' theorem. Let us take a two-dimensional Euclidean space and two arbitrary points A$[a_1,a_2]$ and B$[b_1,b_2]$. Then their distance is d(A,B) = $\sqrt{((a_1 - b_1)^2 + (a_2 - b_2)^2)}$. Avital advances the suggestion of an internal relation between the abstract points (whose

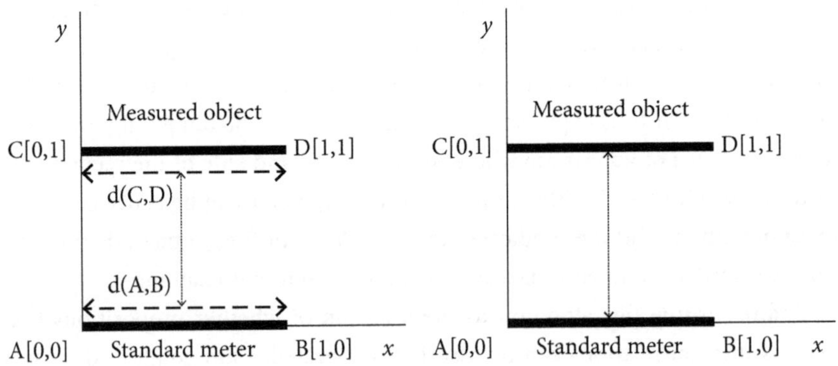

Figure 16.1 Internal relations of measure between the end-points of the rods (*Tractatus* and Avital, 2008) (left) and an internal relation between the lengths of the rods (my proposal) (right).

distance is 1). I propose, however, to consider an internal relation (of identity) between the lengths (whatever they are) of the objects that are being compared. Clearly, if two pairs of points are related by the former relation, their distances are related by the latterrelation and *vice versa.*

If rod S, which is just the standard meter, changes its length as a result of a change in circumstances, e.g., in temperature, one would expect that the unit of length would change. Avital argues, however, that such a change affects all other objects too, for they are in the same space. If, for example, the temperature goes up, such a change in the environment influences other objects besides the standard meter. That is Avital's main point. 'Meanings in this respect are materialized.'[29] The measuring rod must be in the same space as the measured object (this is the maxim of 'same space'[30]) and they have to be subject to the same physical law. This ensures that whatever the changes of circumstances are, the relative ordering of spatial objects according to their lengths remains the same. Hence, Avital can conclude: 'The rod being sampled extends and shrinks in tandem with the objects belonging to the sample as so does the Metre, as this is materialized in the form of the chosen rod; hence, the measures it gives are *independent* of the changing circumstances.'[31]

I think that it is misguided to invoke Euclidean space at this point. Such a consideration grants too much to Kripke's analysis. Only if we 'sublime' our space into an ideal Euclidean space, can we then consider extending and shrinking the standard meter. Avital is right in his critique of Kripke that all changes in every spatial object must be regarded in relation to the standard meter, and not to an abstract space. Avital, however, needs this abstract space in order to enable the possibility of the changing of the standard meter, although this possibility is not detectable.

My proposal is to discard the idea of abstract space and consider the standard meter to be unchanging all of the time. Moreover, the standard meter must be taken to be unchanging even if its extending and contracting were governed by different physical laws than other objects are. It might be changed by human action; e.g., someone might cut a part of it off. Even in this case, we have to regard the standard meter as unchanged if we want to meet all the requirements of the role (of the standard meter).[32] We cannot argue at this point that objects in space and time are subject to the same law as regards their longitudinal variability. It is possible, after all, that the same change of circumstances causes the shrinking of one object and the extension of another. Raising the temperature from 0°C to 3.99°C would simultaneously cause the contraction of a water column and the extension of a mercury column.

To sum up, for Avital there is an internal relation of measure between the end-points of all objects that are one meter long. Then, by derivation, there is an internal relation of having the same length between the lengths of all objects that are one meter long. I propose to begin with this latter kind of internal relation, and not to consider the idea of Euclidean space beyond our visible space.

16.5 What can be said about the standard meter

It should now be clear from the previous discussion what it means for an object to be one meter long. The situation of an object being one meter long amounts to the object's length being internally related to the length of the standard meter. If we consider rod *S*, which is currently the standard meter, then to say that it is one meter long would entail expressing an internal relation between its length and its length. This means expressing that its length is identical with itself. Such a reflexive use of an internal relation is suspect and possibly meaningless. Following Cora Diamond's paper,[33] I can see precisely at this point what is problematic about saying that the standard meter is one meter long.

Diamond points out Wittgenstein's distinction between the transitive and intransitive use of sentences containing the word 'particular' in his *Brown Book*: 'On the one hand, we may say, it is used preliminary to a specification, description, comparison; on the other hand, as what one might describe as an emphasis.'[34] Let us illustrate this distinction by Diamond's examples:

> 'This rod has a particular length, namely 39.37 inches.'
> 'This rod has a particular length,' said, for example, when one is concentrating on the thing's length, and not going on to specify the length or to compare it in length with anything else.[35]

The first sentence relates the length of the rod to something else, namely to the standard inch. A comparison is also being expressed between the lengths of the rod and that of the standard inch. No such comparison is being expressed in the second sentence. So the former sentence is an example of a transitive use, the latter of an intransitive use (of the word 'particular'). I want to add that an internal relation in the transitive use of sentences is also being expressed. The word 'particular' is, of course, an example here; this distinction also applies to other words or terms including the word 'meter' or 'one meter long.'

Philosophical confusion may arise when we confuse these two sorts of word uses: 'There are many troubles which arise in this way, that a word has a transitive and an intransitive use, and that we regard the latter as a particular case of the former, explaining the word when it is used intransitively by a reflexive construction.'[36] Following Wittgenstein's diagnosis, we have to look carefully at the reflexive use of words and examine whether this is rather a case of their intransitive use. The idea behind this is that 'We often use the reflexive form of speech as a means of emphasizing something. And in all such cases our reflexive expressions can therefore be "straightened out."' Wittgenstein's examples are: 'If I can't, I can't' or 'I am as I am.' These sentences can be 'straightened out' into intransitive uses meaning 'I can't do something' or an emphasis on the way that I am. Wittgenstein's next example is closer to our subject: 'Suppose to the question, "What's a kilogram?" I answered, "It is what a litre of water weighs", and someone asked, "Well, what does a litre of water weigh?"'[37] In order to straighten out these sentences, we have to realize that the expression 'weight of a litre of water' is used intransitively in this dialogue, which means that its meaning cannot be given within this language-game. Following this definition of kilogram, the situation of an object weighing one kilogram amounts to the object's weight being internally related to the weight of a liter of water (by the relation of having the same weight). Thus, this case is perfectly analogous to the case of asking how long the standard meter is. We can now formulate the following tentative maxim of logical analysis: a reflexive use (a special case of a transitive use) of a word should be straightened out into an intransitive use. Or so it seems.

Diamond, however, does not see 'anything wrong with representing a non-comparison as a special case of a comparison; if it does lead to some philosophical problem, it will be particularly important not to try to get rid of the problem by simply ruling out such representations.'[38] On the basis of this advice, Diamond has to explain why we should retain transitive uses of the expression 'one meter long' even in reflexive cases and not try to convert them to intransitive uses.[39] The core of her argument is based on her conviction that 'we can imagine comparisons of length which we do not actually carry out.'[40] Hence, she admits that we can compare the meter rod with an imaginary or counterfactual situation in which the rod has been heated and become longer.[41] Even worse, Diamond admits that: 'We can easily imagine a situation in which we wake up one morning and find that the rod that we have been using as a standard appears to have become longer or shorter.'[42] There is, of course, nothing wrong with the mere *appearance* of such a change. Confusion may arise, though, if one takes (or interprets) this appearance as a real change to the standard rod. But, as I have argued above, there are two possibilities: The first is that such a change is possible only after the rod has been deposed from the role of the standard meter. From that moment onwards, the standard would be some object or objects surrounding the former standard rod against which the change in the standard rod was detected.[43] The second possibility is that we would have to reconstruct the situation along Kripke's lines, because 'we have separated the length of the rod from the length "one meter."'[44] Then, however, we would not be comparing the standard meter with the same rod in a counterfactual situation in which it has been heated, but its actual length with its length after it had been heated. After all, this means that the standard is not the rod, but its length at the moment of establishing the standard, i.e., at the moment of baptism. This is pretty much Kripke's point. Diamond, then, insists on allowing a reflexive use of the expression 'one meter long,' for in her view, it is possible that it becomes a genuine transitive use involving a real comparison.

By now, it should be clear that the sentence '*A* is one meter long' involves a comparison of rod *A* and the meter rod, and it expresses the internal relation between the lengths of these two rods. The reflexive case 'The meter rod is one meter long' (which would involve a comparison of the standard meter with itself) should be straightened out into an intransitive use. This, however, means that the meaning of the phrase 'one meter long' cannot be defined in this very same language-game. If it were possible, the phrase would be used transitively. Since the sentence is not meaningless, the meaning of the phrase 'one meter long' must come from elsewhere. It must be a rule (or a hinge proposition) of this language-game which is inherited from another language-game (which I called preparatory) where the meaning of the phrase 'one meter long' is to be defined. It can be defined in various ways, e.g., by an ostensive definition ('This rod is one meter long') or transitively using another unit of length ('One meter is 39.37 inches') or—again transitively—as the distance travelled by light in a vacuum during the time interval of 1/299 792 458 of a second.[45]

17

Aspect-seeing and philosophy of psychology

Wittgenstein used the duck-rabbit figure[1] to show an example of a rare phenomenon which makes the expression 'something is seen as something else' meaningful in everyday language. That led him to distinguish between the 'continuous seeing' of an aspect and the 'dawning' of an aspect:

> Only through the phenomenon of change of aspect does the aspect seem to be detached from the rest of the seeing. It is as if, after the experience of change of aspect, one could say 'So there was an aspect there!'[2]

However, aspects may change without achieving this specific experience, e.g., someone can fail to experience the ambiguity of the figure. Aspect-blind can recognize that something is an ambiguous figure without being able to experience it. They cannot speak of aspects, but something has changed which Wittgenstein calls the 'conception' or 'way of taking' (Auffassung): 'If there were no change of aspect then there would only be a *way of taking*.'[3] Aspect-blind people cannot see aspects but only various conceptions. If they want to report an aspect, they have to employ a conception. Thus: 'An aspect is admittedly called a conception, but a conception can persist without the persisting of an

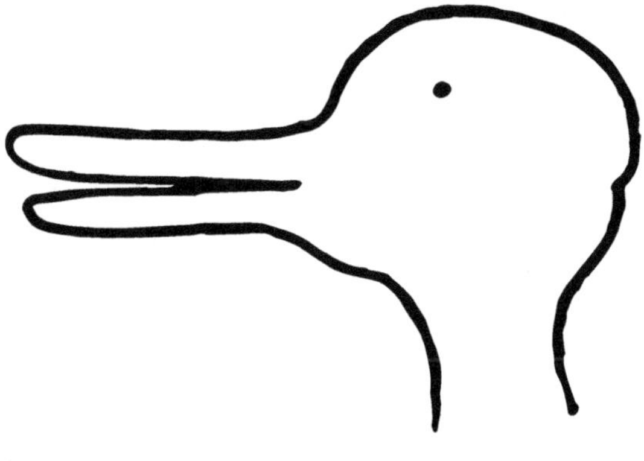

Figure 17.1 The duck-rabbit

aspect.'[4] The aspect and the conception have the same expression in language. The statement 'It's a duck' can stand either for (an exclamation of the dawning of) an aspect or only for (a report of) a conception.

Equipped with this distinction, we can now analyze the concept of aspect more precisely. Wittgenstein says: 'what I perceive in the dawning of an aspect is not a property of the object, but an internal relation between it and other objects.'[5] This is the one and only occurrence of the expression 'internal relation' in the final version of the *Philosophical Investigations* and so we have to investigate this remark very carefully. First of all, it is difficult to infer what the objects involved are. Ter Hark considers three possibilities:

> (i) One object is the geometrical constellation, the other is either the duck or the rabbit. (ii) One object is the duck, the other is the rabbit. (iii) One object is the change of aspect, the other is either the duck or the rabbit.[6]

Ter Hark argues against (i) as follows: (a) the duck-rabbit can be identified independently of the duck or the rabbit and (b) the duck-rabbit is not necessary to describe the aspects. Therefore, there has to be an external relation between the duck-rabbit and the duck or the rabbit. These objections are valid only if the constellation is seen neither as a duck, nor as a rabbit.[7] But then the duck and the rabbit would stand for conceptions, and not for aspects, and thus there would be no relation at all, neither internal nor external. Ter Hark concludes in favor of (iii). Surely there must be an internal relation between the experience of the change of aspect and the conceptions involved. But this is not the relation Wittgenstein means. The quotation above implies that one term in the relation is the perceived object, i.e., the duck-rabbit. This consideration rules out the second possibility as well. The formulation (i) should, however, be refined so that in the dawning of the aspect an internal relation is perceived between the perceived object (i.e., the duck-rabbit) and the duck-aspect or the rabbit-aspect respectively.

Here is another version of this remark: 'By noticing an aspect one perceives an internal relation ~~(between objects)~~.'[8] The internal relation does not really hold between objects (perhaps that is why Wittgenstein struck 'between objects' out), but between concepts that are involved in their descriptions. The reason is expressed at the beginning of Chapter 10. Any talk of internal relations between objects has to be understood as talk of internal relations between concepts describing these objects.[9] The experience of the change of aspect is not involved in the internal relation, although one perceives the internal relation *owing to* (durch) the experience. Rather, it consists in noticing the new and previously unnoticed aspect. Let me slightly modify the example. Instead of the duck-rabbit we now have a chaotic tangle of lines which we have no actual concept of (i.e., we possess no description for precisely *this* tangle of lines, for *this* shape). After a while, however, we notice that there is a rabbit in the tangle of lines:

> The expression of the dawning of an aspect is: 'Now it's *this*—now it's *that*.' The expression of noticing the rabbit in the tangle of lines is: 'There is a rabbit here.' We have not noticed something and now we do; there's nothing paradoxical about this.[10]

Where is the internal relation in this scenario? If we possess no description of the tangle of lines, there is nothing to relate it to. We can, however, say that after noticing the rabbit-aspect in the tangle, we can perceive an internal *property* of the tangle. We could call this the property of *rabbitness*.

Let me be completely clear about the internal relation in aspect-seeing: the expression of the dawning of an aspect is as follows: 'Now I am seeing *A* as *B*.' An internal relation is perceived between concepts *A* and *B*.

I would now like to emphasize a connection between the concepts of internal relation and organization. There are many kinds of internal relations and many kinds of aspects. In seeing-as, we are dealing with aspects of organization: 'One *kind* of aspect might be called "aspects of organization."'[11] In one of his manuscripts, Wittgenstein notes in a cryptic remark: 'The internal relation of structures is the organization which generates the one from the other.'[12] We can infer that in an internal relation, one term is *organizing* the other.

Next we have to look carefully at reflexive cases of such an internal relation. What could it possibly mean when *A* is seen as *A*? Wittgenstein is very clear about this question: 'It would have made as little sense for me to say "Now I am seeing it as…" as to say at the sight of a knife and fork "Now I am seeing this as a knife and fork."'[13] Or: 'I cannot try to see a conventional picture of a lion *as* a lion, any more than an F as that letter.'[14] Therefore a reflexive case of the internal relation of seeing *A* as *A* makes no sense. I cannot see a knife as a knife, a lion as a lion or an *F* as an *F*.[15] These cases can be *straightened out* into the sentences 'I see a knife,' 'I see a lion,' or 'I see the letter *F*.'[16]

17.1 Fitting

The concept of fitting (passen) is briefly discussed in §11.3. Two objects fit together if a single description holds for both. If a piston and a cylinder fit together, then a single description must hold for their shapes. The same point can be made with pieces of a jigsaw puzzle: they fit together if they have (at least in part) the same shape. This means that there is an internal relation between objects that fit together or, more precisely, between their shapes.

In this section, I want to focus on a different kind of fitting which is predominant in Wittgenstein's latest texts. Let us call it, tentatively, fitting underlined—or rather conditioned—by a certain experience, by a feeling. As stated above in the case of aspect-seeing, one perceives an internal relation *owing to* the experience of a change of aspect. But in which sense do we mean 'owing to'?

In Wittgenstein's later remarks on the philosophy of psychology, the expression 'to fit' is intended as a substitute for the concept of psychological association.[17] Psychological association should be understood causally and thus as external, but fitting, by contrast, should be understood formally and thus as internal. Wittgenstein shows that two phenomena can fit together in numerous examples. The name Schubert fits together with Schubert's works,[18] Beethoven's face fits together with his *Ninth Symphony*,[19] the word 'Goethe' fits together with its atmosphere and with the color yellow,[20] my long-familiar furniture fits together with my room[21] or two motives *necessarily* fit together in a musical composition, two figures fit *naturally* together in a poem.[22] Now, the gist of these examples is that these connections are not psychological associations, despite the fact that psychological associations and other causal connections might occur here as well.[23] These objects do not need to fit together as long as they are conceived of as isolated objects. They are, rather, phenomena that fit into the whole of our experience: '*That* is how this piece fits into the world of our thoughts & feelings.'[24] If two things fit together and, hence, are internally connected, then they make up a whole.[25] Let me illustrate this kind of feeling by analyzing a longer, dense remark:

> Look at a long familiar piece of furniture in its old place in your room. You would like to say: 'It is part of an organism.' Or 'Take it outside, and it's no longer at all the same as it was', and similar things. And naturally one isn't thinking of any *causal* dependence of one part on the rest. Rather it's like *this*: I could give this thing a name and say that it is shifted from its place, has a stain, is dusty; but if I tried taking it *quite* out of its present context, I should say that it had ceased to exist and another had got into its place.
>
> One might even feel like this: 'Everything is part and parcel of everything else' (internal and external relations). Displace a piece and it is no longer what it was. Only in this surrounding is this table this table. Everything is part of

> everything. [I believe Hegel meant something like this.] Here we have the inseparable atmosphere. And what is anyone saying, who says this? What sort of method of representation is he proposing? Isn't it that of the painted picture? If, for example, the table has moved, you paint a new picture of the table *with* its surrounding.[26]

Wittgenstein describes a common experience here: one is used to a certain arrangement of everyday objects, e.g., to an arrangement of furniture in one's own room. The furniture may be arranged completely randomly without any aesthetic consideration, or it may be done by someone else without taking into account the feelings of the occupant of the room. It does not matter whether the pieces of furniture fit together like pieces of a jigsaw puzzle.

In the second part of the remark, Wittgenstein presents two interconnected ideas, at least on my reading: (i) We *might* have a *feeling* of the unity of our experience which can be expressed as:

> (104) Everything is part and parcel of everything else.

(ii) Objects as phenomena are what they are only within the world of our feelings, i.e., in (felt) relations to other objects. Focusing on the first idea, we may notice a certain resemblance to the notion of 'feeling' or the 'feeling base' in Bradley. For Bradley, a feeling that is given in immediate experience is—or at least can be—so rich that it can give us a sense of its identity with the whole or Absolute.[27] A feeling can transcend immediate experience towards the Absolute. In Bradley's words:

> [Immediate experience] is a positive non-relational non-objective whole of feeling. Within my immediate experience falls everything of which in any sense I am aware, so far at least as I am aware of it.[28]

This claim has to be understood in the context of Bradley's theory of judgment. If one makes a judgment about one's immediate experience (e.g., 'This is my table'), one has to focus on a certain part of reality. Relations to other parts of reality enter into this judgment as well. (The table is what it is only in its familiar place, in its surroundings.) Although we can try to abstract all the relations out of the judgment, the 'feeling [...] remains after relations have been abstracted out of it.'[29] Feeling is in this sense a *feeling base* which cannot be abstracted, because it is non-relational or even non-conceptual. The feeling base thus transcends all experience.

I do not claim that Wittgenstein was influenced by Bradley here. My point is rather that both thinkers pertain to the same kind of philosophical intuition. Can we say, accordingly, that Wittgenstein was an adherent of monism like Bradley? We have to go back to Wittgenstein's method of analysis as elaborated in §1. Wittgenstein's aim was to differentiate, to show what our experience is, what it is like and what form it takes. In short, his aim was to analyze phenomena. This analysis may take into account our—rather indeterminate—feeling that everything is part and parcel of everything else. Wittgenstein, however, introduces this kind of feeling with the preamble 'One might even feel like this.' This simply means that people might have this feeling. One of the tasks of the philosophical analysis is to qualify (104). The actual question is whether it is really the case that for any two single phenomena we might experience a feeling that they fit together or that one is an aspect of the other. Wittgenstein's reflections show that this is not the case: we cannot imagine certain combinations of colors;[30] we feel aesthetic discomfort with certain combinations of phenomena.[31] We have a feeling of unity that ultimately turns out to be differentiated. Bradley would say that we experience differentiated reality which turns out to be ultimately a unity.

Wittgenstein ascribes to Hegel the idea that objects are what they are only in their familiar surroundings. I do not want to overemphasize this casual remark. Here is my brief suggestion regarding what Wittgenstein might have been referring to in Hegel. In the 'Sense-Certainty' chapter of *Phenomenology of Spirit*, Hegel provides a complicated argument that every demonstrative act indicates our immediate experience, every 'This' is always mediated by a universal. When we try to point out a single thing, we realize that:

> The *Here pointed out*, to which I hold fast, is similarly a *this* Here which, in fact is not this Here, but a Before and Behind, an Above and Below, a Right and Left. The Above is itself similarly this manifold otherness of above, below, etc.[32]

Consider an object that we want to point out as 'Here' or 'This.' We can refer to this object as the object in front of something else, above something else, to the left of something else, etc. Every ostensive 'This' means 'this thing I am pointing at' or 'this thing before me,' etc. Every demonstrative act indicating an object is, hence, dependent on the object's relations to other objects one may point at. In Wittgenstein's terms: every demonstrative act occurs against a background of demonstrative practices.[33] Without this background, knowledge would be impossible. What appears at the outset to be the most immediate and certain knowledge ('the *richest* kind of knowledge' in Hegel's wording) proves to be, in fact, a very low ('the most abstract and poorest') kind of knowledge. Knowledge is, hence, mediated by universality, by our shared (and thus universal) practices.

What, then, has the status of the most certain and immediate knowledge in this scenario if it is not a single intuition? Hegel, in adopting his characteristic synthetic stance, says that if anything about the sense-certainty is maximally immediate knowledge, it is the sense-certainty as a whole:

> Thus it is only sense-certainty as a *whole* which stands firm within itself as *immediacy* and by so doing excludes from itself all the opposition which has hitherto obtained.[34]

If one strives (as Hegel does, but Wittgenstein does not) for the most adequate knowledge (of an object), one has to take into account all other objects and relations to it. Wittgenstein says that if one takes an object in isolation, one may have a feeling that the object 'is part and parcel of everything else,' that it fits into our experience. For Hegel, such an object (when taken in isolation) will be incomplete and will stimulate a feeling of *desire*.[35]

There is a neat summary of the 'Sense-Certainty' chapter by Philip Kain: 'Sense-certainty is as opposed to a doctrine of internal relations as anything can be.'[36] Sense-certainty is an account of knowledge that is founded on single intuitions, single demonstrative acts, and single objects as its most certain and immediate elements. It is the most utterly pluralistic and atomistic account of knowledge. Sense-certainty is equivalent to the doctrine of external relations.

The main argument of the 'Sense-Certainty' chapter is merely that the doctrine of external relations is an inadequate account of knowledge. Wittgenstein gives virtually the same argument against the doctrine of external relations as Hegel does. 'Sense-Certainty' is, however, only the first chapter of the *Phenomenology*, and Hegel still has to produce many more arguments in order to establish the doctrine of internal relations. Wittgenstein does not follow Hegel in this respect.[37, 38]

17.2 Metaphor as seeing-as

In this section, I shall develop the claim made earlier that in seeing *A* as *B*, an internal relation is perceived between the concepts *A* as *B*. Many authors have noticed a link between metaphor and perception. Aristotle says in his *Poetics* 'to make metaphors well is to observe what is like [something else].'[39] The most significant recent studies on this topic, by Max Black and Donald Davidson, conclude that metaphor is to be likened to *seeing-as*. Davidson furthermore mentions Wittgenstein's 'duck-rabbit' and maintains that 'seeing as is not seeing that.'[40] In the metaphor '*A* is *B*' subject *A* is thus *seen as* predicate *B*. Certainly, such a comparison may be conceived of as a metaphor as well. The seeing-as in a metaphor should be similar or somehow analogous to the seeing-as in visual perception.

My intention here is to elaborate an account of how such an analogy is to be conceived. How far does the analogy between these two similar structures go? Or are we misled by that analogy? These are the general questions about philosophical inquiry which Wittgenstein asks himself in his *Blue Book*.[41]

Seeing-as has, in my view, several characteristics. First, aspect-seeing is *holistic*. Aspects of the ambiguous figure have to be mutually exclusive: one can successfully see it either way, but one can never see it both ways at once just as one cannot see one part of the picture under one aspect and another part under the other aspect. Second, a concrete instance of seeing-as can be triggered by a literal statement. The statement 'It's a duck' can cause one to see the figure as a duck. Aspect-seeing has, thus, a certain *causal* feature. These causal and holistic characteristics of aspect-perception are to be transposed to the metaphor. However, there are some problems which hold this immediate transposition back. There are metaphors concerning abstract terms which cannot be literally *seen*. How can justice be seen as a blind woman with a set of pendulum scales? Another difficulty is the author's intentional use of the ambiguous duck-rabbit figure. Would it mean that all metaphors are ambiguous in our analogy as well?

There are three items: the duck, the rabbit, and the duck-rabbit figure. What therefore corresponds to them in our analogy? Let me first discuss an account by Marcus Hester.[42] He claims that in Wittgenstein's example we are given the duck-rabbit and the problem is to see the duck and the rabbit in it. In the metaphor, on the other hand, we are given the duck and the rabbit and the problem is to see the duck-rabbit. In the metaphor '*A* is *B*,' the concepts (or images of) *A* and *B* should blend in order for us to discover the common *Gestalt* between them. For example, in Keats' metaphor of his imagination as a monastery[43] both elements should merge into a single image which can be seen as imagination or a monastery. This resembles Francis Galton's process of *composite photography* in which several portraits are merged into one in order to reveal common qualities of the group.

Hester's account cannot deal with abstract terms: how can we merge an image of imagination with an image of a monastery? It cannot be an image which will have the common properties of both terms, *viz.* properties common to both imagination and a monastery. There are no such properties for most metaphors. This is the question from the very beginning and Hester's account gives us no answer to it. Furthermore, both aspects are mutually exclusive and so the merged image cannot be seen both ways *simultaneously*, for then the holistic trait of the aspect would not be preserved.

Another account of the analogy has been offered by Roger White:

> We may […] regard the metaphorical sentence as a 'Duck-Rabbit'; it is a sentence that may simultaneously be regarded as presenting two different situations; looked at one way, it describes the actual situation, and looked at the other way, an hypothetical situation with which that situation is being compared.[44]

We are supposed to take the abovementioned metaphor of Keats, in analogy to the duck-rabbit ambiguity, as presenting in one reading the imagination (that is, the actual situation) and in another reading a monastery (a hypothetical situation). The holistic trait of the aspect remains preserved here. But the recipient will not be dubious about the two aspects. Both of them are given together with the duck-rabbit. And now we are told that both situations, i.e., both aspects, should be compared. What the analogy also shows is that in the metaphor '*A* is *B*' both the terms should be compared. If all three elements are already given, why should the reader compare the situations? I do not want to deny that White gives a plausible explanation of such a comparison, but this explanation is not a consequence of this analogy.

Nevertheless, both accounts share, in my view, the same defect: two situations/aspects are given which should be compared or merged. But we do not know how. Furthermore, both authors do not use Wittgenstein's subsequent reflections about the dawning of an aspect and about the role played by concepts in perception. A dawning of an aspect is for Wittgenstein 'half visual experience, half thought,' it is 'an amalgam of the two.'[45] These considerations have to be employed in our analogy.

We have to get rid of the intentional ambiguity of the duck-rabbit figure. A spectator does not need to know about the ambiguity of the figure. They might consider it at first as a duck and only later on experience the change of aspect. In such cases they might say: 'Now I see this duck as a rabbit' or, more metaphorically, 'This duck is now a rabbit.' Anyway, we do not need to suppose that a spectator would identify the whole figure as a duck-rabbit at all. They would initially conceive the figure as a tangle of lines.[46]

I propose analyzing this analogy as follows: subject *A* of the metaphor '*A* is *B*' corresponds to the duck-rabbit and predicate *B* is one of the aspects, e.g., the duck. We already know that in seeing *A* as *B*, an internal relation is perceived between *A* and *B*. Then what is perceived in the metaphor '*A* is *B*' is an internal relation between subject *A* and predicate *B* insofar as they are both perceived and thought of. Moreover, a conceptual relation is perceived between the terms involved which has an irreducible subjective side as well. This means that in the metaphor, the predicate *B* organizes the subject *A*. In our example above, the concept of a monastery organizes the concept of Keats' or even someone else's imagination.

Due to the notion of an aspect, the causal as well as the holistic feature of the seeing-as is preserved in the analogy. The first consequence for my theory of metaphor is that metaphors cannot be fully paraphrased in literal language because of the subjective experience of the change of aspect. Furthermore, any internal relations cannot be expressed. The consequence is that a secondary metaphorical meaning cannot be expressed in the metaphor. The main objection against theories of metaphorical meaning is that they are reducing the aspect to a conception and leaving aside the subjective experience of the change of aspect. On the other hand, there are theories that see a function of the metaphor in the evocation of an emotive or perlocutionary effect. They are reducing the aspect just to its subjective component, leaving the linguistic component aside. Furthermore, if the point of a metaphor were an experience of the change of aspect, then only an external relation would be perceived in the metaphor here, because the experience is a concrete event which is causally linked to the metaphor.

The aim of my analysis here has been to demonstrate that elaborating Wittgenstein's notion of the seeing of an aspect allows a useful analogy between seeing-as and metaphors. Let me conclude with a paraphrase of Aristotle: to make metaphors well is to observe internal relations.[47]

18

Aesthetics and art

There is a certain duality in Wittgenstein's reflections on both aesthetics and the theory of art. On the one hand, aesthetics and art exist in a cultural context. They belong to the language-game which Wittgenstein calls 'culture.' His account is then, in this sense, normative and *institutional*. To recognize an object (or a phenomenon) as a work of art at all, it needs to be internally related to the culture of its time. This only means that any work of art has to follow some rules. I will call this aspect of art its *transitive understanding*. On the other hand, beauty and art are also about expression. A work of art displays an extraordinary talent, in which even a genius may transgress traditional rules. In this sense, Wittgenstein's account of art is *expressive*. If a work of art is thus conceived of as an expression, it does not convey or refer to something else. Following Wittgenstein, I will call this aspect of art *intransitive understanding*.

18.1 Transitive understanding: Culture

The understanding of a work of art is manifested in a response or resonance to it. Let me call this *aesthetic reaction*. The fact that people understand a work of art becomes apparent when they respond to it in a particular manner. In this sense, one could say that they respond *correctly*. The concept of aesthetic correctness is indeed central to Wittgenstein's aesthetics. A work of art is correct or right as long as it follows common aesthetic rules (concerning, for instance, harmony, composition, or ideal proportions).

The aesthetic reaction is not just limited to predicates like 'nice' or 'pretty' which Wittgenstein regards rather as interjections.[1] Such simple aesthetic judgments, which are used by children or by less educated people, are replaced by more complex judgments which need a deeper context (which may be provided by education). Wittgenstein calls the context for aesthetic judgments 'culture.' I want to take culture as a language-game, although the only explicit evidence for this claim is less reliable: 'What belongs to a language game is a whole culture.'[2] This suggestion is justified by the fact that Wittgenstein uses the notion of a language-game as a context. For additional evidence, we can focus on Wittgenstein's remarks from the *Zettel*[3] that deal with music. In §164 Wittgenstein explores how the expression 'expressive playing' can be explained. For such an explanation, one needs to be educated in a particular *culture*. I take §175 as Wittgenstein's denial that musical themes (or works of art more generally) have any intrinsic aesthetic features. A theme is always embedded in the context; it 'makes an impression on me which is connected with the things in its surroundings—e.g., with our language and its intonations; and hence with the whole field of our language-games.' Thus, based on these remarks, it is sufficiently justified and indeed fruitful to speak of culture itself as a language-game. After all, the label 'culture' as such is not that important. We would lose nothing by simply talking of a language-game with aesthetic expressions.

To produce a correct aesthetic reaction to a work of art presupposes acquaintance with an (actual) culture. Wittgenstein uses the term 'culture' very loosely here. I shall examine how an aesthetic judgment is involved in it. One can understand culture as a network of connections.[4] A work of art fits (passt zusammen) into this network due to its correctness. An aesthetic judgment is supposed to express this fit.[5] As already elaborated in §§11.3 and 17.1 above, this fitting expresses an internal relation. Two things or phenomena fit together if there is an internal relation between them, or more precisely, if there is an internal relation between their forms. In the same vein, Wittgenstein employs the distinction between motive or reason and cause in this context: 'There is a "Why?" to aesthetic discomfort not a "cause" to it.'[6] Or: 'an aesthetic explanation is not a causal explanation.'[7] And again, this suggests that an aesthetic explanation seeks to express an internal relation, and not a causal relation which is, of course, external.

Now back to the investigation of aesthetic reactions to a work of art. They, the work of art and any reaction to it, must fit together; there must be an internal relation between them. Such a reaction need not be a verbal one; it can simply be a gesture or even another work of art. One could find a fitting musical accompaniment for a poem, or a fitting dance figure for a melody.[8]

One may now ask how a correct aesthetic reaction to a work of art can be identified (or become known). This would be the same as asking how to find a missing part from a whole phenomenon. The answer lies in, or can be deduced from, Wittgenstein's account of aspect-seeing. The phrase 'to see (or hear) something as something else' is used in art very often, e.g., 'You have to hear these bars as an introduction.'[9] Such aspect-perceiving, or the possibility of an eventual change of aspect is, says Wittgenstein, essential in aesthetics.[10] The phrases 'see as' and 'fit together' are closely related. If something is seen as another thing, then both things fit together.[11] A phenomenon is, however, not seen as another thing all the time. The aspect has to dawn and in such dawning of an aspect one perceives an internal relation. The correctness of an aesthetic reaction, therefore, can be affirmed in the dawning of the aspect and in the related astonishment or surprise (Staunen).[12] These reflections lead us to the next tentative conclusion: an aesthetic reaction expresses an aspect of a work of art.

As we know from §17, in aspect-seeing, the perceived object must be organized. To organize a phenomenon means seeing that its parts fit together in a particular way, namely *correctly*. Now we have to distinguish the following. Parts of a work of art fit together (I shall call this fitting *immanent*). This fitting is the basis of the fitting together (what I call the *transcendent* fitting) of the work of art and the reactions to it. An aesthetic reaction is correct insofar as it expresses an aspect of the work of art. An aesthetic judgment reveals to us an internal relation between the work of art and other objects, by which we understand, as noted, that they share a common form. But what are these *other objects*? I want to suggest that they are other works of art. This enables us to regard complex aesthetic reactions as works of art.

The fact that there is an internal relation between two objects—two works of art—implies that they are, or could be, parts of a whole. They are a total work of art (*Gesamtkunstwerk*), one might say. There are many kinds of aesthetic reaction to a work of art and so they can be internally related to a variety of phenomena. These reactions can be very simple ('It's nice!') or significantly more complex. A reaction can reveal, for example, a deep affinity between two artists, e.g., between Brahms and Keller.[13] More precisely, a network of such connections is what Wittgenstein calls a *culture*. It is the total or ultimate work of art. The sole culture *in toto* prescribes the rules for itself. An object becomes a work of art insofar as it expresses (or is used as an expression of) an aspect of the culture. This does not mean that every work of art has to meet all the rules of the convention, but that these rules have an impact on the aesthetic reactions to a work of art, especially to an object's being taken as a work of art at all.[14]

If we take culture as the praxis with art and the sum of all works of art, then the internal relations within a culture are all that matters. In this sense, Wittgenstein's aesthetics is institutional.

18.2 Intransitive understanding: Expression and genius

The preceding section can be taken as describing the first step in our analysis of the language of aesthetics and art. In this first step, we had to distinguish between internal and external relations. What makes an object a work of art is the object's internal relation to its culture. However, in this section, our concern will be the reflexive cases of internal relations. This takes up the second step of the analysis. The point of departure is Wittgenstein's critique of Tolstoy's theory of art:

> There is much that could be learned from Tolstoy's false theorizing that the work of art conveys 'a feeling'.—And you really might call it, if not the expression of a feeling, an expression of feeling, or a felt expression. And you might say too that people who understand it to that extent 'resonate' with it, respond to it. You might say: The work of art does not seek to convey something else, just itself.[15]

Suppose one is forced to answer questions like 'What is this picture supposed to mean?' or 'What does this melody seek to convey to us?' If there is really nothing that one may point at, then a reflexive construction may help. A work of art seeks to *convey* or *express itself*—or it just means itself, it refers to itself. These formulations are reflexive cases of internal relations. The key issue is: either the work of art is a medium for grasping something else or it just exists for itself.[16] The something that is supposed to be grasped may take various forms: for instance, it may be a feeling as Tolstoy (and the Expressive theory of art) suggests; it may be a hidden message (in structuralist accounts) or a political action (in Marxism). Wittgenstein is opposed to all these views of art. A work of art expresses itself. But the *maxim of no reflexive uses of internal relations* urges us to get rid of this vague reflexive construction.[17] However, the question is how to straighten it out and give a positive account of art.

One model of this straightening out may be what Wittgenstein calls *intransitive understanding*. He applies this label to pictures, but we can broaden it to works of art in general.[18] Wittgenstein writes in the *Philosophical Grammar*:

> If I say: 'I understand this picture' the question arises: do I mean 'I understand it *like that*'? With the '*like that*' standing for a translation of what I understand into a different expression? Or is it a sort of intransitive understanding? When I'm understanding one thing do I as it were think of another thing? Does understanding, that is, consist of thinking of something else? And if that isn't what I mean, then what's understood is as it were autonomous, and the understanding of it is comparable to the understanding of a melody.[19]

I argued in §9.3 that a picture has to depict something else. If it does not, it is not a picture at all (like a map that is identical with the territory it depicts). We usually speak of understanding a picture when we recognize what it represents. Pictures in art or works of art in general may represent something (a still life represents a particular scene, for instance), but their representing role is not essential to this kind of understanding. A theme in music does not represent anything. If we look aesthetically at real (and not depicted) things like a landscape or a flower, we do not ponder what they represent. In art we are interested in the things themselves. Wittgenstein quotes Goethe's exclamation in this context: 'Don't look for anything behind the phenomena; they themselves are the theory.'[20] This is why this kind of understanding is *intransitive*.

What, then, is art all about? Why are we interested in works of art at all? The work of art is 'an expression of [a] feeling, or a felt expression.' The very act of expressing or grasping it is a matter of experiencing it. Or as Johannessen puts it: 'the understanding sought here is a way of *experiencing*.'[21] Works of art are expressions of feeling in the way that a smile is an expression of joy. Works of art are usually, however, much more complex. Nobody is tempted to say that by smiling one is conveying a feeling of joy. Analogously, Sophocles' *Oedipus Rex* or Beethoven's *Fifth Symphony* cannot be said to be conveying the feeling of the inexorability of fate. Wittgenstein can thus say that works of art 'give us pleasure, occupy our minds'[22] but without conveying these feelings.

The next model of intransitive understanding concerns the expression 'meaning.' Even this expression demonstrates the ambiguity between transitive and intransitive uses. Wittgenstein imagines the situation of being impressed by a bed of pansies:

> I could have used the expression 'Each of these colour patterns has meaning'; but I didn't say 'has meaning', for this would provoke the question, 'What meaning?', which in the case we are considering is senseless. We are distinguishing between meaningless patterns and patterns which have meaning; but there is no such expression in our game as 'This pattern has the meaning so and so'.[23]

Hence, we can use the word 'meaning' transitively as '*X* has the meaning so and so.' The expression 'so and so' stands for an explanation of meaning. Such an explanation is actually a rule which expresses an internal relation. Intransitive uses of the expression 'meaning' are close to aesthetics. What, then, is the intransitive meaning of 'meaning'? The following classification given by Severin Schroeder may be helpful here. He identifies three ways to use 'meaning' intransitively (although they may overlap): 'denoting (1) value, (2) a specific *Gestalt*, or (3) an (apparent) appropriateness.'[24] 'Meaning' may be used to highlight the (typically personal) value of something: 'This tune has meaning for me' or even 'Life has meaning.' In these contexts, 'meaning' is used intransitively without implying that the meaning is so and so. Expressing a specific *Gestalt* seems to indicate a transitive use of an internal relation. 'I see this picture as a duck' expresses a duck-aspect of the picture, which amounts to expressing an internal relation between the shape of this picture and the shape of a duck.[25] But we can also find a specific *Gestalt* or aspect, for example, in a tune while knowing it is not really there:

> we say 'This tune says *something*', and it is as though I had to find what it says. And yet I know that it doesn't say anything such that I might express in words or pictures what it says. And if, recognizing this, I resign myself to saying 'It just expresses a musical thought', this would mean no more than saying 'It expresses itself'.[26]

But how can we see an aspect of an object and suspect that this aspect is not really contained in that selfsame object? The aspect is not part of its *meaning*, although the object means something. A plausible explanation is that various aspects are switching (dawning and receding), which involves a feeling of astonishment as mentioned a few pages previously.[27] The object means this at one moment and that at another moment. Now a few words about Schroeder's third intransitive way of using 'meaning.' Something is *appropriate* if it fits into its surroundings (i.e., its *transitive understanding*) or if its parts fit together. Noticing such appropriateness is, in fact, akin to the noticing or dawning of an aspect. This is the case of *immanent* fitting as mentioned in the previous section 18.1.

In this chapter, we have so far focused on the receptive side of art, that is to say on the explanation of how and why art is perceived and apprehended. Now we are going to focus on the productive side of art. How do works of art emerge? If the work of art forms an aspect of an actual culture, how, then, can it be explained that this culture can undergo a change? What is the source of these cultural dynamics? Wittgenstein admits that there are works of art that cannot be judged only according to their correctness. He calls such works of art *tremendous*.[28] Impressionist paintings were first judged disparagingly because they did not follow the academic rules of the period. However, such negative attitudes endured for less than a generation, and impressionist works then became the canon of subsequent art movements. A work of art is called tremendous because it occupies and forms a tremendous part of a culture. Although such works of art express aspects of the culture, they contribute to the culture in a different way.

My suggestion is that tremendous works of art enrich a culture with new rules. An artist who has the *talent* to enforce new rules is—in the Kantian sense—a genius.[29] 'Genius is the talent in which the character expresses itself,'[30] says Wittgenstein. This reference to character is a crucial point that goes beyond the institutional conception of art.[31] The enrichment of a culture with new rules does not happen all at once. New rules are, at first, only implicitly incorporated in the works of artistic geniuses, and it takes some time before they are recognized and thus become a part of culture. After this happens, another language-game, 'culture,' is played, for every language-game is defined by its rules.

Culture is embedded in our very form of life.[32] Each child eventually manages to integrate its primitive expressions of pain into complex language-games. Nevertheless, one needs to have talent to master the complex language-game of *culture* and to transpose one's feelings into this extraordinary language-game. To express common feelings in our language, we do not need to introduce new rules. But by contrast, it may happen that the prevailing culture cannot satisfy the artist's demands, which is precisely why new rules are then introduced.

However, every artist needs to address the usual rules of their culture and they may indeed violate *some* of these. If they violated *all* the rules of their culture, we would have no reason to regard their products as works of art. They must express, through their art, the aspects of their culture. In this sense, a work of art should be understood as a model of culture.

A work of art stands in two main relationships—in a vertical relationship to our feelings and life, and in a horizontal relationship to other works of art within the language-game 'culture.'[33] If the horizontal relationship is accentuated, Wittgenstein's conception of art is institutional; if we emphasize, on the other hand, the vertical relationship, one can instead understand art as being expressive.

V

Conclusion

My interpretation of Wittgenstein's writings is now complete. In this concluding Part V, I want to finish by recapitulating the main principles and insights that have driven my interpretation. I want to resist formulating any general theory extracted from Wittgenstein's philosophy. However, if my interpretation is admissible, its main principles do coincide with the main principles of Wittgenstein's logical and grammatical analysis of language. These principles remain mostly tacit in Wittgenstein's texts. Nevertheless, some quite explicit formulations of these principles can also be found.[1] These principles, or rather their guidelines, are:

I To insist on the distinction between internal and external relations in the depth grammar.

II That reflexive cases of internal relations are in fact those cases of direct expression where no relation at all is expressed.

The first principle goes back to Frege's distinction between concepts and objects. It is to be found throughout Wittgenstein's writings, while the second principle manifests itself mainly in Wittgenstein's later philosophy. In the following chapters, I am going to look back at the topics discussed above in the light of these principles. The following chapter addresses why we express internal relations at all. Expressions of internal relations are far from nonsensical. They express current or proposed logical or grammatical rules. The final chapter will discuss the *maxim of no reflexive uses of internal relations*. It will be indicated there that this maxim is analogous to Bradley's insistence that all relations must be both internal and external.

19

Internal relations as imperatives

Having distinguished between internal and external relations, we can ask for what actual reasons do we express internal relations. Expressions of internal relations do not depict any states of affairs and they are not moves in language-games. I am strongly opposed to the view (maintained by some resolute readers) that expressing an internal relation is plain nonsense. Internal relations say something about the logic or grammar of our language. This statement is, however, also ambiguous, as internal relations express both what the logic or grammar of our language *is* and what it *ought to be*. Expressing an internal relation can function as a kind of reminder to someone who is not aware of the logic of our language or it can function as a stimulus to improve our logic or grammar. In short: expressing an internal relation has normative force and can also be taken as an imperative.

Here is an outline of how such imperatives may work. Let us turn first to the *Tractatus*. In the logically adequate language which is outlined in the *Tractatus*, it is impossible to express any internal relation by means of a proposition. Formulating an internal relation in a proposition is an indication that we have not yet reached a logically adequate language. In §7.1 I stated that the signs for relations ought to be eliminated from our logical notation in favor of an internal relation within the signifying fact. This idea is further elaborated in §7.2 where I give an example of how a logical relation between two states of affairs can be incorporated into our logical notation. The very possibility of expressing an internal relation (a logical implication, for example) can be taken as a direction to improve our manner of expression so that it comes closer to a logically adequate language.

Another example of this method is given in §9.1. Expressing an internal relation (or a property, in this case) invites us to coordinate the combinatorial powers of names and objects. Some internal relations can thus be converted into propositional variables. A similar idea is elaborated in §9.3. It is demonstrated there how the supposed expression of the internal relation of depicting between a proposition and a fact can be transformed into a propositional variable.

It is obvious that once an order is fulfilled, it does not need to be repeated. By the same token, once the task of internal relations is achieved (i.e., once they are incorporated into logical grammar), they *can be* left behind.[1] But there is something else on top of that. Since an internal relation modifies the very language in which it is expressed, it cannot be expressed in this modified language. Hence, once the task of internal relations has been achieved, these relations *are* left behind, for there are no propositions that express them.

What is different, then, in Wittgenstein's later work? A striking difference is that nothing prevents us from expressing internal relations, even if there is a surveyable representation of the grammatical rules. We can express internal relations in order to remind someone of actual grammar, to change an existing rule, or to introduce a new rule. Expressing an internal relation is, however, not a move in a language-game. Let me go through some such reminders and imperatives case by case.

My first case concerns the situation of teaching someone an existing grammatical rule, e.g., teaching the name of a thing. In §10.3 I distinguished between the language-game of teaching and the language-game of applying a rule. The sentence

(105) This is called *X*

expresses an external relation in the former game and an internal relation in the latter. If we take these two language-games as a single language-game, (105) would be seen as ambiguous because it expresses both an internal and an external relation. There is nothing wrong here if we are aware of such an ambiguity. This sentence can be employed in the process of teaching as a reminder of the rule: 'You don't know what this is called, do you? It's called *X*.'

Next, we can slightly modify our scenario. Now we want to introduce a new rule, e.g., a name for a newly designed object (that is termed *baptizing*). The verbal expression may be the same as in the previous case or more explicit:

(106) From now on, this shall be called *X*.

Both (105) and (106) express an internal relation. The difference between them is that the former sentence is used as a reminder of an existing rule and the latter one as an imperative that establishes a new rule. This schema is totally universal; it works for every rule. What comes next are some special cases of this schema, *viz.* the rules concerning the standards of measure and color concepts.

In §15.2, I pointed out that the sentence 'This is red' can mean 'There is a red square' or 'This color is called red.' There is an ambiguity here between describing (expressing an external property) and naming (expressing an internal property). Expressing an internal property means, in fact, expressing a rule. And again, 'This color is called red' can be used to remind someone of an existing rule or to introduce a new rule. Something analogous can also be said about standards of measure.[2] 'This rod is one meter long' can mean 'This rod is as long as the standard meter' or 'This rod is the standard meter.' The latter sentence expresses an internal relation. It can inform someone about the actual standard or it can be used for proclaiming a new standard of measure, meaning roughly 'This rod shall be the standard meter.'

Color concepts and standards of measure are, thus, introduced by means of paradigmatic samples. The same is true of numerals, i.e., concepts for numbers. We can give meaning to the numeral 3 by the following definition:

(107) The list | | | means 3.

As stated in §14.2, the list | | | serves in this sense as a yardstick. The numeral 3 is a substitution or, rather, an abbreviation for the list | | |. The same schema applies here. (107) can be used in a teaching process to point out the existing rule for the numeral 3,[3] or it can be used as an imperative to introduce the meaning of '3.'

Mathematical propositions are statements of internal relations. Expressing such a proposition (e.g., that 68 + 57 = 125) says that this statement is a rule within our system of arithmetic. Although mathematical conjectures may have the same surface form as mathematical propositions, they express external relations. They can be confirmed or refuted empirically or heuristically. Mathematical propositions have, therefore, a normative force over mathematical conjectures. We can express a mathematical proposition in order to say that some conjecture is true or false—or that its empirical or heuristic confirmation is correct or incorrect.

Proving a new mathematical proposition is tantamount to introducing a new rule. What was only a conjecture (expressing an external relation) then becomes a mathematical proposition (expressing an internal relation) through its proof. Mathematical proofs aim to integrate mathematical conjectures into the system of already-proven mathematical propositions. The mathematical proof is a calculation that functions as a paradigmatic sample here. The proof says that this proposition shall be a mathematical proposition from now on, which means it shall be connected with our system of mathematics. A mathematical proposition is, thus, like an order, and its proof is like the fulfillment of the order.

This is the first cluster of cases illustrating how expressions of internal relations are used. All these cases are variations on the teaching situation (reminding of an existing rule or introducing a new rule). The second cluster of cases is related to aspect-seeing. Such expressions of internal relations are underlined by a certain experience, typically by a feeling. Suppose someone reported an experience of the change of an aspect:

(108) Now I see this picture as a duck.

This is an exclamatory sentence. However, we can use it in the imperative mood as:

(109) See this picture as a duck!

Expressed in either of these ways, both sentences imply that the experience of the change of aspect is possible, including an internal relation between the shape in this picture and the shape of a duck. This means that there is a smooth transition between these shapes, which can also be expressed as a case of one shape organizing the other. The experiencing of such a transition is, however, not a *private* feeling of its being possible. It is shown in our praxis. The imperative sentence (109) and the indicative sentence (108) both claim that our praxis is such that it allows a smooth transition between these shapes, amounting to experiencing an internal relation between them.

This universal scheme has several instances which I am going to sum up in turn. The first case (discussed in §15.3) is about experiencing mixtures of colors. Experiencing orange as a mixture of red and yellow amounts to *seeing* orange *as* reddish yellow or *as* yellowish red. This means that a smooth transition between these internally related colors can be experienced.

The second instance of this scheme concerns the making of a metaphorical statement. Consider Keats' metaphor (already mentioned above):

(110) My imagination is a monastery.

This metaphor can be rephrased into the form of an aspect expression:

(111) My imagination can be *seen as* a monastery.

Here, the poet is expressing his feelings about a certain state of his imagination. He expresses an internal relation between the concepts of his imagination and a monastery that is backed up by his experience. Again, this amounts to saying that the concept of a monastery organizes the concept of Keats' or the reader's imagination and that there is a smooth transition between them.

Paul Ricoeur said that a metaphor could be taken as a *poem in miniature*. A metaphor is, in fact, a small work of art in its own right. What is true of metaphors is also true of works of art in general. A work of art is an aesthetic reaction to other works of art whose totality is called culture. A work of art expresses an aspect of (current) culture. Works of art are thus internally related to culture and a kind of aspect-switching between various works of art can be experienced.

20

The maxim of no reflexive uses of internal relations

Having identified an internal relation expressed in a sentence, the second step in logical analysis is to look at its reflexive use. Let me say some words about the notion of a reflexive relation. A relation *R* is *reflexive* if and only if *R*(*x*,*x*) holds true for every element in its domain. What I have in mind when speaking of a reflexive use of an internal relation is a single case *R*(*a*,*a*). Therefore, it is not enough to say that an internal relation must not be reflexive. To avoid the reflexive uses, one has to say that an internal relation must be *irreflexive*, or rather that it must exclude its reflexive cases from its domain.

The methodological principle that I am calling the *maxim of no reflexive uses of internal relations* says that a reflexive use of an internal relation might be a failed case of emphasis. One should consider whether straightening it out into an intransitive use (where no relation is expressed at all) would make the language-game more plausible. This method is to be found throughout Wittgenstein's writings. Before turning to his own instances of this method, which have been discussed above, I want to provide a simple illustration of why a reflexive case of an internal relation may be nonsensical.

There are signposts near roads that indicate directions and distances to nearby places. Consider now the following situation. Someone who wants to reach place *A* has lost their way. Remember that 'A philosophical problem always has the form: "I simply don't know my way about."'[1] Now, the lost person is, in fact, already in *A* without realizing it. The lost person is looking for direction signs, but cannot find any sign indicating how to reach *A*. Only a reflexive direction sign could be helpful in this situation. There are, however, no such signposts and it makes little sense to set them up. A reflexive direction sign would be a weird way of indicating the name of an actual place; it would simply be a place-name sign. In fact, nothing relational could help them to know their way around. The right thing to do is not to look for a direction sign, but for the lost person to get to know where they actually are. This means they have to look for a place-name sign. They have to 'see what is *right in front of* [*their*] *eyes*!'[2] A reflexive case of an internal relation is analogous to a signpost indicating the way to the very place where the signpost actually is.

Now let us look at Wittgenstein's own instances of the maxim of no reflexive uses of internal relations.

(1) The first example is Wittgenstein's treatment of identity, which is an internal relation par excellence. The sentence '*a* = *a*' or '*a* is *a*' is, as an expression of pure identity, uninformative and useless. In the *Tractatus* 5.473, Wittgenstein offers the sentence 'Socrates is identical' as an example of nonsense. His point here[3] is that the unary predicate 'identical' has a different meaning from a sign for identity. This line of thinking is taken up again in the *Philosophical Investigations* where Wittgenstein offers the sentence 'A thing is identical with itself' as an example of a useless sentence.[4] This example is then subsequently presented in several variations: 'Every thing fits into itself' or 'Every thing fits into its own shape.' We can now restate these sentences in a reflexive way: the form of *A* is (identical with) the form of *A*. These sentences are seemingly not meaningless; they are, however, useless. We can straighten such sentences out into something like 'Every thing has a particular form' and consider whether this straightened-out sentence would be better suited to the speaker's original intention.

(2) The second example concerns the internal relation of depicting, which was discussed in Chapter 9. A reflexive use of this relation amounts to saying that a picture represents itself. In §9.3, I illustrated the point that a picture cannot represent itself with the map-territory relationship. A map that is identical with the territory it represents is useless. It is, in fact, not a map at all, as aptly recounted by Lewis Carroll and Jorge Luis Borges.

(3) The next application of the method: expectation and its fulfillment (namely, the intentional object) are internally related as elaborated in §11.2. There are cases of expectation without any intentional object, e.g., when someone says that they have a feeling of expectation without being able to specify what exactly they are expecting. We cannot say that the object (that is to say, the fulfillment) is in some mysterious way contained within the expectation. That would be as if an expectation referred to itself. Such a reflexive case should be straightened out into a direct expression of the feeling of expectation as argued in §11.4.

(4) A similar scheme is employed in Wittgenstein's critique of the Principle of Sufficient Reason:[5] 'For every fact *F*, there must be a reason why *F* is the case.' If *R* is the reason for *F*, *R* and *F* are internally related. There are, however, some

facts whose reasons are missing or at least are not obvious. One can save the Principle of Sufficient Reason by postulating a reflexive construction saying that the fact is its own reason, e.g., 'This is simply what I do.' This is, again, a reflexive case of an internal relation. Instead of using such reflexive constructions, Wittgenstein is willing to reject the Principle of Sufficient Reason. Facts without reason express grammatical rules. They are *termini ad quem* of a justification.

(5) The next instance of the maxim of no reflexive uses of internal relations is that we cannot say that a paradigmatic sample has the property of which it is a sample.[6] We cannot in the same language-game say that a paradigmatic sample of *X* has property *X*. It is nonsense to say that the paradigmatic sample | | | of the number 3 has three strokes, because 3 is an internal property of this list. We cannot say that the paradigmatic sample of blue is blue. Blue is an internal property of this sample. Finally, we cannot say that the standard meter is one meter long. Being one meter long is an internal property of the standard meter. We have to assign the internal property to the sample in a preparatory language-game which precedes the game of applying the sample. In this way, we can define a rule in one game and apply it in another game.

(6) If seeing *A* as *B* involves expressing an internal relation between *A* and *B*, we have to consider reflexive cases here as well. As indicated in Chapter 17, it makes little sense to say that I see this knife as a knife, or a lion as a lion, or a letter *F* as an *F*. If these reflexive cases mean anything, they have to be straightened out into intransitive cases that express an emphasis: This *really is* a knife. This *really is* a lion. This *really is* an *F*.

(7) Another reflexive construction is saying that a work of art expresses itself. This construction represents, in fact, an intransitive understanding of art. A work of art is a direct expression of a feeling but without conveying or even communicating any particular feeling. By saying that a work of art has meaning, we do not imply that it has the meaning *so and so*. 'Meaning' is used here intransitively without the implication that the meaning is so and so. The intransitive meaning of a work of art may be its value, its specific *Gestalt* or its appropriateness.

(8) I would like now to add one further example, not mentioned by Wittgenstein. In his *Italian Journey*, Goethe makes the following observation: 'The Venetian was forced to become a new creature; and thus Venice can only be compared with itself. The large canal, winding like a serpent, yields to no street in the world [...].'[7] It would make no sense to compare Venice with itself. The point of uttering such a strange sentence is that—as Goethe realized—every attempt to compare Venice with another town must fail. To say that Venice can

be compared only with itself means, in fact, that Venice could not be compared with anything at all. A reflexive use of a comparison is thus straightened out into an intransitive case of a rejection of any possible comparison.

My final reflection is devoted to making some deeper sense of the maxim of no reflexive uses of internal relations. The requirement that an instance of an internal relation not be reflexive demands, in fact, that there must be a difference between its terms. An internal relation is not one of pure identity. The terms of an internal relation are in a certain sense the same (*qua* internal) and in another sense they are different (*qua* relation). The demand for a difference between these terms suggests that there must be an *external* relation between these terms which would account for their difference. Hence, if two terms *a* and *b* are internally related by the relation R_{int}, there must be an external relation R_{ext} ensuring that *a* and *b* are different:

(112) $(\forall R_{int})(\forall a,b)\ ((R_{int}(a,b) \rightarrow (\exists R_{ext})\ R_{ext}(a,b))$

This is also a formal expression of the maxim of no reflexive uses of internal relations. However, even this expression might be misleading due to the nature of the terms *a* and *b*. The expressions '*a*' and '*b*' are *de dicto* in $R_{int}(a,b)$; they are however *de re* in $R_{ext}(a,b)$. This means that internal relations are held between concepts, whereas external relations are held between objects as indicated in §10.2.

The idea behind the maxim is not Wittgenstein's sole invention. Several other philosophers have developed various strategies for how to cope with the paradoxes of identity. Let me mention Fichte's *ground of distinction* (Unterscheidungs-Grund). If two entities are asserted—or 'posited' (gesetzt)—to be the same, they must be different in some respect, i.e., there must be some ground for their difference. This ground lies in the very presupposition that there must be *two entities* posited as identical. If there were only one entity, any positing would make little sense.

Frege, in his seminal paper *On Sense and Reference*, proposes a different solution to the paradox of identity. Why, he asks, is the proposition '$a = b$' of any cognitive value if *a* and *b* refer to the same object? Why does the proposition that 'The Morning Star is the Evening Star' say something substantial if 'the Morning Star' as well as 'the Evening Star' refers to Venus? Frege's solution rests in finding out that the sides of the equation are nevertheless different. They have the same reference, but different senses. 'The Morning Star' refers to Venus as she appears in the morning sky; 'the Evening Star' refers to the same planet as she appears in the evening sky. The idea lingering behind this is similar to that in Fichte. Any statement of identity presupposes some difference in its terms. Any identity, if it should be informative, is only a partial identity (i.e., identity in certain respects and non-identity in certain other respects).

In my view, the clearest expression of this idea is to be found in Bradley. As already discussed in detail in §4.2, for Bradley every relation must be partly internal and partly external. In particular, there are no wholly internal relations. If there were such a relation, we could not distinguish between its terms. They would lose their individuality. Then, however, if there were no distinct terms, there would be nothing to relate.

Let me highlight this affinity between Bradley and Wittgenstein. Bradley argues that every relation must be both internal and external. Endorsing an analytic attitude, Wittgenstein does not say that a single relation must be both internal and external. He insists on distinguishing between internal and external relations. The maxim of no reflexive uses of internal relations says that every internal relation presupposes an external relation that accounts for any difference between its terms.

Wittgenstein's first choice for the motto of the *Philosophical Investigations* was Joseph Butler's 'Everything is what it is, and not another thing.' Wittgenstein did not use this sentence because G. E. Moore had already used it as the motto for his *Principia Ethica*.[8] 'Everything is what it is' is another reflexive construction saying that everything is related to itself. This construction can therefore be straightened out and understood intransitively as placing an emphasis on things themselves as opposed to what they stand for.[9] Then this construction would have a similar sense as Goethe's 'Don't look for anything behind the phenomena; they themselves are the theory.'[10]

Now, everything is *not another thing*. If a thing were (or stood for, referred to, meant) some other thing, these two things would be internally related.[11] But if everything were nothing else, there would be no internal relations. Thus, internal relations do not—in the end, in the final analysis—belong to things; they are not constitutive of things. They are the means of representation of things. Internal relations can be—in an unattainable ideal—simply left behind.

Notes

Preface and acknowledgments

1 TLP 4.123.

2 In the text, I will touch upon a considerable majority of the themes from Wittgenstein's later philosophy. There are, however, themes that I will pass over. The internet/external distinction does not apply in Wittgenstein's treatment of ethics or religion—or I have not found any substantial employment of it there. The distinction does apply, however, to Wittgenstein's thoughts about certainty (the so-called *hinge* propositions that express internal relations whereas proper propositions express external relations). I will address these ideas in §10.3 in more detail without devoting a complete chapter to them.

Chapter 1

1 Russell, 1984, p. 119.

2 Wittgenstein distinguishes between surface grammar and depth grammar: 'In the use of words one might distinguish "surface grammar" from "depth grammar". What immediately impresses itself upon us about the use of a word is the way it is used in the construction of the sentence, the part of its use—one might say—that can be taken in by the ear.—And now compare the depth grammar, say of the word "to mean", with what its surface grammar would lead us to suspect. No wonder we find it difficult to know our way about' (PI §664). Although this metaphor comes from Wittgenstein's later philosophy, it fits the *Tractatus* as well.

3 TLP 4.0031, Ogden/Ramsey's trans.

4 This follows Kuusela's (2011b, p. 134) interpretation of the *Tractatus*: 'Rather than putting forward a theory or a doctrine about logic, or gesturing at ineffable truths, Wittgenstein's goal in the *Tractatus* is to introduce a particular logical notation, a concept-script—or at least an outline of (some central principles governing) such a notation. [...] This notation, the principles of which the *Tractatus*'s purpose is to make understandable, is then the expression of the logical insights of the early Wittgenstein. This means that these logical insights don't find their expression in (paradoxically nonsensical) theoretical true/false assertions. Rather, they are embodied or built into the notation [...].'

5 PI §90.

6 Examples of such an ambiguity that are given by Wittgenstein include the word 'is' which 'figures as the copula, as a sign for identity, and as an expression for existence' (TLP 3.323). In §49 of the *Philosophical Investigations* he gives the example of a sign '*R*' or 'Red' that may sometimes be a word and sometimes a proposition. It may be the name of the color of a colored square or it may be a proposition expressing that there is one red square. See §15.2 for my discussion of this example.

7 These sections draw on my paper Mácha, 2012b.

8 TLP 4.122.

9 Z §458; RPP I, §949. See also Kuusela, 2011a, p. 604.

10 McManus (2006, p. 98) argues that '[i]nternal relations emerge in contexts of misunderstanding.' This sounds correct to me if it means that the distinction is used in order to cope with misunderstandings. McManus argues, however, that the distinction itself is a kind of misunderstanding and that internal relations are meant to be thrown away. Obviously, if there were no misunderstandings, we would not need this distinction. But we cannot use internal and external relations in order to cope with misunderstandings and at the same time think that this distinction itself is a misunderstanding. Cf. Chapter 3 below.

11 MDC, p. 157.

12 In fact, Marx writes in the 'Afterword' to the second edition of his *Capital* the following: 'With him [Hegel] it is standing on its head. It must be turned right side up again, if you would discover the rational kernel within the mystical shell' (Marx, 1967, p. 12).

13 TLP 4.0031.

14 For an illustration of this point see Chapter 8, where I give two main accounts of simple objects: the *de re* (or metaphysical) view and the *de dicto* (or semantic) view. On the former interpretation, Wittgenstein provided an alternative account of modalities that overcame Russell's and Moore's extreme pluralism (and their doctrine of external relations). On the latter interpretation, Wittgenstein provided only a methodological principle, leaving it undecided what the actual forms of reality are.

Chapter 2

1 See §5.1 for arguments that it is self-contradictory.

2 See Hochberg & Mulligan (2004, pp. 7–9) for an overview.

3 See the next chapter.

4 The former alternative is envisaged in §8.1, the latter one, in turn, in §8.2.

5 The notion of internal and external relations has metaphysical commitments if we interpret the *Tractatus* metaphysically (as was done in §8.1).
6 This transition resembles Kant's transformation of metaphysical principles into regulative ones.
7 Frege, 1980, p. xxii.
8 Z §458.

Chapter 3

1 Rorty,1967, p. 337; see also Ewing, 1934, pp. 117–42.
2 M, p. 86.
3 See Chapter 10 for textual support for this shift.
4 I think that Read (1997) did not notice this terminological shift when summarizing 'the "career" of "internal relations" in Wittgenstein's thought [...] as follows: (1) "*Tractatus*" period: Internal relations are important, and ineffable. (2) "Middle period": Internal relations are extended in RANGE somewhat, but after what might be judged to be initial vacillation, Wittgenstein again becomes increasingly inclined against their expression. (3) c. 1933–9: Internal relations largely drop out. (4) Mature philosophy. Internal relations vanish ALMOST TOTALLY [...].' Sodoma (2014) argues on the other hand that the concept of an internal relation shows a line of continuity in Wittgenstein's thinking.
5 Cf. TLP 4.122: 'I introduce these expressions in order to indicate the source of the confusion between internal relations and relations proper (external relations).' See also VW, p. 237; WVC, p. 55.
6 M, pp. 85 and 87.
7 See §§10.2 and 10.3.
8 TLP 4.126.
9 McManus speaks aptly of 'the oxymoronic quality of "internal relation"' (2006, p. 65; cf. pp. 77 and 99).
10 Cf. Fichte's 'ground of distinction' which is discussed in Chapter 20. There might, however, be another reason for taking the terms to be independent entities that is not captured by the internal relation.
11 This consideration can be amended for internal properties. Suppose we predicate of an object X that it has a property p, i.e., $p(X)$. In order to refer to X, it must be a distinct object of thought. But if the property p is an internal one, we cannot think of the object X not having the property p. The problem would be avoided if $p(X)$ expressed an internal relation between the concepts X and p.
12 NB, p. 123.
13 NB, p. 4.

14 TLP 5.5301, Ogden/Ramsey's trans.

15 PI §216.

16 In Part II, I will present and evaluate the various arguments against internal relations given by Bradley, Russell, and Moore. These authors are much more explicit in arguing why internal relations are improper.

17 Diamond, 2002, p. 276.

18 McManus, 2006, p. 62. Cf. a similar statement quoted in footnote 11, Chapter 1, p. 211.

19 Cf. §14.

20 McGinn, 2009, p. 13.

Part II

1 TLP 4.1251, Ogden/Ramsey's trans.

2 See §§7 and 17.1.

Chapter 4

1 Russell, 1912, p. 58.

2 Moore, 1922, p. 1.

3 Cf. Candlish, 2007, p. 42.

4 Cf. Rockmore: 'British idealism, which was unorthodox, does not follow any standard idealist model' (2005, p. 31) and 'They were idealists first and Hegelians, if they were Hegelians [...], only afterwards' (2005, p. 35).

5 Hegel, 1968, p. 235.

6 Cf. Kain, 2005, pp. 4–6.

7 In a letter to Moore dated May 7, 1914, Wittgenstein confesses that he copied his BA dissertation from Bernard Bosanquet, another exponent of British idealism. This dissertation has not survived. Whether or not an exaggeration, this indicates that Wittgenstein might have been directly acquainted with some of the idealists' texts.

8 The expressions 'Appearance' and 'Reality' are capitalized in Bradley's idiosyncratic sense.

9 Candlish, 2007, p. 23.

10 Bradley, 1897, pp. 61, 205, 286, 297, and *passim*.

11 This conclusion is a mistake. Bradley uses the expression 'unreal' in the sense 'not wholly real' while one would expect that 'unreal' or 'not real' means 'not real at all.' I think this misunderstanding underlies the whole debate over relations.

12 Bradley, 1914, p. 252.

13 This account of judgment resembles Quine's meaning holism. Every judgment depends on sense-giving and empirical content, and one cannot distinguish between these two components.
14 Bradley, 1897, p. 544.
15 Bradley, 1897, p. 366. See Ferreira, 1999, p. 20.
16 Bradley, 1914, p. 253.
17 Ferreira, 1999, p. 27.
18 Bradley, 1914, p. 254.
19 Bradley, 1897, p. 173.
20 See Candlish & Damnjanovic, 2011, §2.2.
21 Cf. Candlish, 2007, p. 43: 'Bradley was forced to resort to metaphor whenever it came to setting out what reality is like.'
22 Bradley, 1897, p. 253.
23 See more about Bradley's account of feeling in §17.1.
24 Bradley, 1897, pp. 511, 519, 522, 533, and *passim*.
25 In my discussion, I shall make use of Bradley's later works, for they can be taken as clarifications of his earlier views on relations.
26 Bradley's most famous argument against the reality of relations from *Appearance and Reality* (1897, Ch. III) makes no use of this distinction (although the expression 'internal relation' occurs there; see my explanation below in the main text).
27 Bradley sometimes uses the expression 'intrinsic' instead of 'internal.'
28 See Candlish, 2007, p. 147 for more details. Manser (1982, p. 192) argues that if 'internal' means 'part of the judgment,' then the doctrine of internal relations is tantamount to Frege's context principle. Each part of a judgment is internal to it, i.e., each part has meaning only in the context of the whole judgment.
29 Bradley, 1935, p. 667; see also p. 641: 'Every relation [...] has a connection with its terms, not simply internal or external, must in principle be both at once.'
30 Bradley, 1935, p. 642.
31 Bradley, 1914, p. 291. Cf. also pp. 237f.: 'And the external relations themselves, if they are to be absolute, must, I suppose, be thinkable apart from any terms.'
32 I highlight Bradley's stress on defining the internal/external distinction in terms of their *thinkability* because Wittgenstein used a similar definition in the *Tractatus*. See §6.2.
33 Bradley, 1935, p. 642.
34 We may alternatively postulate a triadic relation R' that aims to relate R, a, and b in the relational fact $R'(R, a, b)$. The argument would be the same as in the case of two dyadic relations $R1$ and $R2$.
35 Bradley, 1897, p. 31.
36 Cf. Ferreira, 1999, pp. 110–16, Vallicella, 2002, and Candlish, 2007, pp. 169–71 for in-depth discussions of this argument.

37 Bradley, 1935, p. 665.
38 Bradley, 1897, pp. 392 and 364.
39 This understanding of the notion of character follows from Bradley's example of a relation between a red-haired man and red-hairedness. If this relation were wholly internal, we 'could from the nature of red-hairedness reconstruct all the red-haired men.' And more generally, if all things were internally related, 'you could start internally from any one character in the Universe, and you could from that pass to the rest' (Bradley, 1897, p. 580).
40 Cf. Ferreira, 1999, p. 116.
41 Bradley, 1935, p. 644.
42 Vallicella, 2002, p. 8.
43 In other words, if all relations were merely internal, all relations would be reducible to properties. This consideration might lead Russell to a critique based on the fact that not all relational statements are reducible to the subject-predicate form. See §5.1.
44 Wittgenstein advocated similar views concerning works of art and culture. See §18.
45 See Ferreira, 1999, p. 118 for more examples.
46 Bradley, 1914, p. 312.
47 Bradley, 1935, p. 667.
48 Cf., for example, Bradley, 1914, p. 176: 'A relation exists only between terms, and those terms, to be known as such, must be objects.'
49 See the example of a relation between a red-haired man and red-hairedness quoted in fn. 39, p. 217.
50 Quoted in Manser, 1982, p. 182.
51 Quoted in Manser, 1982, p. 183.
52 As we will see below, Moore and Wittgenstein offered arguments against the possibility of expressing internal relations.
53 Manser (1982) argues that Bradley's treatment of relations in his early *Principles of Logic* is focused on relations between particulars.
54 In such a scenario, we can consider the relation between Hugo and Hugo's red-hairedness, where Hugo's red-hairedness is a concrete property.
55 Bradley, 1914, p. 226.
56 Bradley, 1914, p. 151.
57 See §10.2.

Chapter 5

1 Russell, 1907, p. 160.
2 The expression 'is grounded in the natures of the related terms' might be taken to mean something similar to Bradley's expression 'is due merely to the character

of the terms.' Schaffer (2010, p. 349) argues that there was one dominant sense of the notion of internality invoked by Bradley, Bosanquet, and Moore. This is Schaffer's formal reconstruction of this notion: R is internal$_{\text{essential}} =_{\text{df}} (\forall x)(\forall y)$ if Rxy then necessarily $((x \text{ exists} \leftrightarrow Rxy)\ (y \text{ exists} \leftrightarrow Rxy))$. (I have simplified Schaffer's definition by considering binary relations only.)

3 The either-or distinction between internal and external relations is salient in Moore's article 'External and Internal Relations' (1919). Internal relations are opposed here to relations that are 'purely' or 'merely' external. Russell in his texts (1903, 1907) also opposes the fact of internal relations being purely or merely external relations on the one hand, and on the other hand he also argues for 'the axiom of internal relations [being] incompatible with all complexity' (1907, p. 168). Does, then, 'internal' here mean 'merely internal' or 'not entirely external'?

4 This reducibility was so important for Russell that he made it the defining characteristic of internal relations. A relation is internal if and only if it is reducible to a property; and it is external otherwise. See Russell, 1918, pp. 140f. Many years later, in 1959, Russell wrote to J. O. Wisdom: 'As for Hegel, I can still understand why people were Hegelian. The matter was concerned with the axiom of internal relation according to which a relation between two terms consists of adjectives of both or an adjective of the whole of which both compose. If this is accepted, the rest of Hegel's philosophy follows, as in Bradley' (Russell, 1959).

5 This conviction is an instance of a broader argumentative strategy of Russell's. He thought that the whole philosophical and logical tradition was flawed in its commitment to the subject-predicate view of propositions and neglected the relational form (and was unable to admit the reality of relations in the end). See, for example, Russell, 1918, p. 127 or Candlish, 2007, pp. 132–6.

6 This equivalence does not hold for Wittgenstein. At TLP 3.1432 he indicates how a relation (regardless of its symmetry) can be eliminated from a relational fact *aRb*. In the fact *ab*, it is said that *a* stands to *b* in a certain relation. The fact *ba* expresses a different relation than the fact *ab*.

7 Russell, 1903, p. 225.

8 See Ferreira, 1999, p. 197.

9 Russell, 1907, p. 163. Cf. fn. 4 above.

10 Bradley, 1935, pp. 670, 672. Quoted in Candlish, 2007, p. 165.

11 Bradley, 1897, Chapter III.

12 We can take these two terms to be synonymous here.

13 But a particular stamp might be more valuable if it is a part of a certain miniature sheet. I am thankful to Maja Jaakson for providing me with this example.

14 Moore, 1919, p. 288.

15 Russell, 1907, p. 154.

16 See Bradley's example of a red-haired man in fn. 39, p. 217.

17 See §4.2.
18 Russell, 1907, p. 161, my italics.
19 Moore, 1919, p. 289.
20 See, for example, Hylton, 1990, p. 121; Proops, 2002; Potter, 2009, p. 13; McGinn, 2006, p. 178.
21 Russell, 1899, p. 143.
22 As we will see, the relation of diversity plays an important role in Wittgenstein's analysis of internal relations. He condemns reflexive internal relations (that is, relations of the form *a*R*a*) to be unintelligible.
23 Quoted in Russell, 1918, p. 142.
24 Russell, 1918, p. 30.
25 For Russell, facts are always complexes; they are unities of two or more simples or other complexes.
26 Proops (2002) wrongly takes Russell to be committed here to the (in this context quite absurd) view that the relation of logical entailment is an external one.
27 Russell, 1984, p. 105.

Chapter 6

1 NB, pp. 116f.
2 There will be one important exception: on what I call the *de re* interpretation of simple objects, Wittgenstein allows for the internal properties of Tractarian objects which determine an object's combinatorial possibilities with other objects. These internal properties are, in effect, relational properties; hence there are internal relations between simple objects. But more about this later in §8.1. The subsequent section 8.2 addresses the competing interpretation of simple objects, which is called *de dicto* and does not require any internal relations between simple objects.
3 NB, p. 9.
4 NB, p. 43; see also TLP 3.24.
5 See §5.
6 The reverse transformation would not work. The conjunction of 'There is *M* here' and 'There is *N* here' does not entail that *M* and *N* are parts of the whole, for one would need set theory and predicate logic.
7 NB, p. 19.
8 NB, p. 19.
9 TLP 4.122.
10 Sentences are among them, for any sentence contains at least one universal.
11 Remarks concerning internal and external relations from the so-called *Prototractatus* do not substantially differ from the ones in the *Tractatus*.

12 TLP 4.123.
13 TLP 4.123.
14 TLP 4.123. See §8.1 for further discussion.
15 VW 2003, p. 238.
16 ROC I, §1; Ms 176, p. 1r.
17 Cf. TLP 6.22.
18 TLP 3.001.
19 TLP 2.225.
20 See Proops, 2002 for arguments in favor of this conclusion.
21 TLP 3.02.
22 TLP 3.03. I use Ogden/Ramsey's trans. here which is closer to the German original: 'Wir können nichts Unlogisches denken.'
23 TLP 4.12.
24 TLP 4.122.
25 TLP 2.15.
26 The notion of an internal relation is ambiguous here, reproducing the ambiguity of the notion of a picture. Internal relations within a *real* picture express its structure, which is an arrangement of its parts. (The red apple is to the left of the jug.) 'Internal' means 'inner' here. Internal relations within a *logical* picture are relations among its logical parts, which are concepts. Internal relations are conceptual relations. An analogous ambiguity is to be found in F. Bradley where 'internal' means *inter alia* 'to be part of' a judgment. Cf. the beginning of §4.2. I am indebted here to Ondřej Beran.
27 NB, p. 19, 25.10.1914.
28 TLP 4.122.
29 TLP 4.1251.
30 Wittgenstein uses the expression 'zeigt sich' (TLP 4.122) here which is translated by Pears/McGuinness as 'makes itself manifest.' Ogden and Ramsey translate it as 'shows itself.' This translation does not obscure the connection between the saying/showing distinction and the external/internal distinction.
31 TLP 4.4611.

Chapter 7

1 TLP 4.122.
2 NB, p. 96.
3 TLP 4.14.
4 TLP 3.1431.
5 TLP 3.1432.

6 WWK, pp. 54f.
7 TLP 3.328.
8 NB, p. 105.
9 See NB, p. 37: 'My fundamental thought is that the logical constants are not proxies.' And also TLP 4.0312: 'My fundamental idea is that the "logical constants" are not representatives.'
10 Landini, 2007, p. 79. This idea is related to the general interpretation of the *Tractatus* which I follow in the present book—namely that Wittgenstein's goal in the *Tractatus* is to outline a logically adequate notation (a *Begriffsschrift*) where all the internal relations are shown. Cf. §1 and note 4 therein.
11 See Potter, 2009, pp. 116f.
12 Cf. Landini, 2007, p. 85: '[T]he logical constants include *all and only* notions with logico-semantic content.' If such notions express a property or a relation, these would be, of course, internal.
13 Following Candlish (2007, p. 130) I use the term 'unreal' in order to indicate Wittgenstein's affinity to Bradley. Wittgenstein, however, does not employ this term. At TLP 2.06 he defines reality as the 'existence and non-existence of states of affairs.' If relations are not parts of states of affairs, they can be conceived of as being unreal. The affinity of both authors is further undermined by their different accounts of substance.
14 This line of thought is taken up in §8.2.
15 TLP 5.135.
16 Landini, 2007, p. 52. For the whole argument, see pp. 40–53.
17 McGinn, 2006, p. 142.
18 '[A] name *is* a name of a *simple*, in virtue of *which* logical relations hold between propositions involving *it* and propositions involving other names; "*a*" names a complex just in case propositions of the form "$\varphi(a)$" imply propositions of the form "$\psi(b)$" for some *b*'s (constituents of *a*); "*a*" names a simple just in case propositions of the form "$\varphi(a)$" do not imply propositions of the form "$\psi(b)$" for any *b*'s. Thus the mutual independence of elementary propositions is a consequence of Wittgenstein's conception of a simple name' (Kremer, 1997, p. 98).
19 'An elementary proposition really contains all logical operations in itself' (TLP 5.47).
20 See Moore, 1919, p. 51; cf. Hylton, 1990, p. 143; Proops, 2002, p. 304.
21 See Hylton, 1990, pp. 143–52.
22 Russell expressed this idea in the 'Introduction' to the *Tractatus*: 'Thus the whole business of logical inference is concerned with propositions which are not atomic. Such propositions may be called molecular' (TLP, Introduction).
23 I understand here that Wittgenstein means that logical constants stand for logical operations such as conjunction, negation, or the Sheffer stroke.

24 TLP 5.122. Consider, for example, the following inference: $(p|q)|(p|q), p|p \vDash q$ (see TLP 5.1311). The truth-grounds of the consequent are, in a definite way, *contained* among the truth-grounds of the antecedent.

25 Cf. McManus (2006, p. 146): 'One might say that logical relations are "internal", in that the deduced proposition is, in a sense, *part of* the proposition from which it is deduced.'

26 Cf. TLP 5.13–5.133.

27 TLP 4.1251.

Chapter 8

1 That certain combinations of objects are impossible follows from Wittgenstein's examples given at 2.0131. Certain objects (specks in the visual field) must have some color; other objects (notes) must have some pitch and so on. It is thus impossible that these objects stand alone in states of affairs.

2 Cf. TLP 2.012ff.

3 See TLP 2.0123.

4 See TLP 2.01231.

5 Schaffer (2010) provides a complex argument that 'failure of free recombination is the modal signature of an integrated monistic cosmos' (pp. 342 and 355). If his argument is sound and if we take the Tractarian objects *metaphysically* as the ultimate constituents of the world, then metaphysical monism follows from the Tractarian ontology.

6 TLP 2.03.

7 Cf. Candlish & Basile, 2013: '[I]t is all but clear that Wittgenstein's logico-ontological atoms can be said to possess a form; surely, they differ from Democritean atoms in that they lack material properties (cf. 2.0331 and 2.0232).'

8 Hacker, 2001, p. 171.

9 Not to be confused with Francis Bradley, whose views were discussed in previous chapters.

10 Bradley, 1992, p. 81.

11 Bradley, 1992, p. 84; see also p. 24.

12 NB, p. 108.

13 I take visual and audial properties of names to be external.

14 See TLP 2.011.

15 TLP 4.123. The context of this remark is discussed in §6.2.

16 It is far from clear whether the shifting use concerns the simplicity of objects. See the next section for another suggestion.

17 NB, p. 62.

18 NB, p. 69.
19 NB, p. 69.
20 NB, p. 64.
21 NB, p. 65.
22 TLP 6.37.
23 Bradley, 1992, p. 81.
24 Cf. fn. 9, p. 221.
25 Cf. Landini (2007, p. 281): 'Wittgenstein's objects (logical atoms) have no logically essential properties at all. Indeed, the Tractarian *Grundgedanke* states that there are no *logical* properties and relations.'
26 Even Bradley (1992, p. 71) admits hesitantly that the semantic sense is more fundamental than the metaphysical one.
27 NB, p. 50.
28 NB, p. 69.
29 NB, p. 69.
30 PR, p. 72.
31 NB, p. 70.
32 See Bradley, 1992, p. 89.
33 NB, p. 60.
34 There is a notebook entry from 1915 'Relations and properties, etc. are *objects* too' (NB, p. 61) and a report by Desmond Lee from 1930 or 1931 (LWL, p. 120).
35 Cf. Johnston, 2009, p. 150.
36 NB, p. 61.
37 The structure of classes might be more fine-grained. We might distinguish among relations with different multiplicities or introduce higher-order predicates and relations.
38 An *a posteriori* account of logical categories is advanced by Johnston (2009) who attributes this account back to Ramsey. Johnston argues, however, that the idea of the elimination of relations (based on TLP 3.1432) is an anachronism in the *Tractatus*. I hope to show that the idea of the elimination of relations can be reconciled with the claim that there are relations among simple objects in a wholly analyzed language.

Chapter 9

1 TLP 4.014, my italics.
2 Cf. Kuusela, 2011a, pp. 614f. for a discussion.
3 TLP 4.016.
4 McManus, 2006, Chapter 7.3; cf. §3 above.

5 McManus, 2006, p. 65.
6 Diamond, 2002, p. 273.
7 A *limitation* as opposed to a *limit*.
8 McManus, 2006, p. 70.
9 If we take names as signs regardless of their symbolizing role, we can combine them in any way. Signs are mere orthographic units. But even thinking like this is misleading. Treating something as a name amounts to conceiving of a sign as belonging to a logical category of names. Hence, we are already considering its symbolizing role—*viz.* names symbolize simples.
10 Cf. TLP 3.334.
11 TLP 3.202.
12 TLP 4.21.
13 Cf. TLP 4.01.
14 TLP 4.22.
15 TLP 5.
16 TLP 4.001.
17 TLP 2.01.
18 TLP 2.
19 TLP 2.06.
20 TLP 1.1.
21 Cf. PR, p. 72 quoted in §8.2 above.
22 TLP 2.04, my italics.
23 Cf. TLP 2.022.
24 See §8.1.
25 NB, p. 53.
26 Bradley, 1992, p. 130. Peter Hacker expresses a similar view. Cf. McGinn, 2006, p. 89.
27 TLP 3.3. There is, however, another remark in the *Tractatus* that advocates of the names-object level fundamentality may invoke to support their case: 'It [a proposition] is understood by anyone who understands its constituents' (4.024). There seems to be a tension among these remarks. I take 4.024 as expressing a sufficient condition of understanding a proposition without touching upon the issue of fundamentality (unlike the context principle at 3.3).
28 TLP 3.203: 'A name means an object. The object is its meaning.'
29 Hacker, 1986, p. 75.
30 We are speaking of symbols here. Symbols are signs with sense. The relation between name and object is internal, because for a given name (taken as a symbol) it is unthinkable that it would have some other sense. The connection between a sign and its sense is arbitrary and thus external.
31 Wittgenstein sometimes speaks of propositions without distinguishing whether they are elementary or complex. Similarly, he sometimes speaks of situations without

distinguishing whether they are *elementary* states of affairs or *complex* facts. We can merge the levels of elementary and complex propositions, because the picturing function of complex propositions is fully determined by the picturing function of atomic propositions.

32 TLP 3.11.

33 TLP 3.13.

34 Wittgenstein gives another example of such a projection: 'In order to understand the essential nature of a proposition, we should consider hieroglyphic script, which depicts the facts that it describes' (TLP 4.016). This explanation suggests that the projection is something natural. From the visual characteristics of a hieroglyphic sign for, e.g., a house, we could determine that the sign represents a house without any prior knowledge. This is, however, not how Egyptian hieroglyphs represent. Most hieroglyphic signs are (like English letters) phonetic in nature, meaning that the sign is read independently of its visual characteristics. The phonological value of a sign is derived from the name of the represented thing by means of the so-called *rebus principle* according to which the representation of, for example, a duck 𓅭 'son' _*zi3_ can stand for 'hard ground' _*s3t.w_ due to their similar phonetic structures (analogously, the numeral '2' can stand for the preposition 'to' in English). Cf. Loprieno, 1995, pp. 12f. We can, thus, take the rebus principle as a peculiar method of projection.

35 My present interpretation follows the main features of Marie McGinn's *anti-metaphysical* reading of the *Tractatus*. Cf. 'The link between the items [the musical score, the musical idea, the music, and the gramophone record] is internal insofar as it is made, in each case, via a rule of projection that enables us, given any one of them, to construct the others from it' (McGinn, 2006, p. 80).

36 TLP 4.031.

37 TLP 2.0121.

38 Cf. TLP 3.02; for a detailed discussion of the notion of thinkability see §6.2.

39 TLP 4.126.

40 This example is also discussed in §§6.2, 10.2, and 10.5.

41 Wittgenstein's interest in measuring may initially originate in his reading of Plato's *Theaetetus* where Protagoras' famous fragment 'Man is the measure of all things' is discussed. Another possible source is Otto Weininger's book *Über die letzten Dinge* (*On Last Things*). The notebook entry 'I have to judge the world, to measure things' (NB, p. 82) is influenced by Weininger, who advanced the idea that man lays down measures of things in their epistemological and ethical aspects. The absolute measure is, for Weininger and for the Wittgenstein of the *Tractatus*, logic. Such measures, Weininger argues, are given by or originate in the biological nature of man. See (Mácha, 2012a) for further details.

42 NB, pp. 32 and 41.

43 TLP 2.1512.
44 See §9.3.
45 TLP 2.131.
46 TLP 2.15.
47 TLP 2.15121.
48 There is an important disanalogy here. A yardstick is one-dimensional and thus has only two end-points. A picture (and a proposition) may have higher multiplicity and more end-points.
49 PR, p. 85.
50 TLP 2.2.
51 TLP 4.023.
52 Cf. Sluga 2002, p. 89. Frege must have been responding to conversations they had had before the war, or possibly to lost letters from Wittgenstein to Frege during the war. Thanks to Jim Klagge for this clarification.
53 Frege, 1956, p. 291. I have altered the translation of the German 'Vorstellung' from 'idea' into 'picture.' From the context of Frege's text it is clear that he means by 'Vorstellung' a mental picture or image.
54 TLP 2.141.
55 TLP 3.02.
56 If a represented situation were real, it would automatically make the proposition true.
57 Cf. PR, pp. 48f.: 'It's easy to understand that a ruler is and must be in the same space as the object measured by it. But in what sense are *words* in the same space as an object whose length is described in words, or, in the same space as a colour, etc.? It sounds absurd.'
58 The pictorial relationship cannot wholly determine the depicted situation, because it is not a perfect identity. The picture and the depicted situation are always identical in a certain respect. This fact does not disturb the internality of this relationship.
59 Cf. TLP 3.11: 'The method of projection is to think of the sense of the proposition.'
60 Frege, 1956, p. 291.
61 Carroll, 1893, p. 169.
62 Borges, 1998, p. 325.
63 We have no evidence that Wittgenstein was familiar with Korzybski's, Carroll's, or Borges' writings.
64 TLP 3.311.
65 Except logical constants. See NB, p. 114.
66 TLP 3.313.
67 Cf. TLP 3.315.
68 NB, p. 65.
69 TLP 3.317.

70 Cf., for example, PI §29.

71 PI §1.

72 BBB, p. 143 and PI §326. See also my discussion of the Principle of Sufficient Reason in §12.1.

73 See PI §29.

74 Cf. PI §§241f.

Chapter 10

1 VW, p. 237.

2 LFM, p. 73.

3 Ms 109, p. 291, 1.2.1931; Ts 211, p. 147.

4 PI II, p. 196.

5 VW, pp. 130–2.

6 VW, p. 237.

7 NB, pp. 116f.

8 PPO, pp. 389f.

9 TLP 4.123.

10 PI §371.

11 Wittgenstein occasionally mentions unthinkability in his conversations: VW, p. 236; WWK, p. 54.

12 See OC §§95ff.

13 This obscurity is obvious in Wittgenstein's later remarks. In *On Certainty* he writes: 'But there is no sharp boundary between methodological propositions and propositions within a method. [...] The lack of sharpness *is* that of the boundary between *rule* and empirical proposition' (OC §§318–19).

14 OC §§96–8.

15 See WWK, pp. 54–5; Ms 108, p. 299; WV, p. 238; ROC I, §1 for various uses of this example.

16 It is not essential that we use a geometrical constellation in this example. We could have taken material objects like two sticks (see ROC I, §1) or two distances ('Strecken,' see WV, p. 238).

17 Wittgenstein uses this example in the following places: WWK, pp. 54–55; WV, p. 238; RFM I, §104, p. 75; ROC I, §1.

18 TLP 4.123.

19 WWK, p. 55.

20 LFM, p. 73.

21 LFM, p. 73.

22 RFM I, §77.

23 Symphony No. 5 (Beethoven) on *Wikipedia*. Available from: http://en.wikipedia.org/wiki/File:Beethoven_symphony_5_opening.svg (accessed March 1, 2013).
24 LWPP I, §156.
25 LWPP I, §155.
26 LWPP I, §158.
27 See LWPP I, §§157–62.
28 See §16 on the standard meter.
29 See §15.2 for a more detailed discussion.
30 Cf. LWPP I, §161 for a variation of this example.
31 LWPP I, §761.
32 For the opposition between the factual and the conceptual, see RPP II, §5.
33 PI §130.
34 Wittgenstein occasionally conceives of language-games as parts of actual practices. See, for instance, PI §654ff.
35 I take language-games primarily to be what Glock calls *fictional* language-games (Glock, 1996, pp. 194–6). Wittgenstein, however, uses the notion of a language-game in other meanings too. Language games can also be actual linguistic activities or even sub-languages of certain communities (like, for instance, the language of science or religion). What counts as a language-game here is determined by our actual practices. The present inquiry is, however, focused on Wittgenstein's method of analysis. In this context, the notion of a language-game is a methodological tool. This is not to say that certain language-games cannot (accidentally) coincide with actual practices.
36 Cf. Moyal-Sharrock, 2004, p. 66.
37 This scenario has not escaped the attention of commentators. See, for example, Hintikka, 1982 or Baker & Hacker, 2005b, p. 62: 'The training activity antecedent to the language-game of §2 [of the PI] is itself a language-game.' There are even different kinds or stages of training which Wittgenstein subsumes under the family-concept 'general training' (BBB, p. 98). Some of these stages may involve testing the application of a rule.
38 The expression 'vertical relation' is from ter Hark (1990, p. 34). The failure to consider vertical relations between language-games is called the 'ground-floor fallacy,' for example, naming and describing within the same language-game.
39 These thoughts draw upon my own paper Mácha, 2013; and see also Smith, 2013.
40 See ROC I, §1 for the most explicit expression of the connection of temporality and the internal/external distinction. See also RFM I, §104 and LFM, p. 166.
41 PG, p. 215. The German original reads: 'Ist die Zeit den Sätzen wesentlich?' (Ms 212, p. 377). I have changed the translation of German 'Sätzen' into 'sentences' instead of 'propositions.' It would be more plausible to translate this sentence by 'Is tense essential to sentences?' in order to highlight the grammatical character of this consideration. I am grateful to Deirdre Smith for emphasizing this possibility to me.

42 Jason Stanley (2000) recently proposed the so-called *binding argument* in order to detect covert variables in the logical form of sentences. If a sentence contains a covert variable, it is possible to bind the variable by an explicit quantifier. So if the sentence

(1) It rains.

contains a hidden temporal variable, so the sentence

(2) Every time John lights a cigarette, it rains.

will bind the presumed variable contained in (1), and the sentence

(3) For every time *t* at which John lights a cigarette, it rains at *t* at the location in which John lights a cigarette at *t*.

will be a natural interpretation of (2) (Stanley, 2000, pp. 415–16).

43 RFM I, §101.

44 Cappelen and Lepore (2005, p. 74) have proposed the application of Stanley's Binding Argument to mathematical propositions like (44). In so doing we get (47). Although there is obviously no hidden variable in (44), there is an explicit bound variable in (47). That is the reason, they have argued, for the failure of the Binding Argument. The argument, however, presupposes that (44) has the same logical form when it is uttered alone as when it is embedded in (47). The point in Wittgenstein's work is that the same sentence may have different forms in different language-games. In certain language-games, (47) is not a plausible elucidation of (44).

45 See RFM, p. 338 for Wittgenstein's treatment of this example.

46 See Donnellan, 1966.

47 The distinction between attributive and referential uses of a definite description applies only to descriptions used *de re* and hence expressing external relations. *De dicto* descriptions, which express internal relations, are used neither attributively nor referentially.

48 This claim is contestable. Necessitarians argue that laws of nature are necessary. But there is no room for monological necessity in Wittgenstein's later philosophy. In a Wittgensteinian framework, one could argue, however, that laws of nature are still contingent but propositions that express them are expressions of internal relations. A law of nature, once discovered empirically, can be hardened into a rule (see OC §96).

49 Here I am indebted to Peter Baumann.

50 BT, p. 77e. See also LFM, p. 75.

51 But there do not need to be things that actually have these colors or shades of color.

52 LWL, p. 57. See also LWL, p. 9; Ms 112, p. 63r; LFM, p. 85.

53 There is no *third* thing in the case of binary relations. There is no *fourth* thing in the case of ternary relations and so on.

54 McGinn, 2000, p. 85. Colin McGinn provides an argument that modal properties are epiphenomenal to causal powers. Whether some of an object's properties are

contingent or necessary makes no difference to its causal powers. 'Only the actual can be causal. [...] The modal is not part of the causal order' (p. 86). The same is true of internal properties and relations that can be said to be epiphenomenal to external properties and relations. Thanks to Modesto Gómez Alonso for this reference.

55 In the *Critique of Pure Reason* (B15) Kant expresses the opposite view. He claims that from the mere conception of a sum of five and seven we *never* obtain the conception of twelve. In order to perform the synthesis, there has to be a *third* thing, which for Kant is the power of intuition.

56 Ms 110, p. 289, my trans. ('Wie kann man kalkulieren daß 3+2=5 ist?!')

57 Cf. BT, p. 67 and my further discussion of numbers in §14.2.

58 Ms 111, p. 111.

59 RFM I, p. 74. I have changed the last word to 'schemas' as 'Schemen' appears in the original typescripts Ts 221, p. 157 and Ts 222, p. 75.

60 Baker & Hacker, 1984, p. 109; see also Hymers, 1996, pp. 598f.

61 Baker & Hacker, 1984, p. 110.

62 See LFM, p. 73.

63 See PI §§79 and 354. See also Glock, 1996, pp. 95–7.

64 See Klagge, 2011, §7 for a detailed discussion.

65 PGL, p. 292.

66 LWPP II, p. 94.

67 Klagge (forthcoming) writes that 'the factors that will or might lead to such a change are unknown to us now.'

Chapter 11

1 The intended state may already be fulfilled without the agent being aware of this. Fulfillment means realizing that the intended state is fulfilled (it may have been fulfilled before as well). It makes no sense to expect that *p* or to have a fear of *p* and at the same time know that *p* is the case. I am thankful to Peter Baumann for bringing this point to my attention.

2 Cf. 'Any "reasonable" expectation is an expectation that a rule we have observed up to now will continue to hold' (PR, p. 294 and PG, p. 231).

3 PR, p. 63.

4 Russell, 1921, §§III and XIII.

5 Russell, 1921, p. 65.

6 Cf. PR, p. 63.

7 Russell, 1921, p. 270.

8 PR, p. 64.

9 See Hymers, 1996, p. 596 for an extended discussion.

10 PR, p. 67.

11 PR, p. 64.

12 PI §445 and PG, p. 140.

13 PR, p. 63.

14 See §11.3 for more about the picture conception (of intentionality).

15 Cf. Ms 109, p. 172; BT, p. 265e.

16 See PG, pp. 161f.

17 See BT, p. 275 for other examples.

18 PG, p. 160.

19 PG, p. 140.

20 BT, p. 284e; see also PG, p. 157.

21 Crane, 2011, p. 21.

22 Crane, 2011, pp. 21f.

23 Crane's demand implies that in order to understand the meaning of a word one needs to know all the connotations of the word (all the descriptions that accidentally refer to the same object). This is an unrealistic account of understanding.

24 BT, pp. 272f.

25 BT, p. 273e.

26 PR, p. 77.

27 Ms 108, pp. 211f.

28 Ms 109, p. 52, my trans. '*p* ist — im strengsten Sinne — das Gemeinsame zwischen Maßstab und Gemessenem.'

29 See §16 for a detailed discussion of the standard meter.

30 PG, pp. 150f.

31 Ms 109, p. 61.

32 Ms 109, p. 61.

33 The metaphor of fitting also plays an important role in Wittgenstein's later reflections on the philosophy of psychology. This role is investigated in §17.1.

34 PI §438.

35 PI §439.

36 PI §439.

37 PI §182.

38 PG, p. 134 and Z §54. See also Ms 108, pp. 211f.

39 PR, p. 71.

40 BBB, p. 20.

41 It would be difficult to imagine a belief or a hypothesis without specifying its content.

42 BBB, p. 20.

43 BBB, p. 21.

44 For the difference between indexes and arguments, see TLP 5.02. Using an expression as an index creates an *opaque context*. If we substitute the name '*B*' with a different co-referring name, the new clause does not need to characterize the same kind of sensations. This is not the case if we use an expression as an application of a function to its argument. See BBB, p. 21.
45 This is, of course, an empirical fact, and Wittgenstein offers only his guess that it is true. The frequency of intransitive uses may vary for different kinds of intentional expressions.
46 BBB, p. 22.
47 BBB, p. 29.
48 BBB, p. 23.
49 PI §§574 and 586.
50 RPP II, §154.
51 RPP II, §§2–5.

Chapter 12

1 As Anscombe (1957) does.
2 LA, pp. 13 and 22; Ms 112, p. 112v; BBB, p. 15; VW, pp. 108–11. I think that Wittgenstein uses the expressions 'reason' (Grund) and 'motive' (Motiv) interchangeably (Cf. BBB, p. 15).
3 Cf. RPP II, §909: 'We remain unconscious of the prodigious diversity of all of our everyday language-games because the outward forms of our language make everything alike.'
4 LA, p. 13. The bracketed postscripts are by James Taylor.
5 See §§10.2 and 10.4.
6 BBB, p. 15. Cf. Ms 113, p. 57r; Ts 302, p. 19; VW, p. 109.
7 Z §437; see also BT, p. 209e. In an earlier form, this remark reads 'internally related' instead of 'grammatically related.' See Ms 113, p. 43r and Ts 211, p. 591.
8 Cf. Ms 115, p. 136.
9 BBB, p. 15. See also BT, p. 296e and Ts 302, p. 19.
10 See §11.2.
11 See p. 99.
12 PI II, p. 224 and RPP I, §631
13 RPP I, §633.
14 See Glock, 1996, p. 76.
15 LA, p. 22.
16 See VW, p. 111: 'the reason is what he specifies. He answers with a *rule*. He could have also given this rule if he had not gone by it.'

17 VW, p. 47. See Ts 302, p. 19.
18 Wittgenstein employed this analogy several times. He considered the first and the second answer at VW, p. 47 and the second and the third one at LA, p. 22.
19 For the critique of causal theories of meaning, see PG, p. 60: 'Meaning, in our sense, is embodied in the explanation of meaning. If, on the other hand, by the word "meaning" we mean a characteristic sensation connected with the use of a word, then the relation between the explanation of a word and its meaning is rather that of cause to effect.'
20 NB, p. 130.
21 BBB, p. 14.
22 See Melamed and Lin, 2011. Their wording is slightly different.
23 Quoted after Melamed and Lin, 2011. The first formulation is from Spinoza's exposition of Descartes' *Principles of Philosophy*, the second one from his *Ethics*.
24 Spinoza's conception of causality is, however, more intricate. He maintains a kind of rudimentary picture theory, namely the view that causal relations between facts presuppose logical relations between propositions that describe these facts. Cause presupposes reason. Facts are, however, not wholly independent for Spinoza; they are not contingently related (in contrast to Wittgenstein's atomic facts). There is an essential union of all events and facts. These two claims imply that all relations are partly internal and partly external. Bradley followed Spinoza in this respect. See §4.2. Thanks to Modesto Gómez Alonso for elucidating Spinoza's account of causality to me.
25 BBB, p. 14.
26 AWL, p. 16.
27 PG, p. 97.
28 BBB, p. 143.
29 PI §217.
30 See Chapter 13 for more details.
31 Cf. §10.3.
32 PG, p. 111.
33 Exodus 3:14.
34 *Ethics*, 3p2s.
35 BT, p. 296e. Cf. Ms 138, p. 23b.
36 The figurative German expression 'der Zahn der Zeit' (literally 'the tooth of time') is usually translated non-figuratively as 'the ravages of time.'
37 Cf. §10.7.
38 PI §193.
39 LFM, p. 196.
40 LA, pp. 15ff.
41 PI §193.

42 LA, p. 15.
43 Cf. Livingston, 2010, §IV.
44 Frege, 1980, §55.
45 See Searle, 1990; cf. Livingston, 2010, fn. 34.
46 Livingston, 2010, fn. 34.
47 RPP I, §§903 and 904.
48 Cf. Hacker, 1996a, pp. 496–503. See Klagge, 2011, pp. 101ff. for an in-depth discussion. This section draws mostly on §8 of Klagge's book.
49 Klagge, 2011, p. 102.
50 §12.1.
51 UW, p. 411.
52 UW, p. 411.
53 RPP I, §906.
54 Wittgenstein might have had in mind Spinoza's psycho-physical parallelism as a reaction to Descartes' dualism of soul and body.
55 Kant, 1987, §69ff. We possess, however, no evidence that Wittgenstein read Kant's *Critique of Judgment*.
56 Kant, 1987, §70.
57 Kant, 1987, §70.
58 Kant, 1987, §70.
59 See, for example, Breitenbach, 2011 for details.
60 I see in this one of the main traits of Wittgenstein's philosophy, which can be summed up by a quotation from *King Lear*: 'I'll teach you differences.' See §1.
61 Davidson, 1963, p. 3. Cf. however Davidson's summary of his paper 'Actions, Reasons, and Causes' where he concedes a substantially weaker claim that rationalizations 'can, and often must, invoke causal connections' (p. xiv). If this is Davidson's position, then there would be no disagreement between Davidson and Wittgenstein on this matter.
62 Davidson, 2001, p. 9.
63 Davidson, 2001, p. 11.
64 AWL, p. 5.
65 Cf. Davidson's acknowledgment of this point. One may 'answer the question "Why did you do it?" with, "For no reason", meaning not that there is no reason but that there is no *further* reason, no reason that cannot be inferred from the fact that the action was done intentionally; no reason, in other words, besides wanting to do it' (2001, p. 6).
66 See p. 119.
67 'Here there are two motives—conscious and unconscious. The games played with the two motives are utterly different' (LA, p. 23).

Chapter 13

1 See Baker and Hacker, 1984 and Kripke, 1982.
2 'Eines ist klar, daß wenn ich der Regel (richtig) gefolgt bin das Resultat zu der Vorlage und dem Ausdruck der Regel in einer internen Beziehung stehen wird, die ich nicht anders ausdrücken kann, als durch die Wiedergabe jener drei Komplexe, weil [...] in dieser Wiedergabe allein schon alles bestimmt ist' (Ms 109, p. 291; my trans.).
3 Ms 116, p. 144, trans. by ter Hark, 1990, p. 47.
4 Baker & Hacker, 1984, p. 72.
5 Baker & Hacker, 1984, p. 100.
6 PI §201.
7 Kripke, 1982, p. 66.
8 See PI II, p. 230 for Wittgenstein's argument. See also PI §142; RPP I, §48; LWPP I, §209.
9 Kripke, 1982, p. 89.
10 Baker & Hacker, 1984, p. 75.
11 Baker & Hacker, 1985, p. 172.
12 Cf. PI §241: '"So you are saying that human agreement decides what is true and what is false?"—It is what human beings say that is true and false; and they agree in the *language* they use. That is not agreement in opinions but in form of life.'
13 Kripke has never wholly explicitly made such an admission. I think, however, that he makes this admission in footnote 19 (1982, pp. 25–6). He attributes to Wittgenstein the 'view that the relation between the desire (expectation and so on) and its object must be "internal", not "external."' This is parallel to the view that 'The relation of meaning and intention to future action is *normative*, not *descriptive*' (1982, p. 37).
14 Kripke, 1982, p. 13.
15 The role of a mathematical proof in general is to show that certain grammatical propositions are not independent: 'A mathematical proof connects a proposition with a system.' LFM, p. 136. See §14.3.
16 Kripke, 1982, pp. 16f.
17 Kripke, 1982, p. 17.
18 Ms 112, p. 113r.; PI §217.
19 Ms 109, p. 93. The English translation is taken from Krüger (forthcoming) and slightly amended.
20 Ms 109, p. 294.
21 The present problem is neatly summarized by Krüger (forthcoming, sec. I): 'On the one hand it is only a game if the signs are used in accordance with a rule; on the other hand it is impossible to determine the use of signs by the expressions of their rules because expressions – of any kind – are interpretable.'

22 Cf. Krüger, forthcoming, §III.
23 PI §219.
24 PI §241.
25 Ms 162b, p. 67v.
26 Cf. PI §240.
27 Cf. Altieri (forthcoming, §IV).
28 These paragraphs draw on a detailed analysis in Krüger (forthcoming).
29 Z §541.
30 OC §151.

Chapter 14

1 Cf. mathematical statements 3 > 2 (§10.2), 50 + 50 = 100 (§10.4), 1597 + 2548 = 4181 (§10.5), 25 × 25 = 625 (§11.2), 68 + 57 = 125 (§13).
2 PPO, p. 390. Cf. also: 'All the errors that have been made in this chapter of the philosophy of mathematics are based on the confusion between internal properties of a form (a rule as one among a list of rules) and what we call "properties" in everyday life (red as a property of this book)' (PG, pp. 476f.).
3 WWK, p. 224.
4 RFM, p. 159.
5 TLP 4.01.
6 PG, p. 268.
7 VW, p. 165.
8 PG, p. 269.
9 Ms 106, pp. 110 and 133.
10 We usually use the sign ∀ for the universal quantifier today.
11 If there were neither equation, nor any relational statement in (83), an internal *property* would be expressed instead.
12 PG, p. 268.
13 For instance, the number π has an infinite expansion which cannot be written down. It can, however, be captured by an infinite converging series which can be described by rules, for example, by the *Leibniz formula* for π.
14 PR, p. 140.
15 PG, p. 332.
16 This is true for material concepts, but not for formal concepts. Cf. Frascolla, 1994, p. 48.
17 AWL, p. 205.
18 PR, p. 307. Cf. also: 'But in what sense is ||||||||||||| the paradigm of a number? Consider how it can be used as such' (RFM, p. 149).

19 WWK, p. 223. See also: 'According to the Frege-Russell abstraction principle the number 3 is the class of all triples' (WWK, p. 221).

20 Cf. PI §1.

21 PR, p. 140. Cf. also: 'Dr. Wittgenstein made a very successful attempt. He began by quoting and criticizing Russell's definition of number, that is, "the class of classes similar to a given class", similarity being defined by means of a 1-1 correlation, and pointed out that Russell confuses the existence of this correlation with the possibility of its existence' (PPO, p. 373).

22 Waismann, 1951, p. 109.

23 BT, p. 410e.

24 WWK, p. 225.

25 PR, p. 141.

26 Cf. RFM, p. 174.

27 'To say "mathematics has the function of grammar" would be false. It has many other functions. But mathematical propositions are of the same kind as grammatical propositions even when they appear to be experiential propositions' (PPO, p. 389).

28 RFM, p. 363.

29 RFM, p. 434.

30 LFM, p. 136.

31 'What a proof really proves is the compatibility of the proposition with the propositions from which one started, the primitive propositions, or rather the incompatibility of the opposite' (LFM, pp. 73f).

32 PR, p. 192.

33 '[A] mathematical proposition only gets its meaning from the calculus in which it is embedded' (LFM, p. 137).

34 PG, p. 371.

35 As of May 2013.

36 PR, p. 204.

37 Cf. §14.1.

38 The same point could be made about the conjecture that the group '7777' occurs in the decimal expansion of π. See PI §§352 and 516; RFM, pp. 284 and 407f.

39 *Contra* Floyd: 'Wittgenstein is not insisting that [...] we do not understand a mathematical proposition until we possess its proof' (2000, p. 244).

40 *Contra* Shanker: a mathematical conjecture is 'a meaningless expression albeit one which may exercise a heuristic influence on the construction of some new proof-system' (1988, p. 230).

41 PG, p. 367.

42 RFM, pp. 159–61.

43 RFM, p. 161.

44 I discuss these paradigms in §§15.2 and 16.

45 LFM, p. 104.

46 Cf. 'The idea that the sequences of strokes in an arithmetical construction, like the figures of a geometrical proof, [can] take the part of *paradigms*, *symbols*, or, in Tractarian terms, *variables*, will develop, in later writings, into the conception of mathematical proof as the picture of an experiment' (Frascolla, 1994, p. 49).

47 RFM, p. 161.

48 RFM, p. 158.

49 See Diamond, 2001, pp. 123–5 for another focused discussion of the idea of depositing something in the archives.

50 PR, pp. 306f.

51 RFM, p. 51.

52 PI §30.

53 RFM, pp. 167f.: 'If I were to see the standard metre in Paris, but were not acquainted with the institution of measuring and its connexion with the standard metre—could I say, that I was acquainted with the concept of the standard metre?

A proof is an instrument—but why do I say "an instrument of language"?'

Chapter 15

1 NB, p. 82, 11.9.1916.

2 For example, colors are certain ranges of the electromagnetic spectrum interacting with the light receptors in the eye.

3 Z §357. Cf. also ROC III, §3: 'Here we have a sort of mathematics of colour.'

4 As argued at the beginning of §14.2.

5 ROC I, §54.

6 NB, p. 118.

7 TLP 4.123.

8 VW, p. 239.

9 RFM, pp. 48, 75f.

10 ROC I, §1.

11 §§6.2, 10.2, and 10.5.

12 The HSV color space represents colors in a three-dimensional cylindrical coordinate system. There are four-dimensional color spaces which of course cannot be presented as spatial objects.

13 ROC I, §22.

14 AWL, p. 143.

15 BBB, p. 14.

16 Cf. §§11.3 and 16, and *passim*.

17 AWL, p. 88.

18 ROC III, §259.
19 Cf. §14.3 where we discuss presuppositions of depositing something in the archives.
20 This is, of course, an idealization of children's learning. They may learn color concepts in some other way than by observing their parents pointing at examples. Such speculative ontogenetic considerations, however, are meant only to illustrate the philosophical point.
21 Cf. BBB, p. 14: 'The rule which has been taught and is subsequently applied interests us only so far as it is involved in the application.'
22 PI §49.
23 AWL, p. 143.
24 This discussion is taken from my own paper (Mácha, 2013).
25 AWL, p. 143.
26 PI §50.
27 PI §50, my italics.
28 BT, p. 342e. Cf. also PR, p. 108.
29 Today, one would call such a color 'purple' or 'magenta.' It is important to note that these reflections are specific to German. 'Purple' has been established as a basic color concept in English for far longer than in German.
30 BT, p. 342e.
31 See §6.1.
32 BT, p. 342e.
33 Here I am indebted to Ondřej Beran.
34 ROC III, §3.
35 PGL, p. 18.
36 BT, p. 343e.
37 Cf. ter Hark, 1990, p. 206.
38 BT, p. 342e.
39 Z §346.
40 Z §359.
41 PI §350.
42 See Lee, 1999, pp. 238f. Following paragraphs draw on Lee's account.
43 PI II, p. 212.
44 ROC III, §63.
45 The concept of aspect-blindness is broader, for it covers non-optical aspects too. Our present concern is limited to aspects of colors.
46 ROC I, §78.
47 Recent empirical research suggests that certain color-blind observers may have their color space extended relative to the norm and are hence able to distinguish color shades that most people cannot. See Mollon et al., 2005.
48 ROC I, §11.

49 In the geometrical model of Hering's opponent theory, red and green are separated by yellow. This fact was widely accepted in Wittgenstein's times. However, recent investigations of the so-called filling-in phenomena (see, for example, Livitz et al., 2011) have cast doubts upon this fact. Reddish green nevertheless seems to be possible, which means that red and green are not opposite colors. This evidence does not disprove Wittgenstein's arguments. The geometry of our color space is, however, different from the one Wittgenstein adhered to.

50 ROC I, §14.

51 ROC I, §14.

52 Cf. Lee, 1999, p. 237.

53 ROC I, §33.

54 Wittgenstein considers other qualities as well, for example, glitter, reflection, mirroring of light, etc.

55 ROC I, §21, Wittgenstein's ellipses.

56 ROC I, §45.

57 Lee, 1999, p. 232.

58 ROC I, §19.

59 Cf. ROC I, §29.

60 The rule might be something like this: 'Every coloured medium darkens that which is seen through it, it swallows light' (ROC I, §30).

61 ROC I, §31.

62 These are among the 'very general facts of daily experience' (RFM, p. 82) or the 'general facts of nature' (PI §142). See fn. 8, p. 236 for further references.

63 ROC I, §32.

64 This might be implied by Alan Lee (1999, p. 239). He thinks: 'the problematic status of white among the colours presents a problem of demarcation between internal and external relations of the colour system.' Once we admit that the distinction is relative to a language-game, the problem vanishes.

Chapter 16

1 TLP 2.1512; see §9.2 above.

2 PI §131.

3 PI §50.

4 By the expressions 'the meter rod,' 'the standard meter,' 'the rod that is the standard meter,' or 'the rod that is just the standard meter' I refer *de re* to the rod in question. I will indicate a *de dicto* reference explicitly by the expression 'the role of the standard meter.'

5 Kripke, 1980, p. 54.

6 See, for example, Loomis, 1999; Pollock, 2004; Baker and Hacker 2005a, pp. 189–99; Dolev, 2007; Avital, 2008.

7 As far as I know, this idea has been suggested only by Fogelin (2002, p. 127): 'To begin with, it may not seem obvious that we cannot say of the standard meter that it is a meter long; indeed, we may be inclined to say the opposite, that it is the only thing that *really* is one meter long.' Fogelin, however, does not attribute this view to Wittgenstein. This idea should not be confused with the related idea that the standard meter is exactly one meter long and all other objects might be one meter long only approximately or with some degree of tolerance (Pollock, 2004, p. 151), (Avital, 2008, p. 337).

8 Kripke, 1980, p. 54.

9 See Loomis 1999, p. 304; Pollock, 2004, p. 153; Baker and Hacker, 2005a, p. 172.

10 The fact that Wittgenstein's definition of the standard meter is timeless will be important later in this chapter where I will discuss the standard meter in connection with the distinction between internal and external relations. See my discussion of the *criterion of temporality* in §10.4.

11 I do not want to stipulate the counterintuitive claim that no object except the standard meter is one meter long. By endorsing the third definition, I want to point out that the sense in which the standard meter could be said to be one meter long is different from the sense in which other objects could be said to be one meter long.

12 One could raise the objection that the length of the meter cannot change, since the current definition of the meter is fixed by the speed of light. The meter is the length of the path travelled by light in a vacuum during the time interval of 1/299 792 458 of a second. One can, however, ask—as physicists actually do—whether the speed of light is constant or changing in time, cf. the so-called *variable speed of light hypothesis*. The philosophical lesson would be the same, although there is no natural intuition with respect to how such a variability could be detected. The general question should be, thus, about whether a physical unit can be defined at all.

13 Definition (III) states that one-meter-long is the unique thing (ιx) that is identical with the standard meter. One-meter-long$_t$ (that is, one-meter-long in a derived sense) refers to everything whose end-points would coincide with those of the standard meter when placed alongside it.

14 Definitions (ii) and (iii)—and their formal counterparts (II) and (III)—require *a possibility* of coincidence, not that the coincidence is actually taking place. These definitions demand that the two rods must be *comparable* not *compared*. This means, however, that the unit of length must be defined in advance. There is a parallel issue about defining the notion of number in Waismann's notes. It is argued here that one 'cannot explain number by means of correlation [...] you can explain it by means of possible correlation, and this precisely presupposes number' (WWK, pp. 164–5). See also PPO, p. 373.

15 To recall fn. 12 above, what is the background against which we could measure the variability of the speed of light? The variability of the speed of light makes sense only if the remaining fundamental physical constants (these are the electron charge and Plank's constant) are fixed. For a detailed discussion see Uzan, 2003.

16 Cf. fn. 12 above.

17 Gert, 2002, pp. 65f.

18 PI §49.

19 Gert, 2002, p. 63.

20 Jolley, 2010, p. 116. Language-games are like geographic regions. There are no facts of the matter as to when we have two different regions or a single one. Thanks to Jim Klagge for this analogy.

21 Cf. Jolley, 2010, p. 116. A close reading of §50 of the *Philosophical Investigations* vindicating the conjecture that the expression 'one meter long' can appear in different meanings is to be found in Gierlinger, 2010.

22 This preparatory language-game does not consist solely in the act of pure ostensive naming. It is more likely that the reference of the expression 'the standard meter' has to be fixed by appropriate training. Moreover, as already noted, the environment in which the standard meter is stored should also be fixed. The preparatory language-game is, thus, rather a complex issue. See §10.3 for details.

23 Formulations of such a definition can be found in Wittgenstein's manuscripts from the early 1930s. *Viz.* Wittgenstein's definitions '1m = die Länge des Pariser Urmeters' or '1m ist die Länge des Pariser Urmeters' (1 m is the length of the standard meter in Paris) from Ms 113, p. 23r; Ms 115, p. 58; Ts 211 p. 569f.; Ts 212, p. 704; Ts 213 (BT), p. 241.

24 WWK, p. 54; see §10.2 above for more examples.

25 See §10.4.

26 TLP 4.023.

27 Avital, 2008, p. 323.

28 The principle of bipolarity states that 'every proposition must be capable of being true, and capable of being false' (Glock, 1996, p. 63). Wittgenstein rejected this criterion explicitly as a 'mythology of symbolism' (Z §211). Sentences that would have been recognized and withdrawn as nonsensical according to the principle of bipolarity are conceived of in Wittgenstein's later work as rules of a game, as part of a kind of mythology. Some sentences are of the form of empirical sentences, but they have been hardened and become rules (see OC §§95–9.) This is the case of the sentence 'Rod S, which is the standard meter, is one meter long.'

29 Avital, 2008, p. 323.

30 Cf. §9.2 where the *maxim of same space* is considered in the Tractarian framework.

31 Avital, 2008, p. 331.

32 In practice, if something like this happened, we would abolish this unit of measure and define a new one. Cf. Dolev quoting Reichenbach: 'if an earthquake should ever throw it [the standard meter] out of its vault and deform its diameter, nobody would want to retain it as the prototype of the meter' (Dolev, 2007, p. 133).
33 Diamond, 2001.
34 BBB, p. 158.
35 Diamond, 2001, p. 110.
36 BBB, p. 160.
37 BBB, p. 161.
38 Diamond, 2001, p. 120.
39 Recall the previous discussion where we could stipulate that the relation *same-length* is reflexive in definition (II'). Yet this move would be drawing a veil over the problem of the possible confusion of transitive and intransitive uses of the expression 'one meter long.'
40 Diamond, 2001, p. 116.
41 As noted in fn. 14, p. 242, the comparison need not *actually* take place; it must be, however, *possible* to carry it out. Diamond's counterfactual situation goes over such a possibility.
42 Diamond, 2001, pp. 120–1.
43 If the standard meter appeared to have become longer or shorter, then there would have to be at least one object that appeared to be unchanged.
44 Diamond, 2001, p. 121.
45 Wittgenstein mentioned this sort of ambiguity at the beginning of *The Blue Book*: 'I point this out to remove, once and for all, the idea that the words of the ostensive definition predicate something of the defined; the confusion between the sentence "this is red," attributing the colour red to something, and the ostensive definition "this is called 'red.'"' (BBB, p. 2). See also PI §37 where Wittgenstein varies this argument with the sentence 'That is blue,' which is at one time a statement about an object (a case of predication) and at another time an ostensive explanation of meaning: 'That is called "blue."'

Chapter 17

1 Figure 17.1, see PI II, p. 194 or Ms 144, p. 39.
2 Ts 229, p. 228; RPP I, §415.
3 Ms 137, p. 9b; RPP II, §436.
4 Ms 132, p. 182, my trans.
5 PI II, p. 212; Ms 137, p. 128a.

6 Ter Hark, 1990, pp. 182f.

7 Cf. Jantschek, 1996, fn. 75.

8 Ms 138, p. 5a, my trans. 'Man [~~erkennt im Aufleuchten eine~~ | nimmt durch das Bemerken] des Aspekts eine interne Relation ~~(von Objekten)~~ wahr.' The strikeouts are Wittgenstein's.

9 LFM, p. 73.

10 LWPP I, §520.

11 PI II, p. 208.

12 Ms 127, p. 215, my trans.

13 PI II, p. 195.

14 PI II, p. 206.

15 We can imagine an extraordinary language-game in which these sentences were nevertheless meaningful. Then, of course, no straightening out would be necessary.

16 This section draws on my book (Mácha, 2010, pp. 138–42) and my paper (Mácha, 2009).

17 Cf., for example, RPP I §337.

18 PI II, p. 215.

19 RPP I, §338.

20 Ms 131, p. 149.

21 RPP I, §339.

22 CV, p. 65; Ms 134, p. 78.

23 LWPP I, §76.

24 CV, p. 65; Ms 134, p. 78.

25 RPP I, §341.

26 RPP I, §339. The parenthesis in square brackets occurs only in an earlier manuscript Ms 131, p. 154.

27 Cf. Ferreira, 1999, pp. 10, 86 and *passim*.

28 Bradley, 1914, p. 189.

29 Ferreira, 1999, p. 120.

30 Cf. §15.3.

31 Cf. §18.

32 Hegel, 1968, p. 64.

33 Here is a 'Wittgensteinian' summary of the 'Sense-Certainty' chapter by Willem deVries (2008, p. 74): 'Hegel's argument brings to the fore the fact that there are no lone isolated demonstrative acts, and therefore no lone isolated intuitions. Every demonstration, and therefore every intuition, is the determinate act it is because it occurs within and against a background of demonstrative practices that license and indeed ultimately demand the normative assessment of the individual demonstrative acts.'

34 Hegel, 1968, p. 62.

35 Cf. Kain, 2005, p. 45: 'If the doctrine of internal relations is correct and the reality of things involves the totality of their relations—the absolute—then to cut things off from the absolute will create in them an absence or lack, which in those things with consciousness will stimulate desire.'

36 Kain, 2005, p. 27.

37 Cf. Taylor, 1975, p. 143 for a statement of an explicit similarity between Hegel's and Wittgenstein's arguments.

38 Section 17.1 draws on my paper (Mácha, 2014).

39 Aristotle, 1987, 1459a.

40 Davidson, 2001, p. 263.

41 Cf. BBB, p. 28.

42 Hester, 1967, p. 179.

43 'My imagination is a monastery, and I am its monk.' *Letter to Percy Bysshe Shelley*, August 1820.

44 White, 1996, p. 115.

45 PI II, p. 197.

46 Cf., for example, Ms 137, p. 14b; Ms 144, p. 47.

47 This section draws on my own paper (Mácha, 2009).

Chapter 18

1 LA, p. 3.

2 LA, p. 8.

3 Z §§157–75.

4 'Culture' might be on a list of expressions that Wittgenstein borrowed from Spengler. Indeed, Wittgenstein sometimes uses the expression 'culture' in Spengler's sense, i.e., as opposed to 'civilization.' (See Ms 109, pp. 204f.; Ms 110, pp. 12f.; Ms 136, p. 18b; Ms 183, p. 46; Ts 211, p. 157.) I want to place emphasis on the fact that in Wittgenstein's conversations on aesthetics, the expression 'culture' is used in a slightly different (although related) sense as a context for aesthetic judgments that can also take place within Spengler's civilization.

5 RPP II, §501.

6 LA, p. 14; see LS §908.

7 LA, p. 18.

8 Cf. Ms 137, p. 20b where a gesture and a dancing figure are taken as simple explanations of a musical phrase.

9 Z §209.

10 LS §634.

11 *Viz.* LS §654: 'If I see it *this* way, it fits *this*, but not *that*.' The seeing 'this way' is a variation of aspect-seeing. See §17 above or the quotation at the beginning of §18.2.

12 See PI II, p. 199 where the German expression 'Staunen' is translated as 'surprise.'

13 It is not obvious (at least for me, not being familiar with Keller's works) what Wittgenstein could have in mind when he says this. In Ms 183, p. 59, he writes that the same principles of good and right (from the period) are embodied in the works of these artists. Hence, due to these principles, there is an internal relation between these works. There is an extensive commentary on their affinity: 'I often found that certain themes of Brahms were extremely Kellerian' (LA, p. 32). This could simply mean that they lived at the same time or in the same culture of the time. Such a relation is external. Nevertheless, there might be something hidden in this utterance. It might express a similarity between the works of the artists that is difficult to describe. Wittgenstein likens this to a similarity between two faces that is not obvious at first but can quickly be found. Such a relation would be internal.

14 Once again, no artist can break all rules at the same time: 'You can say that every composer changed the rules, but the variation was very slight; not all the rules were changed' (LA, p. 6).

15 CV, p. 67.

16 Saying that a work of art just exists for itself is another reflexive construction. It seems that language itself is trying to impose this on us.

17 Insisting on this reflexive construction can lead to absurdities. Schroeder reports Tolstoy's response to the question of what he meant by his novel *Anna Karenina*. He responded that 'if he were to put into words what he meant to express by his novel, he would have to write down the whole novel again' (Schroeder, 2001, p. 225). It would be absurd for Tolstoy to have to write out the novel again to satisfy his questioner. If we resist the temptation to hunt for hidden meanings in art, we can then direct our attention to the work's real aesthetic values, its appropriateness and its aspects.

18 See Johannessen, 1994 for a detailed analysis of Wittgenstein's account of intransitive understanding in philosophy and art.

19 PG, p. 79.

20 RPP I, §889.

21 Johannessen, 1994, p. 237.

22 PI §524.

23 BBB, p. 179.

24 Schroeder, 2001, p. 224.

25 See Chapter 17.

26 BBB, p. 166.

27 Wenzel (2010) connects this Wittgensteinian aspect-switching with the Kantian 'free play' of imagination and understanding which is central to Kant's aesthetics.

28 LA, p. 8.

29 Ms 162b, p. 22.

30 Ms 136, p. 59a.

31 This idea is embodied in Özlem, 2010.

32 In the context of *The Brown Book*, the expressions 'culture' and 'form of life' are very close. See Glock, 1996, p. 125.

33 Instead of two relationships, we can speak of two tendencies or movements in the history of art. Art movements that preferred the horizontal relation to culture are called 'academism,' 'classicism,' and the like. Romantic, revolutionary, or avant-garde art movements strived rather for an expression of feelings. One can see this point more clearly if we consider extreme examples of these tendencies. It is sometimes said that works of academic art are without feeling and that expressive works of art are destructive or rude.

Part V

1 I have in mind Wittgenstein's talk of 'the confusion between internal relations and relations proper' in the *Tractatus* (4.122, see §6.2 above) and the very first paragraph of the *Remarks on Colour*.

Chapter 19

1 Cf. the remark by McGinn quoted on p. 15.

2 See §16.3.

3 I remember having learned the meaning of '3' by reference to a paradigmatic sample consisting of three pears.

Chapter 20

1 BT, p. 310e.

2 CV, p. 44.

3 TLP 5.4733.

4 PI §216.

5 Cf. §12.1.

6 For Plato, ideas are kinds of paradigmatic samples (although immaterial ones). Now, an idea exemplifies the very property of which it is a sample. So the idea of good is good to the highest extent, and the idea of beauty is beautiful to the highest

extent. But this poses a problem as Plato himself recognized in the third man argument. The maxim of no reflexive uses of internal relations is a way of avoiding this problem.

7 Goethe, 2008, p. 123.

8 Reported in Kreisel, 1978, p. 13. Kreisel slightly misquotes Butler when he writes: 'Everything is what it is, and nothing else.' The correct phrasing is: 'Everything is what it is, and not another thing.' This is the phrasing Moore gives in his *Principia Ethica* (Moore, 1903, §123).

9 Most commentators have interpreted Wittgenstein's fondness for this epitaph as an expression of his anti-reductionism.

10 RPP I, §889; see §18.2.

11 Hegel would say that everything is indeed something else; everything 'is the unity of itself and its opposite' (Hegel, 1977, p. 220).

Bibliography

Altieri, Ch. (forthcoming). Doubt and Display: A Foundation for a Wittgensteinian Approach to the Arts. In S. Greve and J. Mácha (eds), *Wittgenstein and the Creativity of Language*. London: Palgrave Macmillan.

Anscombe, G. E. M. (1957). *Intention*. Oxford: Blackwell.

Aristotle (1987). *Poetics I*. Trans. R. Janko. Indianapolis: Hackett Publishing.

Avital, D. (2008). The Standard Metre in Paris. *Philosophical Investigations* 31(4), 318–39.

Baker, G. P. and Hacker, P. M. S. (1983). *Wittgenstein: Meaning and Understanding*. Oxford: Blackwell.

Baker, G. P. and Hacker, P. M. S. (1984). *Scepticism, Rules and Language*. Oxford: Blackwell.

Baker, G. P. and Hacker, P. M. S. (1985). *Wittgenstein: Rules, Grammar, and Necessity – Volume 2 of an Analytical Commentary on the Philosophical Investigations*. Oxford: Blackwell.

Baker, G. P. and Hacker, P. M. S. (2005a). *Wittgenstein: Understanding and Meaning. Volume 1 of An Analytical Commentary on the Philosophical Investigations. Part I – Essays*. Oxford: Blackwell.

Baker, G. P. and Hacker, P. M. S. (2005b). *Wittgenstein: Understanding and Meaning. Part II: Exegesis §§1–184*. Second edition. Oxford: Blackwell.

Black, M. (1962). *Models and Metaphors*. Ithaca: Cornell University Press.

Borges, J. L. (1998). On Exactitude of Science. In *Collected Fictions*. Trans. by A. Hurley. New York: Viking.

Bradley, F. H. (1897). *Appearance and Reality*. Second edition. London: George Allen & Unwin.

Bradley, F. H. (1914). *Essays on Truth and Reality*. Cambridge: Cambridge University Press.

Bradley, F. H. (1935). *Collected Essays*. Oxford: Clarendon Press.

Bradley, R. (1992). *The Nature of All Being. A Study of Wittgenstein's Modal Atomism*. Oxford: Oxford University Press.

Breitenbach, A. (2011). Kant on Causal Knowledge: Causality, Mechanism and Reflective Judgment. In K. Allen and T. Stoneham (eds), *Causation and Modern Philosophy*. Abingdon: Routledge, pp. 201–19.

Candlish, S. (2007). *The Russell/Bradley Dispute and its Significance for Twentieth-Century Philosophy*. New York: Palgrave Macmillan.

Candlish, S. and Basile, P. (2013). Francis Herbert Bradley. In E. N. Zalta (ed.), *The Stanford Encyclopedia of Philosophy* (Spring 2013 Edition), [online]. Available from:

http://plato.stanford.edu/archives/spr2013/entries/bradley/ (accessed November 27, 2013).

Candlish, S. and Damnjanovic, N. (2011). The Identity Theory of Truth. In E. N. Zalta (ed.), *The Stanford Encyclopedia of Philosophy* (Fall 2011 Edition), [online]. Available from: http://plato.stanford.edu/entries/truth-identity/ (accessed August 22, 2013).

Cappelen, H. and Lepore, E. (2005). *Insensitive Semantics: A Defense of Semantic Minimalism and Speech Act Pluralism*. Oxford: Blackwell.

Carroll, L. (1893). *Sylvie and Bruno Concluded*. London: Macmillan.

Crane, T. (2011). Wittgenstein on Intentionality and Mental Representation. In A. Reboul (ed.), *Philosophical Papers Dedicated to Kevin Mulligan* [online]. Geneva, pp. 1–30. Available from: http://www.philosophie.ch/kevin/festschrift/ (accessed April 9, 2013).

Davidson, D. (1963). Actions, Reasons and Causes. *Journal of Philosophy* 60, 685–700; reprinted in *Essays on Actions and Events*. Oxford: Clarendon Press, 2001 and quoted thereafter.

Davidson, D. (2001). What Metaphors Mean. In *Inquiries into Truth and Interpretation*. Oxford: Clarendon Press.

Diamond, C. (2001). How Long Is the Standard Meter in Paris? In T. McCarthy and S. C. Stidd (eds), *Wittgenstein in America*. Oxford: Clarendon Press, pp. 104–39.

Diamond, C. (2002). Truth before Tarski: After Sluga, after Ricketts, after Geach, after Goldfarb, Hylton, Floyd, and van Heijenoort. In E. H. Reck (ed.), *From Frege to Wittgenstein: Perspectives on Early Analytic Philosophy*. New York: Oxford University Press, pp. 252–79.

Dolev, Y. (2007). Mission Impossible and Wittgenstein's Standard Metre. *Philosophical Investigations* 30(2), 127–37.

Donnellan, K. (1966). Reference and Definite Descriptions. *Philosophical Review* 75, 281–304.

Erbacher, C. (2012). Can One Sentence Say What Another Sentence Can Only Show? Perspectives on the Discussion of *Tractatus Logico-Philosophicus* 4.1212 ('Was gezeigt werden kann, kann nicht gesagt werden') in the Light of the Literary Features of the work. *Wittgenstein-Studien* 3(1), 81–93.

Ewing, A. C. (1934). *Idealism: a Critical Survey*. London: Methuen.

Ferreira, P. (1999). *Bradley and the Structure of Knowledge*. Albany: State University of New York Press.

Floyd, J. (2000). Wittgenstein, Mathematics and Philosophy. In A. Crary and R. Read (eds), *The New Wittgenstein*. London: Routledge, pp. 232–61.

Fogelin, R. J. (2002). *Wittgenstein*. 2nd edn. New York: Routledge.

Frascolla, P. (1994). *Wittgenstein's Philosophy of Mathematics*. London and New York: Routledge.

Frege, G. (1956). The Thought: A Logical Inquiry. *Mind* 65(259), 289–311.

Frege, G. (1980). *The Foundations of Arithmetic*. 2nd rev. edn. Trans. L. Austin. Evanston: Northwestern University Press.

Garver, N. (1994). *This Complicated Form of Life. Essays on Wittgenstein.* Chicago and La Salle: Open Court.

Gert, H. J. (2002). The Standard Meter by Any Name is Still a Meter Long. *Philosophy and Phenomenological Research* LXV(1), 50–68.

Gierlinger, F. (2010). Darstellungsweisen. Eine Notiz zum §50 der Philosophischen Untersuchungen. *Papers of the 33rd International Wittgenstein Symposium.* Kirchberg am Wechsel: ALWS, pp. 101–3.

Glock, H.-J. (1996). *A Wittgenstein Dictionary.* Oxford: Blackwell.

Goethe, J. W. (2008). *Letters from Switzerland and Letters from Italy.* Trans. A. J. W. Morrison. Rockville: Wildside Press.

Hacker, P. M. S. (1986). *Insight and Illusion. Themes in the Philosophy of Wittgenstein.* Rev. edn. Oxford: Clarendon Press.

Hacker, P. M. S. (1996a). *Wittgenstein: Mind and Will. An Analytical Commentary on the Philosophical Investigations, Volume 4.* Oxford: Blackwell.

Hacker, P. M. S. (1996b). *Wittgenstein's Place in Twentieth-Century Analytic Philosophy.* Oxford: Blackwell.

Hacker, P. M. S. (2001). Naming, Thinking, and Meaning in the *Tractatus*. In *Wittgenstein: Connections and Controversies.* Oxford: Oxford University Press, pp. 170–90.

Hegel, G. W. F. (1968). *The Logic of Hegel.* Trans. W. Wallace. Oxford: Oxford University Press.

Hegel, G. W. F. (1977). *Phenomenology of Spirit.* Trans. A. V. Miller. Oxford: Oxford University Press.

Hering, E. ([1872] 1964). *Outlines of a Theory of the Light Sense.* Cambridge, MA: Harvard University Press.

Hester, M. (1967). *The Meaning of Poetic Metaphor.* Paris: Mouton.

Hintikka, J. (1982). A Dialogical Model of Teaching. *Synthese* 51(1), 39–59.

Hochberg, H. and Mulligan, K. (2004). Introduction. In H. Hochberg and K. Mulligan (eds), *Relations and Predicates.* Frankfurt am Main: Ontos, pp. 7–9.

Hylton, P. (1990). *Russell, Idealism, and the Emergence of Analytic Philosophy.* Oxford: Clarendon Press.

Hymers, M. (1996). Internal Relations and Analyticity: Wittgenstein and Quine. *Canadian Journal of Philosophy* 26(4), 591–612.

Jantschek, T. (1996). Wittgenstein über Sehen und Sehen-als. *Wittgenstein Studies* 2.

Johannessen, K. S. (1994). Philosophy, Art and Intransitive Understanding. In K. S. Johannessen, R. Larsen and K. O. Åmås (eds), *Wittgenstein and Norway.* Oslo: Solum Forlag, pp. 217–49.

Johnston, C. (2009). Tractarian Objects and Logical Categories. *Synthese* 167(1), 145–61.

Jolley, K. D. (2010). Measurable Confusion?: Wittgenstein's Meter-Stick and Beyond. *The Pluralist* 5(2), 105–40.

Kain, P. J. (2005). *Hegel and the Other: A study of the* Phenomenology of Spirit. Albany: State University of New York Press.

Kant, I. (1987). *Critique of Judgement*. Trans. W. S. Pluhar. Indianapolis/Cambridge: Hackett Publishing.

Klagge, J. (2011). *Wittgenstein in Exile*. Cambridge, MA: MIT Press.

Klagge, J. (forthcoming). Wittgenstein, Science, and the Evolution of Concepts.

Kreisel, G. (1978). The Motto of 'Philosophical Investigations' and the Philosophy of Proofs and Rules. *Grazer Philosophische Studien* 6, 13–38.

Kremer, M. (1997). Contextualism and Holism in the Early Wittgenstein: From *Prototractatus* to *Tractatus*. *Philosophical Topics* 25(2), 87–120.

Kripke, S. (1980). *Naming and Necessity*. Oxford: Blackwell.

Kripke, S. (1982). *Wittgenstein on Rules and Private Language*. Cambridge: Harvard University Press.

Krüger, W. (forthcoming). The Determinacy of Sense and Meaning. Some Notes to Wittgenstein's 'Philosophical Considerations' (Ms 110: 214) from the Early 1930s for the Background of his *Philosophical Investigations*.

Kuusela, O. (2011a). The Development of Wittgenstein's Philosophy. In O. Kuusela, and M. McGinn (eds), *Oxford Handbook of Wittgenstein*. Oxford: Oxford University Press, pp. 597–619.

Kuusela, O. (2011b). The Dialectic of Interpretations: Reading Wittgenstein's *Tractatus*. In R. Read and M. A. Lavery (eds), *Beyond the Tractatus Wars*. New York: Routledge, pp. 121–48.

Landini, G. (2007). *Wittgenstein's Apprenticeship with Russell*. Cambridge: Cambridge University Press.

Lee, A. (1999). Wittgenstein's *Remarks on Colour*. *Philosophical Investigations* 22, 215–39.

Livingston, P. (2010). Wittgenstein, Turing, and the 'Finitude' of Language. *Linguistic and Philosophical Investigations* 9, 215–47.

Livitz, G., Yazdanbakhsh, A., Eskew, R. T. Jr., and Mingolla, E. (2011). Perceiving Opponent Hues in Color Induction Displays. *Seeing Perceiving* 24(1), 1–17.

Loomis, E. (1999). Necessity, the A Priori, and the Standard Meter. *Synthese* 121(1), 291–307.

Loprieno, A. (1995). *Ancient Egyptian. A Linguistic Introductiuon*. Cambridge: Cambridge University Press.

Mácha, J. (2009). Metaphor: Perceiving an Internal Relation. *Papers of the 32nd International Wittgenstein Symposium* [online]. Kirchberg am Wechsel: ALWS, pp. 235–6. Available from: http://wab.uib.no/ojs/agora-alws/article/view/1586/1622 (accessed June 30, 2013).

Mácha, J. (2010). *Analytische Theorien der Metapher. Untersuchungen zum Konzept der metaphorischen Bedeutung*. Berlin: LIT Verlag.

Mácha, J. (2012a). Language Meets and Measures reality. In J. Padilla Gálvez and M. Gaffal (eds), *Doubtful Certainties: Language-games, Forms of Life, Relativism*. Heusenstamm: De Gruyter, 2012, pp. 121–8.

Mácha, J. (2012b). On the Idea of Analysis in the Late Wittgenstein. *Papers of the 35th International Wittgenstein Symposium*. Kirchberg am Wechsel: ALWS, pp. 105–7.

Mácha, J. (2013). Vertical Relations of Language-games. *Papers of the 36th International Ludwig Wittgenstein Symposium*. Kirchberg am Wechsel: ALWS, pp. 242–4.

Mácha, J. (2014). Fitting, Feeling and What Hegel Meant. *Papers of the 37th International Ludwig Wittgenstein Symposium*. Kirchberg am Wechsel: ALWS, pp. 181–3.

Majetschak, S. (2007). Kunst und Kennerschaft. *Wittgenstein-Studien* 15, 49–68.

Manser, A. R. (1982). Bradley and Internal Relations. In G. Vesey (ed.), *Idealism Past and Present*. Cambridge: Cambridge University Press, 181–95.

Marx, K. (1967). *Capital*. Vol. I. New York: International Publishers.

McGinn, C. (2000). *Logical Properties. Identity, Existence, Predication, Necessity, Truth*. Oxford: Clarendon Press.

McGinn, M. (2006). *Elucidating the* Tractatus. *Wittgenstein's Early Philosophy of Logic and Language*. Oxford: Clarendon Press.

McGinn, M. (2009). Wittgenstein and Internal Relations. *European Journal of Philosophy*, 18(4), 495–509.

McManus, D. (2006). *The Enchantment of Words. Wittgenstein's* Tractatus Logico-Philosophicus. Oxford: Clarendon Press.

Melamed, Y. and Lin, M. (2011). Principle of Sufficient Reason. In E. N. Zalta (ed.), *The Stanford Encyclopedia of Philosophy* (Fall 2011 Edition), [online]. Available from: http://plato.stanford.edu/archives/fall2011/entries/sufficient-reason/ (accessed April 21, 2013).

Mollon, J. D., Bosten, J. M., Robinson, J. D., and Jordan, G. (2005). Multidimensional Scaling Reveals a Color Dimension Unique to 'Color Deficient' Observers. *Current Biology* 15, R950–R952.

Moore, G. E. ([1903] 1968). *Principia Ethica*. Cambridge: Cambridge University Press.

Moore, G. E. (1919). External and Internal Relations. *Proceedings of the Aristotelian Society* 20, 40–62.

Moore, G. E. (1922). *Philosophical Studies*. New York: Harcourt and London: Kegan Paul.

Moyal-Sharrock, D. (2004). *Understanding Wittgenstein's* On Certainty. Basingstoke & New York: Palgrave Macmillan.

Özlem, F. (2010). Wittgenstein on Art and Creative Imagination: 'How to Understand "Genius" as Courage in Talent and Character Manifested Through Talent.' In *Papers of the 33rd International Ludwig Wittgenstein Symposium* [online]. Kirchberg am Wechsel: ALWS, pp. 245–246. Available from: http://wab.uib.no/ojs/agora-alws/article/view/1665/1781 (accessed June 30, 2013).

Pollock, W. J. (2004). Wittgenstein on The Standard Metre. *Philosophical Investigations* 27(2), 148–57.

Potter, M. (2009). *Wittgenstein's Notes on Logic*. Oxford: Clarendon Press.

Proops, I. (2002). The Tractatus on Inference and Entailment. In E. Reck (ed.), *From Frege to Wittgenstein: Essays on Early Analytic Philosophy*. Oxford: Oxford University Press, pp. 283–307.

Read, R. (1997). The Career of 'Internal Relations' in Wittgenstein's Work. *Wittgenstein Studies* 2.

Read, R. (2012). *Wittgenstein among the Sciences*. London: Ashgate.

Rockmore, T. (2005). *Hegel, Idealism, and Analytic Philosophy*. New Haven: Yale University Press.

Rodríguez-Consuegra, F. (1996). Russell's Perilous Journey from Atomism to Holism, 1919–1950. In R. Monk and A. Palmer (eds), *Bertrand Russell and the Origins of Analytical Philosophy*. Bristol: Thoemmes Press, pp. 217–44.

Rodych, V. (2011). Wittgenstein's Philosophy of Mathematics. In E. N. Zalta (ed.), *The Stanford Encyclopedia of Philosophy* (Summer 2011 Edition) [online]. Available from: http://plato.stanford.edu/archives/sum2011/entries/wittgenstein-mathematics/ (accessed May 14, 2013).

Rorty, R. (1967). Relations, Internal and External. In D. M. Borchert (ed.), *Encyclopedia of Philosophy.* 2nd edn. Farmington Hills: Thomson Gale, 2006. Vol. 8, pp. 335–45.

Russell, B. ([1899] 1990). The Classification of Relations. In N. Griffin and A. C. Lewis (eds), *The Collected Papers of Bertrand Russell, Vol. 2: Philosophical Papers, 1896–99.* London and Boston: Unwin Hyman, pp. 136–46.

Russell, B. ([1903] 1938). *The Principles of Mathematics*. New York: W. W. Norton.

Russell, B. ([1907] 1910). The Monistic Theory of Truth. In *Philosophical Essays*. London: Longmans, Green, pp. 150–69.

Russell, B. (1912). *The Problems of Philosophy*. New York: Henry Holt and London: William and Norgate.

Russell, B. ([1918] 2010). *The Philosophy of Logical Atomism*. London/New York: Routledge.

Russell, B. (1921). *The Analysis of Mind*. London: George Allen & Unwin.

Russell, B. (1959). Russell to J. O. Wisdom, 15 August 1959, *Bertrand Russell Archives*. Hamilton: McMaster University, box 5.55.

Russell, B. ([1984] 2000). Theory of Knowledge: The 1913 Manuscript. In K. Blackwell and E. R. Eames (eds), *The Collected Papers of Bertrand Russell, Vol. 7: Theory of Knowledge: The 1913 Manuscript*. London: Routledge.

Schaffer, J. (2010). The Internal Relatedness of All Things. *Mind* 119, 314–76.

Schroeder, S. (2001). The Coded-message Model of Literature. In R. Allen and M. Turvey (eds), *Wittgenstein, Theory and the Arts*. London: Routledge, pp. 210–28.

Schulte, J. (1990). Ästhetisch richtig. In *Chor und Gesetz*. Frankfurt am Main: Suhrkamp, pp. 73–88.

Searle, J. (1990). Is the Brain a Digital Computer? *Proceedings and Addresses of the American Philosophical Association* 64, 21–37.

Shanker, S. F. (1988). Wittgenstein's Remarks on the Significance of Gödel's Theorem. In S. G. Shanker (ed.), *Gödel's Theorem in Focus*. London: Croom Helm, pp. 155–256.

Sluga, H. (2002). Frege on the Indefinability of Truth. In E. H. Reck (ed.), *From Frege to Wittgenstein: Perspectives on Early Analytic Philosophy*. New York: Oxford University Press, pp. 75–95.

Smith, D. (2013). Language Games in Ts-310 – a Heuristic Method for Philosophizing, *Papers of the 36th International Ludwig Wittgenstein Symposium*. Kirchberg am Wechsel: ALWS, pp. 387–89.

Sodoma, K. A. (2014). 'Denk nicht, sondern schau' – Interne Relationen und die Kontinuität in Wittgensteins Philosophie. *Papers of the 37th International Ludwig Wittgenstein Symposium*. Kirchberg am Wechsel: ALWS, pp. 264–66.

Stanley, J. (2000). Context and Logical Form. *Linguistics and Philosophy* 23, 391–434.

Taylor, Ch. (1975). *Hegel*. Cambridge: Cambridge University Press.

Ter Hark, M. (1990). *Beyond the Inner and the Outer*. Dordrecht: Kluwer.

Ter Hark, M. (2004). 'Patterns of Life': A Third Wittgenstein Concept. In D. Moyal-Sharrock (ed.), *The Third Wittgenstein*. Aldershot: Ashgate, pp. 125–43.

Uzan, J.-P. (2003). The Fundamental Constants and their Variation: Observational Status and Theoretical Motivations. *Reviews of Modern Physics* 75, 403–55, [online]. Available from: http://link.aps.org/doi/10.1103/RevModPhys.75.403 (accessed November 15, 2011).

Vallicella, V. (2002). Relations, Monism and the Vindication of Bradley's Regress. *Dialectica* 56(1), 3–35.

Vries, W. A. de (2008). Sense-certainty and the 'This-such.' In D. Moyar & M. Quante (eds), *Hegel's* Phenomenology of Spirit. *A Critical Guide*. Cambridge: Cambridge University Press, pp. 63–75.

Waismann, F. (1951). *Introduction to Mathematical Thinking: the Formation of Concepts in Modern Mathematics*. Trans. J. Benac. New York: F. Ungar.

Wenzel, C. H. (2010). On Wittgenstein's Notion of Meaning-Blindness: Its Subjective, Objective, and Aesthetic Aspects. *Philosophical Investigations* 33(3), 201–19.

White, R. (1996). *The Structure of Metaphor*. Oxford: Blackwell.

Index

Lightning Source UK Ltd.
Milton Keynes UK
UKHW050724040521
383089UK00003BA/77

9 781350 01437